"Though the sewing craft is well established, there are still many individuals who want to learn, or who wish to improve their present ability. For these, many facilities are available. . . . But, all too often, these facilities are inconvenient, too expensive, or are designed only for the expert. . . . The publication of this compact, inexpensive book on sewing is intended to solve all the problems for such persons. Here is a book which can be as useful in the hands of the novice as to the experienced sewer."

From the *Introduction* by Dr. Henrietta Fleck,
Chairman, Department of Home Economics,
New York University

*Other books by Sylvia K. Mager and N. H. Mager*

*The Complete Letter Writer
*A Guide to Better Living
†A Guide to Tropical Fish
†The Household Encyclopedia
†The Office Encyclopedia

*Published in a *Permabook* edition.
†Published in a *Washington Square Press* edition.

# A COMPLETE GUIDE TO HOME SEWING

BY

SYLVIA K. MAGER

INTRODUCTION BY

DR. HENRIETTA FLECK

A POCKET CARDINAL® EDITION published by

POCKET BOOKS, INC. • NEW YORK

A COMPLETE GUIDE TO HOME SEWING

A Pocket *Cardinal* edition

1st printing........February, 1952
13th printing..........April, 1965

This original Pocket *Cardinal*® edition is printed from brand-new plates made from newly set, clear, easy-to-read type.
Pocket *Cardinal* editions are published by Pocket Books, Inc., and are printed and distributed in the U.S.A. by Affiliated Publishers, a division of Pocket Books, Inc., 630 Fifth Avenue, New York, N.Y. 10020.
Trademarks registered in the United States and other countries.

L

*CONTENTS*

# *INTRODUCTION*

SEWING is an art as old as mankind. Transmitted by women from century to century, it has never lost its utility or its charm. Mother taught daughter; neighbor taught neighbor. As an attainment, it constitutes, for women and men alike, a lore all its own. The woman of yesterday, were she able to look in on methods and implements today, would be amazed at the singular progress which has been made to improve quality and artistic effect.

Though the sewing craft is well established, there are still many individuals who want to learn, or who wish to improve their present ability. For these, many facilities are available. Courses are offered by schools, department stores, and sewing machine manufacturers. Magazines frequently devote many of their pages to some aspect of clothing. Many books have been written on the subject. But, all too often, these facilities are not available in the locale of the person desiring them, they are inconvenient, too expensive, or are designed only for the expert.

The publication of this compact, inexpensive book on sewing is intended to solve the problem for such persons and should indeed be a boon to all who are interested in the subject. Here is a book which can be as useful in the hands of the novice as to the experienced sewer.

For the beginner there is a chapter on first projects. An individual can progress with confidence from less complicated problems to the more involved until she is a competent sewer. And there need be no limit to the age of the beginner. "Beginner" may or may not connote youth. Many a woman has learned to sew at an early age, as soon indeed as she could handle the sewing machine with comfort and safety. Other women have learned when they were the age of grandmothers. Fortunately, this is a skill which can bring satisfaction at any age. Therefore, it is hoped that this book will encourage many women to try their hands at this fascinating occupation.

For the experienced sewer, there is a wealth of material in this book. She has only to refer to the section in which she has a special interest at the moment, such as collars, pleats, sleeves and the like and a possible solution will be revealed to her.

A singular advantage in this book is the comprehensive coverage of all aspects of sewing. If a person is interested in the selection of a pattern for a new spring dress, how to mend a tear in a coat, the use of the buttonhole attachment on her sewing machine, or the best choice of fabric for pajamas, the information is readily available.

In connection with the extensive treatment of the subject, it is well to consider that the book does not have to be read from cover to cover to find the answer to any such problem. The index is alphabetical and so inclusive that it becomes a valuable aid in finding the answer to your question. Not only is this a book of instruction, it is a sort of sewing encyclopedia as well. Yet the book is not filled with endless repetition. Rather than repeat a process monotonously, a cross reference is made to a full description of a given process to aid the reader in turning to it.

The large number of well selected and appropriate descriptive illustrations in the book are among its most valuable features. They were especially made to assist the sewer through each step in the process, as though an expert were standing at her shoulder, explaining each move. They are a kind of security against failure. When diagrams are combined with the simple, clear-cut, step-by-step instructions, even the faint-hearted should find new incentives to learn.

The section on equipment is particularly valuable. Present-day equipment is a far cry from the bone needle and other simple implements of the primitive age. Modern sewing machines operate safely and easily and have numerous attachments for many of the complicated operations, formerly done by hand. And, there are many other tools available to the homemaker, which promote ease of construction. This book elaborates on the kinds of equipment, their use, and care. The equipment of today is truly labor-saving and has eliminated endless hours which our ancestors spent over the needle.

Methods have also changed and this book is an exponent of the latest trends. Every reasonable effort has been made to streamline construction processes. Diligent use of pressing, pinning, and sewing machine attachments, have overcome the former tediousness of sewing. Many short cuts in construction, such as gathering on the machine, are indeed a boon to the home sewer, and are well developed in this book.

Women are not only blessed with modern equipment and methods but the improvement of the fabrics with which they work is notable. Science has made many contributions to the kinds and quality of textiles to be used in clothes and home furnishings. No longer do mothers have to put in large seams and hems to guard against shrinkage. Our grandmothers were often sorely tried with fabrics that raveled easily, pulled out of shape, puckered, or faded. The array of textiles available to homemakers today is a veritable treasure chest.

This book has a section on the selection of fabrics for definite purposes, that should prove especially helpful.

With modern methods, equipment, and fabrics to serve as inspiration, what woman can find any reasonable excuse to discourage her from sewing? But if there is one, let her consider some of the arguments in favor of learning to sew and the self-improvement associated with good sewing.

There are few families today that do not welcome an opportunity to increase their income. Again and again, women have told me of the savings which have been derived from sewing for their household. This includes making clothes for various family members, according to their needs and interests, as well as making furnishings for the home.

Specific ways to effect savings are listed here. Toweling can be bought by the bolt and hemmed at home. Home alterations of a store-purchased garment are noticeably lower in cost. Slip covers, table mats, and curtains made at home are preferable to ready-made and can be much less expensive. Sewing play clothes for the children from remnants purchased at reduced prices makes for real thrift. What homemaker has not been made happy by the contrast in her budget between home-sewed and store-purchased items? The savings can sensibly be used for other useful purposes—recreation, travel, books, and the like.

But aside from the practical aspects of sewing there are the less tangible to consider. There is the deep sense of satisfaction gained from having done something useful by one's own effort. However small, or however difficult, the making of something new, such as a blouse, a playsuit, or a shirt, leaves lasting contentment. And then, to see these garments worn by family members, and to realize their appreciation, adds to the delight.

There is no doubt that satisfactions of this kind are closely related to the development of personality. For example, the high school student who can wear better clothes because she makes them herself, and has more, because of the savings she is able to achieve, can go about with more self-confidence and a deeper sense of security. At the same time she inspires admiration and respect from others. This applies similarly to the homemaker who sews her own slip covers and curtains.

Sewing can be an integral part of homemaking and by taking it in stride, rather than making it a special task to worry about, it can lend itself to improved family morale and cooperation. In visits to families, repeatedly I have heard stories which confirmed this. Briefly, here are a few of the comments I have heard. A mother of a twelve-year-old boy told me that her son was disgusted and unhappy over his "sissy-like" room. Only a small expenditure was needed for stout materials for upholstery and curtains. The removal of feminine things made the room take on a masculine look. Improved family relations resulted.

A certain Mr. Brown needed a darkroom for his hobby, photography. So his wife made inexpensive black curtains for a small room in the basement. A high school student helped her grandmother make a traveling dress for a trip to see her new grandson. Harold was interested in sailing, but couldn't afford to buy a boat. His father helped him to make a boat and his mother sewed the sails for him. A grandmother won status with her family by doing the mending for a nominal charge, which in turn contributed to her sense of independence. In other words, sewing is not only a means for less expensive living, but constantly contributes to a family's welfare and happiness.

May this book open the door to many hours of happy sewing for you.

Dr. Henrietta Fleck,
*Chairman, Department of Home Economics*
*New York University*

## *PREFACE*

HUNDREDS of books about sewing have been written in the past generation. Each of them has a point of view. Each tries to be best from that viewpoint.

This book has several viewpoints.

It tries to teach sewing according to the most widely accepted, most modern teaching method, as far as a book can be adapted to that method.

It tries to introduce the short cuts and manufacturing techniques developed by an industry that has made America the best-dressed nation in the world at the least comparative cost.

It tries to cover the large subject of sewing in a comparatively small space so that this book may be produced at a cost sufficiently low to make it available to everyone.

It tries to give you information of the type that will help you judge better the workmanship of the clothes you buy, and take better care and have longer use of all your clothes.

It tries to show you how sewing can be simple, interesting and relaxing, as well as money-saving.

The author has relied in good part upon the assistance of many members of the New York City school system and wishes to express her appreciation for the advice and cooperation of the teachers and students who took time to teach and to learn from the projects set forth in this book. She is also particularly indebted to Mrs. Rita Rosenberg and Mrs. Drucella Lowrie for their editorial assistance and to the Consumers Research Division of the American Viscose Corporation for the use of their material on style selection.

# A COMPLETE GUIDE TO HOME SEWING

# 1. *BEGINNING TO SEW*

ONE of the greatest pleasures and most happy experiences people can have is in creating something beautiful and useful by themselves. Sewing satisfies your unfulfilled desires by giving you an opportunity to design, and to play with colors and textures for your family and your home. Making a skirt or a dress is a stimulating experience that will cause you to feel very proud of having created something wearable and useful, and of having saved money over the price of a bought article.

Sewing requires patience and planning. Many people who start to sew want to get finished too quickly. They seem to forget that haste makes waste and that if it's worth doing at all, it's worth doing well. In school, teachers discover that the boys do much better in sewing than the girls because they first read the pattern thoroughly, almost as though it were a blueprint in one of their shop classes.

A first principle is to proceed slowly and carefully. Know what you are going to do before you do it. There is no pleasure in ripping, and careful planning and a clear notion of the steps involved will prevent frayed nerves and a feeling of frustration. There is no profit in throwing away something half finished because you are weary of ripping and redoing. Sewing is practical work and you will have a tremendous sense of satisfaction if you are enthusiastic and are willing to be patient. Nothing succeeds like success, so practice first to develop confidence. Have your mind free of worries and get your other chores out of the way before you start to sew. Make a date with yourself to sew and prepare to enjoy yourself.

Be sure to choose styles that you know look well on you

and that you will want to wear. And by all means pick a material that you really like. You will naturally not want to start with a fabric that is very expensive, but you can find something pretty and to your taste in an inexpensive material.

Be sure to start with good equipment. It pays for itself many times over in better workmanship, time-saving, and ease of working. Selection of equipment will be discussed more fully a little later on, but perhaps you will want to turn to p. 4 now to see what you will need. Sit on a chair with a back and remember that good posture prevents quick tiring. Good light is a first and foremost requirement for your comfort. Place your light carefully to avoid glare and shadows and to prevent eyestrain. Ventilate your room properly. Get all your equipment together and have it nearby and handy before you start to work.

Don't try to work in a very tiny space. Make sure that you have room to work easily. Your dining table, protected with pads, makes a good cutting table. If you possibly can, sew in a place in which you can leave the unfinished work neatly arranged ready to pick up the next time you're going to sew.

Start with a simple project (see Chapter 8) or a garment with only a few pattern pieces. You want to get good results without struggling too hard the first time. Later on, you can try more difficult patterns. You will do well to choose patterns that you can use several times. Many give directions for more than one item, for example: a dress and jacket, or a skirt, blouse, and bolero all in one pattern. For your first experience with a pattern, you will find it easier to work with a printed rather than a perforated one.

Learn something about the fabrics you will use. For your first try, buy a closely woven material that will not ravel too readily. Probably a cotton fabric is your best bet for an initial garment. Cultivate an awareness of fashion changes and try to learn to visualize what fabrics will best create the effect you want to get.

Enthusiasm and a desire to be successful are your tickets to success. Have fun!

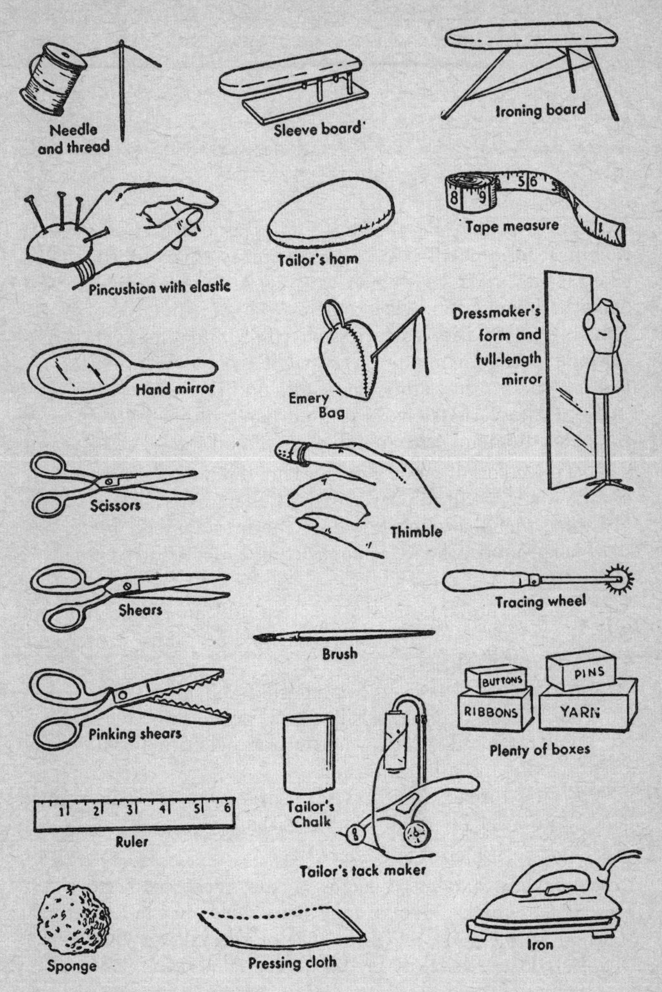
Needle
and thread
Sleeve board
Ironing board
Pincushion with elastic
Tailor's ham
Tape measure
Hand mirror
Emery
Bag
Dressmaker's
form and
full-length
mirror
Scissors
Thimble
Shears
Tracing wheel
Brush
Pinking shears
BUTTONS
PINS
RIBBONS
YARN
Plenty of boxes
Tailor's
Chalk
Ruler
Tailor's tack maker
Sponge
Pressing cloth
Iron

# 2. *SEWING EQUIPMENT*

THE cave woman of prehistoric times used a fishbone with a hole in it for a needle, and a tough animal sinew for thread. In like fashion, modern women can sew with only a needle and thread. However, in order to achieve high standards of workmanship, with the least possible time and effort, it is important to have as many of the right tools as you can afford.

First choose the right size needle and thread for your sewing job. The various charts printed here will help you in your selection. Remember to match your thread to:

1. The color of your fabric. The thread on the spool is darker than it will appear when stitching. Match one strand of thread, not the whole spool, to the fabric. With prints, use the background color. Use contrasting threads for basting.

2. The kind of fabric:

—*Cotton* thread is used for cotton and linen, and mercerized thread, a shiny cotton, is also used for some wools, and for plastic type fabrics.

—*Linen* thread is used for tailoring and millinery.

—*Silk* thread is used for silk, wool, rayon, and velvet.

—*Nylon* thread, used primarily for nylon material, needs a fine needle and a light tension.

—*Elastic* thread, sewed with a large machine stitch, may be used in order to get adjustable gathers.

3. The needle size. See chart.

*Needles* are sold in packages of one size or assorted sizes. Too long or thick a needle may leave holes in your material. Sharpen a dull point by pushing it in and out of your emery bag, but do not leave it in the emery all the time or it may

## FABRIC, THREAD AND NEEDLE CHART

| Kind of Material | Hand Needle | Cotton Thread | Silk Thread | Machine Needle | Machine Stitch |
|---|---|---|---|---|---|
| Heavy coating and suiting; canvas, duck, tarpaulin, upholstery fabric | 3-4 | 8-10-12 | E buttonhole twist | ccarsest 19 | 8 |
| Awnings, denim, bed ticking, sailcloth, drapery fabric | 4-5 | 16-20-24 | D-E | coarse 18 | 10-12 |
| Muslin, heavy cretonne, khaki, velveteen, twill, gabardine, corduroy, madras | 5-6 | 30-36-40 | C-D | medium coarse 16 | 12 |
| Cotton prints, cambric, gingham, percale, sheer wool, taffeta, chintz, poplin, faille, flannel, firm silk | 6-7 | 50-60-70 | B | medium 14 | 14 |
| Lawn, dimity, voile, chiffon, rayon sheer, thin silk | 8-9 | 80-90 | O-A | medium fine 11 | 16-18 |
| Chiffon organdie, georgette, batiste, net, marquisette, ninon, fine lace | 10-11 | 100-120 | 00-000 | fine 9 | 20-22 |

rust. You will find size 6 and 7 needles, and size 60 thread, your best bets for ordinary sewing. Betweens, crewels, millinery needles and sharps are names given to various types of needles. Use only good steel needles that are suitable for the fabric being sewed on.

Select slender, smooth, sharp pointed *pins* about one inch long. These do not leave marks after you have pulled them out. The finest pins are called dressmaker's pins or silk pins. Sizes 5 and 6 are best for general use. Have a pincushion for your pins, with an elastic to go around your wrist so that both hands are free. Or keep pins in a box lined with wax paper to prevent rust.

Challenge yourself to learn to wear a *thimble,* and practice until you sew better and more easily with one than without.

Choose a light-weight thimble of silver, celluloid or chrome that fits your middle finger without pressure and without leaving any color on your fingers.

Get a *tape measure* with numbers on both sides, each series running in the opposite direction. Have a metal tab on one end and roll the tape up when it is not in use. A six-inch ruler, especially the transparent type, will often be more convenient to use and a 36-inch yardstick has special uses for measuring material, long straight lines, and hems. For all kinds of measuring, you will need gauges that you make out of cardboard or that you buy.

*Scissors* are less than six inches long and have both handles of the same size. They are used to cut in hard to get at places, and to snip short threads.

*Shears* are more than six inches long and have different size handles, the larger being for the fingers, the smaller for the thumb. If you can choose only one, choose shears of medium weight, about eight inches long.

*Pinking shears* cut with saw-tooth edges and are good for finishing seams.

Keep your cutting tools well sharpened, and use them properly, that is, only for cutting fabric and thread. Use a very inexpensive pair to cut paper or for household purposes. The scissors sharpener will keep points sharp for you.

A *tracing wheel* is handy for marking guide lines through several layers of material, on cotton, linen and heavy silk.

*Tailor's chalk* marks distinctly and comes in several colors. It is easily brushed off and is used very frequently to mark sewing lines, pattern perforations, and alteration lines.

*Pressing* is a part of sewing, and for good sewing results you must learn to press as you sew. The following equipment is useful.

1. Electric iron with a rubber-covered cord. A steam iron is very handy and convenient. Have a stand for your iron unless it is one of the late models which require none.

2. Ironing board well padded with removable slip covers

for ease in laundering, and a sleeve board for ironing sleeves and for short seams, darts, tucks.

3. Tailor's cushion, a ham-shaped pad good for pressing curved seams. You can make this yourself with two cloth ovals about 18 inches long and some stuffing.

4. Press cloths of gingham, canvas or cheesecloth for delicate fabrics.

5. Basin and sponge to moisten fabric, for smooth ironing.

6. Small brush to raise nap on fabrics.

7. Paraffin for smoothing irons and salt for cleaning them.

8. Velvet board is used to press napped fabrics. The fabric is placed right side down, on the wire bristles sticking up from the board. The material is steamed and pressed as always, but the bristles prevent flattening of nap.

Other useful equipment is:

1. Full-length mirror and a large hand mirror to enable you to see the rear view.

2. A dress form for ease in fitting. Many on the market today are adjustable.

3. Large cutting table or cutting board to fit on table.

4. A good supply of findings: snaps, hooks and eyes, buttons, rickrack, bindings, elastic, ribbon, etc.

5. Orange stick for smoothing out creases, pushing corners out.

6. Embroidery hoops.

7. Tweezers to pull out threads caught in machine stitching, if you do not have a modern machine in which the bobbin holder is easily removed.

8. Needle threader to help you thread needle easily.

9. Tailor's tack maker.

10. Dressmaker's carbon paper may be used to transfer markings from pattern to fabric. It comes in many colors but it is advisable to use white or yellow. When using it on a thin fabric, try it first on a scrap to make sure that the marks do not show through on the right side.

11. A tailor's mitt is useful for the final operations. Use it

to press curved seams, darts, and sleeve caps. The mitt is put on the narrow end of the sleeve board and the garment is steamed over it.

Make your sewing easier and more pleasant by planning a sewing corner for yourself. Arrange your equipment in handy boxes for ease in using. If you can manage a chest of drawers, so much the better. Remember that you can sew with a minimum of equipment and add as you go along. Keep scraps of material for practice at first and ends of thread for basting. Handle your patterns carefully so that they may be used over again.

Old belts, buttons and trimmings may come in handy when you least expect them to. Arrange them in labeled boxes and jars, with such labels as garment scraps, trimming fabrics, yarn, fur, ribbons, etc. Put away only clean fabric. Take advantage of sales and put away remnants for future use. Try to develop a system for greatest efficiency.

# 3. *BASIC STITCHES*

To THREAD your needle, cut the thread at an angle so that you will have a pointed end to put through the needle eye. If you need a knot, form it according to these directions:

1. Hold the end of the thread between the thumb and the first finger of the right hand. With the left hand, hold the thread about 2 inches from the end.
2. Bring thread around end of first finger, cross ends and hold in place with thumb.
3. Roll cut end into center of loop and continue rolling loop off end of finger.
4. Draw loop into a knot and pull down to the end of the thread.

To sew we push the needle in and out of the material with our thimble. Practice making small and large stitches and learn to conserve your energy by taking several stitches before pulling the needle all the way out of the material. We end a line of sewing by going over the last stitch two or three times or by taking a small backstitch, as in basting.

Master the art of the thimble and practice holding the needle so that the eye end fits into one of the little depressions in the thimble and you are able to push the needle through the cloth with the side of the thimble.

While this chapter is basically for reference, it will pay you to stop a moment and develop at least a nodding acquaintance with the various stitches described. Practice each stitch so that when called upon to do it, you will not have to stop in the middle of doing something else to develop skill.

*Basting* is a temporary type of stitch used to hold two or more pieces of material together. Begin with a knot, put the needle through the material from the wrong side to the right, take a tiny backstitch for security, baste as described below, and end off with a tiny backstitch or with two or three small stitches perpendicular to the basting line.

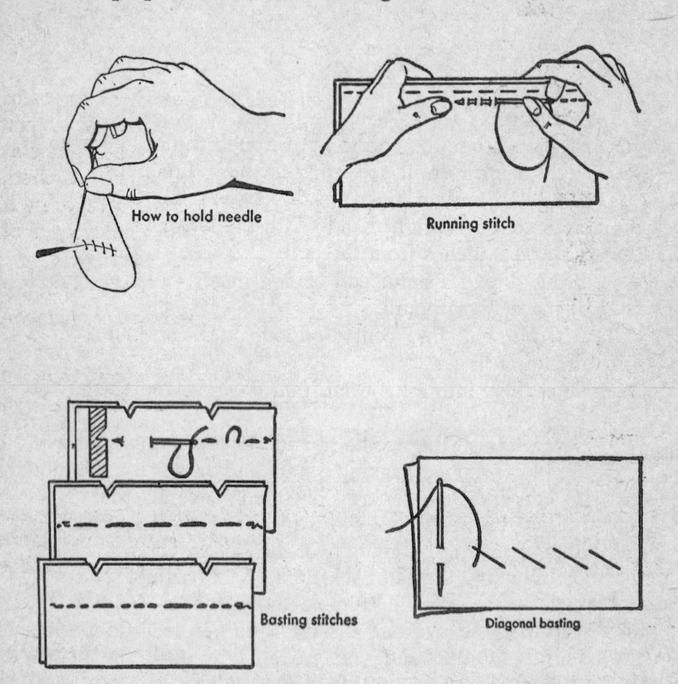

How to hold needle

Running stitch

Basting stitches

Diagonal basting

1. Even basting. Make your stitches ½ inch long and the spaces between stitches the same. This is a firm basting which is accurate and which will not pull out easily when fitting garments.

2. Uneven basting. Stitches are ½ inch to ⅝ inch long with ¼ inch space between. It is good as a guide line.

3. Diagonal basting. Used to prevent slipping of material when inserting zippers or putting in coat linings. Slant stitches on right side from bottom to top, come through to wrong side, hold needle in a straight line and pull out to right side again directly below where you originally inserted needle.

4. Dressmaker basting. Take one long and two or three short stitches.

5. Alteration or slip basting. This is used to baste seams where the garment has been fitted right side out or when you have to match plaids or stripes. Fold top material under at the proper place, and pin this fold to the place to be matched. Make a stitch through the turned-in edge of the fold, draw it through and make a short stitch through the under layer of material.

*The running stitch* is a tiny, even basting stitch used for gathering, shirring, mending. It can be used where a strong stitch is unnecessary.

*Gathering* is not a stitch but is rather an effect. Make a row of running stitches, but at the end, do not fasten. Leave a piece of thread about four inches long, and, holding this tightly, push the material back gently so as not to break the thread. Wind the thread around a pin to hold.

*Shirring* is the effect gotten by two or more rows of gathering. Make two or three lines of running stitches not more than ¼ inch apart and, holding all the ends together, gather and fasten threads around a pin.

*Gauging* is used to bring a large amount of material into a small space. Do two or three lines of uneven basting, making sure that corresponding stitches lie directly in line, one above the other. Pull up threads as in gathering and shirring.

*Backstitching* is the strongest handmade stitch. Take a tiny running stitch, go back to the end of the stitch, through to the wrong side, and out again to the right side at a distance from the end of the last stitch equal to one running stitch. Continue going back and under, being sure to work in a straight line.

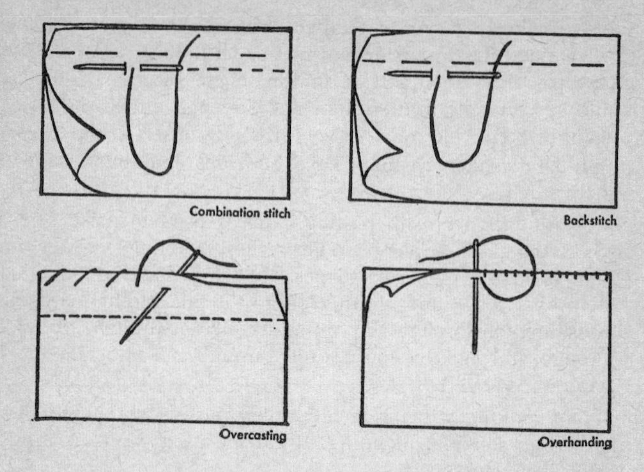
Combination stitch

Backstitch

Overcasting

Overhanding

*A half backstitch* is made by making one running stitch, going back, under, and out again as described above, except that you leave a space equivalent to two running stitches, and follow up by going back the equivalent of one running stitch. On the right side, then, the work looks like a series of running stitches. Like the combination stitch, below, it is used where you need a stitch stronger than a running stitch, but not as strong as a backstitch.

*A combination stitch* is two running stitches followed by one backstitch. It is stronger than a straight running stitch, but not as strong as backstitching.

*Overcasting* is used on fabric edges to prevent raveling. Make stitches slanting from right to left on the right side and have needle point towards your left shoulder as you come through from the wrong to the right side again. Overcasting can also be done quickly on the modern zigzag type of machine.

*Overhanding* is a stitch used to make flat, strong, invisible seams. Baste the two folds to be joined together and, holding the cloth firmly as you sew, make tiny, practically invisible stitches perpendicular to the seam line on the right side, and slanted on the wrong side. The same effect can be obtained by using a short zigzag machine stitch.

In *hemming,* turn in the edge of the fabric ¼ inch, then turn second time, and baste to under fabric. Make small slanting stitches from right to left, *catching* only a thread or two of the under material. A bias hemming tape may be stitched on to avoid turning hem under. Blind hemming is done like hemming but with larger stitches through the fold and only one thread on under side. The work is invisible on the right side. This too can be done more rapidly with the new zigzag

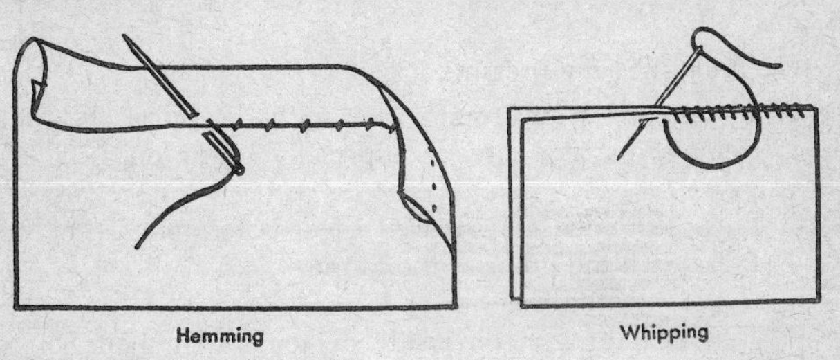

Hemming

Whipping

machines and is especially recommended when considerable hemming is to be done. *Slip stitching* is done for very fine work and is invisible on both sides. Take up one thread on under side of fold and one on under side of fabric.

*Whipping* is done to get a fine finished edge. Roll edge to be whipped a little at a time, wrong side facing you, hold roll tightly, and make tiny slanted stitches that pass under, not through the roll.

*Pressing.* It is most important to realize that pressing is a part of sewing, not an "extra." We might even say that pressing immediately after stitching is the difference between the work of an amateur and an expert. Never attach one part of a garment to another before the seams, darts, tucks, pleats, etc., are pressed.

Pressing is different from ironing in that, in pressing, we do not push the iron along the material. Instead, we use pressure and steam. That is, we raise the iron, set it down firmly, lift the iron again and set it down firmly at the next part to be pressed.

For most fabrics, it is better to press on the wrong side. Cotton may be pressed on the right side, but wool, silk and rayon may become shiny, and napped fabrics will have their pile or nap crushed if pressed on the right side.

In most cases, we need press cloths for pressing, unless we have a steam iron. A sponge is used for dampening the press cloth. Some workers prefer a small paintbrush to moisten seams.

General rules for pressing are:

1. In pressing seams, open seam with the tip of the iron.
2. Remove basting threads, especially heavy ones, before pressing.
3. Press all folded and creased edges before edgestitching.
4. Press with the grain of the fabric.
5. Never rest the iron on the fabric.
6. Test heat of iron on inside of hem or on belt before pressing.
7. Avoid stretching parts of the garment while pressing. Be especially careful with curved and bias edges.
8. In general, press seams from the bottom up or towards the center. (Waistline seam is an exception.)
9. Press gathered sections by putting tip of iron up into gathers. Do not press them flat.
10. To shrink out fullness in wool, as in a sleeve cap, press with the side of the iron parallel to stitching line, first on seam side, then on sleeve side of stitching, with iron close to, but not touching, the stitching. A smooth molded effect can be gotten as all fullness is shrunk out.

You will find a list of pressing equipment needed on pp. 6-7. Set up your ironing board when you start to work. Remember that your motto is "Stitch and press."

# 4. *THE SEWING MACHINE*

Operating a sewing machine is comparatively simple. Anyone can learn to do it well and proficiency is merely a matter of practice. You will get the most satisfaction and pleasure out of sewing if you own your machine and learn to use it well. Machines may be operated either by electric motor or by foot treadle. Practice first on paper and then on cloth. See p. 37 for practice suggestions if you are a beginner.

The upper part of the machine is called the head, and the large wheel on the right is the balance wheel. This is connected to the drive wheel, underneath the table, by a belt, and the two wheels turn together. The balance wheel is turned towards you to make the needle go up and down.

The presser foot (3) holds the material in place as you sew, and is lifted and lowered by means of the foot lifting lever (6). The needle, which falls between the toes of the presser foot, is inserted into the needle bar (5) and tightened in place with a small screw. The needle must be inserted properly, straight up into the needle bar, with grooved side to right or left, depending on your machine.

MACHINE PARTS

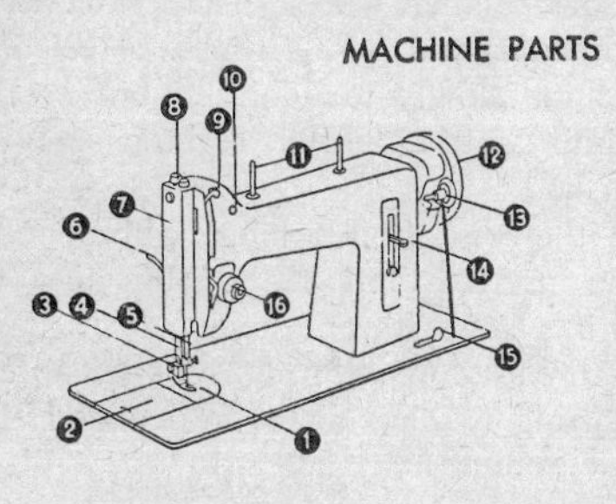


1. Needle plate
2. Sliding plate
3. Presser foot
4. Presser bar
5. Needle bar
6. Foot lifting lever
7. Front plate
8. Presser bar regulating nut
9. Take-up lever
10. Thread guiding nut
11. Reel bearers
12. Wheel
13. Bobbin winder
14. Stitch regulating scale
15. Bobbin winder tension
16. Upper thread tension

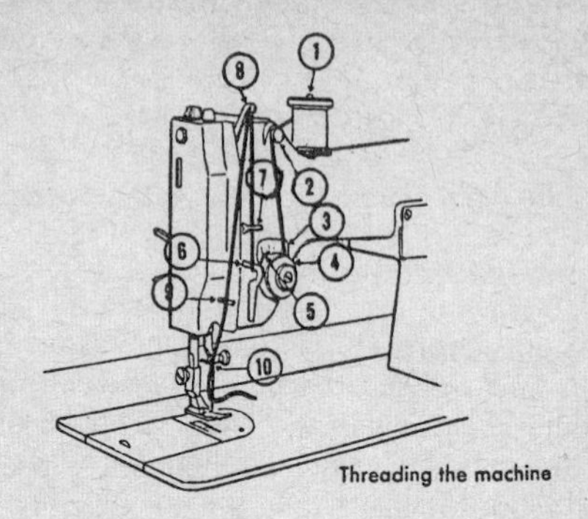

Threading the machine

Notice the other parts on the picture. The machine is usually threaded in this order: spool pin, (1), thread guide (2), tension disks (3, 4, 5) and spring (6), take-up lever (8) at highest point, thread guides (7, 9), needle (10). The needle is always threaded from the side on which the last thread guide is, along the groove into the hole. Check your manual for exact details for your machine.

Use the same kind and size thread on the bobbin as on top of the machine, except for special effects. To wind the bobbin, wind some thread around it by hand until there is enough tightness so thread does not slip off, insert bobbin into bobbin winder, put thread on spool pin. Loosen the large screw in the center of the balance wheel so that needle no longer goes up and down, push winder into place back against wheel, run machine slowly to wind bobbin evenly, not so full that it fits into shuttle tightly. Tighten screw in balance wheel when finished.

In old type treadles, there is often a long bobbin and a shuttle into which it is inserted. Put the bobbin into the shuttle, holding the top in place with one finger of left hand. With right hand, pull thread down through slit to bottom where it catches in a spring and up again into center. Put shuttle into shuttle case, point first, flat side up. Pull up

underneath are caught under the new thread and not left loose to tangle and cause the new thread to break.

Learn to treadle smoothly with both feet flat on treadle, left foot in upper left corner, right foot in lower right corner. Turn balance wheel with hand and the treadle will begin to move. You must continue the movement with an even pressure of the feet to get a uniform, back and forth, motion. Stop by putting hand on the balance wheel. Learning to treadle without jerking the wheel back is most important and fundamental. Practice treadling before you thread the needle until you can always get the balance wheel to go in proper direction—in most machines, towards you. If the wheel goes the wrong way, the thread will break and you will have to rethread your needle and start your line of stitching again. Practice on paper first and then on cloth. Use the following types of designs to practice on the machine: straight lines, circles, mazes, wavy or scalloped lines, crossed loops as in flower petals, and any other design that appeals to you. Work on double thickness of paper.

Be sure to remove the belt from the wheel when opening or closing the machine, if your machine requires this. Put belt in proper position again before starting to stitch. If belt breaks or is too loose, open the metal hook with pliers. Cut off a piece of the belt, punch a hole in one end and clamp the hook back. The sewing machine company will sell you an instrument which has pliers, special cutter and hole punch combined.

On electric machines, the secret is to get the machine operating at the speed you want. You must practice pressing the foot button or knee lever till you can make the machine crawl at an even tempo. If you can work it slowly, you can work it fast. The upper thread is threaded in way similar to that described above. For bobbin thread, place bobbin in case, holding thread forward or back according to machine, catch the thread in slot and then pull it in the opposite direction to catch in notch. Reversing the direction of the thread gives proper amount of resistance. The bobbin may have detachable bobbin case latch into which bobbin fits. Bobbin is inserted into bobbin case and thread pulled up as above.

Always be sure the machine is wiped clean before you start to stitch.

At all times, start to stitch with a practice piece of fabric to be used for garment. Select proper size needle and thread (see table, p. 5). Never allow a stitch to be taken without cloth under the needle. Watch beginning and end of stitching lines for this. Stitch a short line and check size of stitch and tension. Stitch regulator at right will change size of stitch by your moving the lever up and down or turning dial. In most machines, the higher the number, the smaller the stitch. Twelve stitches per inch is usual regulation but shorter stitches are used for finer fabric and longer stitches for heavier cloth and for plastics and nylon. If stitch length isn't specified on the stitch control, stitch a short distance, measure off an inch and count the number of stitches in the measured inch.

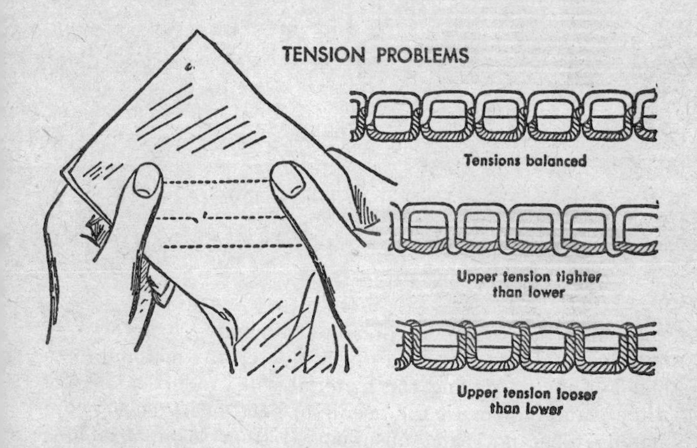


Tension is correct when both sides of the stitch look the same. This is because upper and under threads loop in center of material. If loops appear on the top, the upper tension is too tight and is pulling the under thread, or the bobbin tension is too loose. If loops appear on underside, the reverse is true. Bottom tension is regulated by a tiny screw and is best done by someone with experience. In general, plan to adjust upper tension only, by turning screw or numbered dial to right to make tension tighter, to left to loosen. If a tension is too tight, the thread will break. Always have presser foot down when you loosen or tighten tension.

When starting to stitch, see that take-up is at highest point, and both threads are back through toes of presser foot. Hold these threads loosely for the first few stitches to prevent bunching of the thread. Put down needle and presser foot,

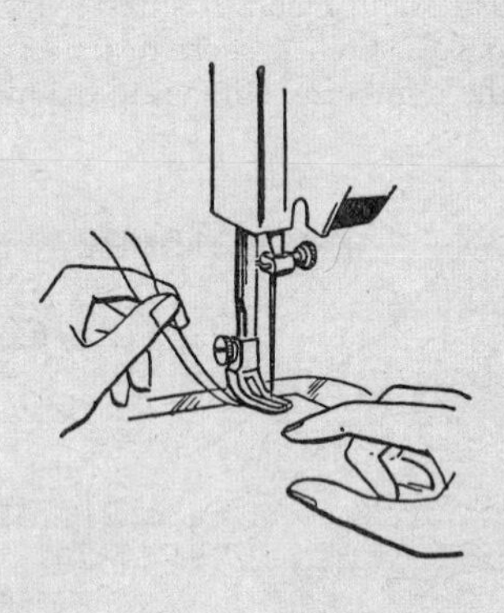

guide material with light pressure of hand. Do not pull or hold material taut; the feed dog will keep the material moving. Pushing or pulling the material will produce imperfect stitches and may cause the needle to bend or break. See that material does not hang unsupported from sewing machine table. In general it is best to stitch with the seam at the right-hand side of the goods. This is more convenient for the right-handed worker and keeps the material from being crushed and wrinkled in the limited space under the head. For this reason the seam guide is attached to the plate at the right of the feed dog.

To remove work from the machine, stop machine by putting hand on balance wheel, bring take-up lever to its highest point, raise presser foot, pull work back, not forward, and cut threads on machine cutter behind presser foot, or with scissors. Leave enough thread from needle and bobbin so that you can start to stitch again without having needle become unthreaded.

A machine kept clean, oiled, and correctly adjusted should produce perfect stitching. If there is any difficulty in securing good results, consult the summary of machine troubles and their possible causes below, and make the adjustments indicated.

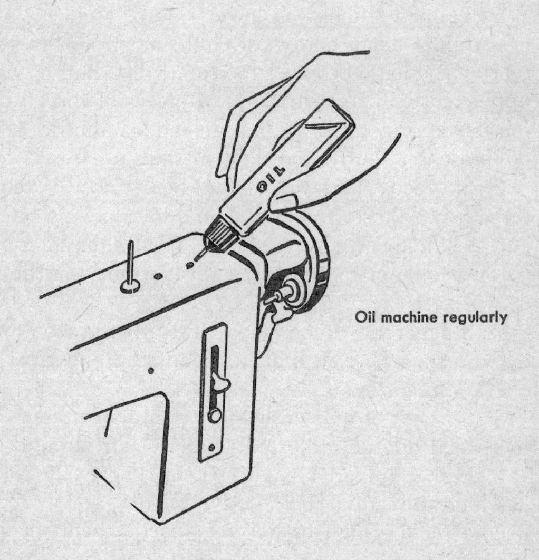

Oil machine regularly

These are some common machine troubles and their causes:

1. Tangled thread at beginning:

–bobbin too full or bobbin thread wound in wrong direction.

–under thread not drawn up or both threads not pulled back under presser foot.

–improper oiling or cleaning of machine.

2. Jammed machine: threads jam bobbin case.

3. Machine runs hard: lack of oil; thread wound around wheel and treadle bearings; gummed oil or dirt in bearings; tight bearings; belt too tight; bobbin winder against wheel or belt during stitching.

4. Imperfect stitches (looped stitches on top of cloth or upper thread lies straight along top of cloth): upper tension too tight or lower too loose; bobbin incorrectly threaded; dirt, lint, or rust between upper tension disks; dirt, lint, or pieces of thread under lower tension spring.

5. Looped stitches on lower side of cloth or lower thread lies straight along bottom of cloth: incorrect threading, upper tension too loose or lower too tight; dirt, lint, or rust between upper tension disks; dirt, lint, or pieces of thread under lower tension spring; dirt, or lint in end of shuttle or bottom of bobbin case; shuttle too tight in shuttle carrier.

6. Skipped stitches: needle bent; needle too small for thread; needle set too high or too low; needle set wrong side out; needle incorrectly threaded; needle too long or too short; oil on needle or too much on shuttle race; shuttle point blunt or worn.

7. Staggered stitches: too little pressure on presser foot; take-up spring weak, broken, or missing; incorrect adjustment of take-up spring.

8. Stitches of uneven length: improper pressure on presser foot; feed dog not adjusted properly; dirt around feed works.

9. Upper thread breaking: poor, knotty, or rotten thread; machine threaded incorrectly; needle set wrong side out; needle set too high or too low; needle bent; needle too fine

for thread; needle threaded incorrectly; needle rubs against presser foot, needle plate, or shuttle; rough or sharp places on shuttle or eye of needle; upper tension much too tight; in long-shuttle machine, not enough clearance between shuttle and shuttle cradle.

10. Lower thread breaking: poor, knotty, or rotten thread; lower tension much too tight; bobbin case or shuttle threaded incorrectly; burr or sharp edges on needle plate; bobbin wound too loosely or too tightly; bobbin wound too full; bobbin wound unevenly; rough or sharp edges on bobbin shoulders; rough or sharp edges on lower tension spring; dirt or thread in shuttle cavity so bobbin cannot turn freely; packed lint in shuttle or bobbin case.

11. Material not feeding through machine correctly: stitch-length regulator turned too far so feed is not acting; dirt under needle plate around feed dog; incorrect setting of feed dog; incorrect pressure on presser foot; bent presser foot or feed dog.

12. Bobbin won't wind correctly: drive wheel on winder not bearing heavily enough on handwheel or belt; rubber tire on bobbin-winder wheel loose, oily, or worn; thread guide on winder bent so thread piles up at one end of bobbin; cam wheel that operates thread guide not turning freely or incorrectly set.

13. Clutch not releasing handwheel: handwheel bearing gummed; clutch bound with thread or gummed with dirt, thread, or oil; incorrect assembling.

14. Handwheel hard to turn or set: thread jammed in shuttle race; thread or dirt in bearings; bearings rusted or gummed; bearings too tight.

15. Runs noisily: lack of oil; loose bearings; shuttle loose in its carrier; loose bobbin case.

16. Puckers in cloth: Seam puckers—one or both tensions too tight; side puckers—dull needle.

17. Needle breaking: pulling the material while stitching; needle too long or set too low; presser foot incorrectly attached; failure to raise needle before removing material.

# 5. *MACHINE ATTACHMENTS*

Use the instruction book that comes with your sewing machine for exact instructions for using individual attachments. Some are very easy and are attached to the machine and used almost as easily as the regular presser foot. Others are more complicated, but all can very easily be learned if you take the time to concentrate on them. An evening spent with the ruffler is not too much time really to learn how to attach it, and how to use it for the various purposes for which it is intended. Be sure to concentrate on how to get started, how to end off, how to work the attachment at corners, what to do at seam joinings, how to pull bobbin thread up.

With the development of the new zigzag machines, it is possible to achieve most of the desired results without the use of attachments.

*The cloth guide* is used to help you to sew a straight line the desired distance from the edge of the fabric. A screw changes the position of the guide for narrower or wider spacings.

*Hemmers* come in various widths so that you may get the desired size. The adjustable hemmer can be adjusted, as its name indicates, for different size hems. The foot hemmer turns the raw edge of the material twice and stitches a narrow hem about ⅛ inch. The biggest problem for the beginner is how to hold the fabric at the proper angle as it is drawn through the hemmer. With very thin material, allow thin paper to feed through the hemmer with the fabric.

*The binder* encases the edge of the fabric with binding and stitches it flat. The end of the binding is cut on the diagonal, then inserted and pulled through the scroll of the

MACHINE ATTACHMENTS

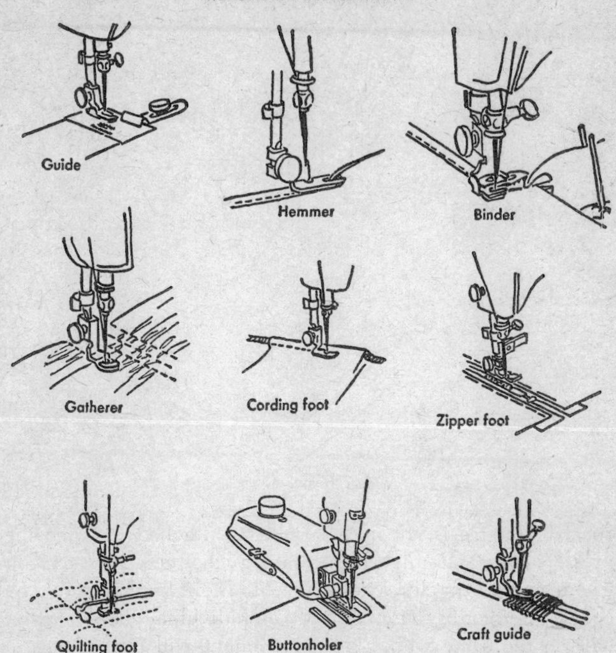


binder. The edge of the fabric is held firmly in the slot, for, if it slips, the binding may not catch it. If you have a zigzag machine, you will find that the zigzag stitch holds the binding more securely in place, and may also furnish a more decorative effect. Binders usually take width #5 binding, but multiple slotted binders now take other widths.

*The gatherer* will make gathers of varied fullness, depending on the size stitch you are using. A longer stitch will increase fullness. Very lovely effects are gotten on sheer fabrics.

*The cording foot* is an indispensable attachment for which

MACHINE ATTACHMENTS

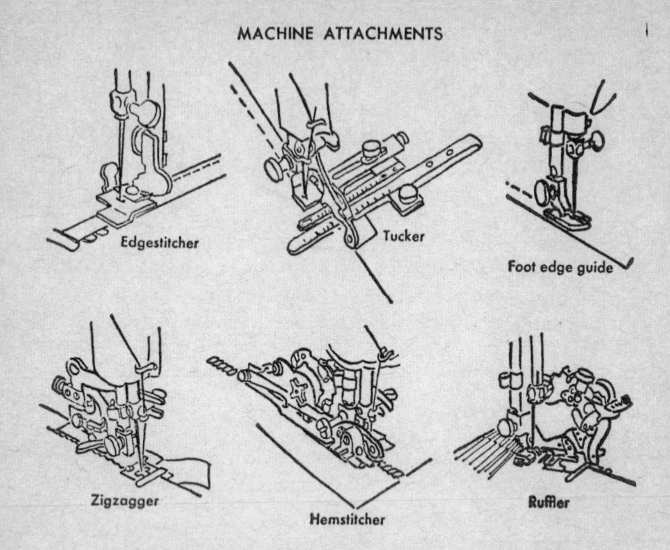


special practice is not necessary. It is attached just like the presser foot, and might be called a one-toed presser foot. There are two styles available, with right or left toe. The choice of either of these is strictly an individual one, for either will do the same work. This attachment will enable you to insert cording into a strip of bias so that the stitching is very close to the cord. It can also be used for inserting zippers, although there is also a zipper foot.

*The buttonholer,* though a rather expensive attachment, will pay for itself many times over if you are going to sew a lot, especially if you are going to sew for children. The attachment has a series of templates which are changed as you desire a change in the size of the buttonhole. The buttonholes may be adjusted for the length of the hole, the number of stitches, the height or depth of the stitches, and the cutting space between stitches in the center of the buttonhole. A razor or a very sharply pointed pair of scissors is used to cut the buttonholes after the stitching is complete. A very strong buttonhole may be made by stitching around twice.

Buttonholes can also be made with a zigzag machine without any attachments. Unlike buttonholes made with the attachment, these buttonholes can be made to any length, and can be corded to add strength.

*The zipper foot* was designed to enable the worker to sew very close to the metal of the zipper. It has an adjustable slide feature that allows you to stitch on either side of the metal.

*The quilting foot* is short and has turned-up edges in front so that padded parts of the quilting can easily slip under the quilter. A guide bar enables you to space evenly between lines of stitching.

*Craft guide* is used to make all kinds of trimmings and edgings. There are two steel prongs, with a slot in the middle, attached to a handle. Yarn, braid, ribbon, or tubing is wound around the prongs and fastened at one end with a paper clip. The guide spaces the trimming material and feeds it evenly under the presser foot as you stitch in the slot. An instruction sheet comes with the craft guide and gives full instructions for its use, even to making rugs.

*The edgestitcher* stitches edges together with very little overlap. It is used for making pin tucks, for piping with ribbon or braid, or for applying lace.

*The tucker* helps you to get tucks of even width and even spaces between tucks. The first tuck is creased by hand, and, as the tucker stitches it, the place for the second tuck is marked.

*The fagoter* imitates hand fagoting. Thread or yarn is wound around the prongs of the fagoter and is stitched to position over paper. The fabric is stitched over this, and the paper torn away.

*The zigzagger* makes a zigzag stitch whose length and width may be easily varied. This kind of stitch is very useful for appliqué work by machine, for applying lace, for monograms and other decorative effects. Since the zigzagger catches various levels of the thread, it gives a firm hold and prevents raveling.

The difference between the zigzag attachment and the zigzag machine is basic. The attachment moves the fabric from side to side; in the zigzag machine the needle moves from side to side. Thus the width of the stitch may be varied as you sew to produce many novel effects.

*The hemstitcher* separates the threads of the fabric and overcasts them into position. The hemstitching thus gotten is durable and accurate. If it is cut through the center, a picot edge results. Hemstitching is frequently done on table linens and as a decorative note for women's clothes.

*The ruffler* is an attachment which looks a lot more complicated than it really is. With a little practice, you will be able to make ruffles, pleats, group pleats and gathered effects that are beautifully professional in appearance. Keep the ruffler well oiled.

*The walking presser foot* is an ingenious device that enables the seamstress to stitch together two fabrics of unlike textures without slipping or stretching, thus keeping the fabrics on grain and preserving the true lines of the fashion design. The presser foot is particularly useful when stitching garments that require use of facings, interfacings, or linings. For example, if the surface fabric is a hard-to-handle velvet and the lining a satin fabric, the walking presser foot will keep the two fabrics perfectly aligned. Unlike the ordinary presser foot, the two toes of the walking presser foot move independently. The left moves in unison with the feed of the sewing machine while the right holds the material firmly in position during the stitching.

# 6. *SELECTING A SEWING MACHINE*

THE sewing machine you select will be a treasured tool for many years. The ordinary machine you will see is the lockstitch machine which has been essentially unchanged since 1900. A recent development has been the zigzag machine which was adapted from industrial machinery. Another type of machine makes a chain stitch.

The lockstitch machine makes ordinary stitches "locked" into the material. In such machines the needle moves in a straight line, up and down. Various sewing operations may be performed by adding attachments which may be inserted quite easily. These are described on pp. 24-28.

The zigzag machine, first introduced in Europe, in addition to doing ordinary jobs that a sewing machine is called upon to do, can perform a variety of other operations, such as sewing on buttons and embroidering. It operates with a needle which moves from side to side. This makes it possible to do not only the ordinary sewing jobs which a lockstitch machine can do, but also many operations which must usually be done by hand. By moving the lever which regulates the sidewise length of the stitch, and the lever which regulates the length of the stitch, the zigzag machine may be made to create a wide variety of decorative stitches, sew on buttons, make buttonholes of any length, do blind stitching, hemstitching, monogramming and appliqué sewing without attachments. Some of the decorative stitches are shown in chapter 34 (p. 192).

Three American manufacturers make most of the machines sold in this country—Singer Sewing Machine Co., White Sewing Machine Co. (which also makes Domestic and Sears

Kenmore) and the Free-New Home-National group (a merger of various companies which makes the Free Westinghouse and private brands for stores like Macy's and Montgomery Ward). Many imported machines are considered at least equal to those made in America. Among the most popular are the Necchi (Italian), Elna (Swiss), Anker (German), Pfaff (German) and the British Singer. One foreign-made machine is rated "best buy" by Consumers Union. All of them have some features not found in American-made machines.

Also introduced by European sewing machine manufacturers to the American market are machines with a free (cylindrical) lower arm, which are especially useful for darning or for sewing tubular articles, such as socks, sleeves, and pants legs.

Here are some hints on what to look for when you buy your sewing machine:

1. Your machine should be a round-bobbin, lockstitch machine. Do not buy a long shuttle machine, which uses a long bobbin, because such machines vibrate excessively.

Your machine should run quietly and without vibration.

There are chain-stitch machines on the market which sew without a bobbin. Chain stitching ravels out and is, therefore, not suitable for sewing where strength and permanence are required.

2. A modern sewing machine should have at least the following features:

a. A lever for sewing forward and reverse.
b. A numerically calibrated (measuring) tension, which makes adjustments of thread simpler, and prevents breaking of thread.
c. A hinged pressure foot for sewing over heavy seams and pins.
d. A simple drop feed adjustment to permit darning and embroidery.
e. A self-releasing automatic bobbin winder.

3. While not essential, your machine should, if possible, also have a snap-out hook case for easy cleaning, and should have the bobbin case so placed that the machine does not have to be tilted over to replace the bobbin.

4. Servicing for your machine should be easily obtainable. Almost all American machines and the more widely advertised European types are sold and serviced all over the United States.

Of the leading foreign makes, the Necchi and Elna machines use standard needles. On the Necchi and Pfaff machines, the parts which need most frequent replacement are interchangeable with those of standard American makes.

The miracle of modern engineering has found its way into the sewing room with the new zigzag, twin-needle, and swing-needle machines, and automatic devices which make even the beginning seamstress an artist. In addition to a regular straight stitch, some machines produce a zigzag stitch of varying widths and lengths. The zigzag has many practical uses as well as decorative ones. It is particularly useful to sew on buttons, make buttonholes, sew lace, join lace to an insertion or ribbon, make appliqué designs, do quilting, roll hems, apply binding, and do various mending jobs.

Before the automatic machines, decorative effects were accomplished by moving by hand the lever which widened or narrowed the stitches. Now endless versions of decorative stitches are possible through the use of disks or cams which move the lever automatically. Thus, when the stitch length is regulated to bring the stitches close together, a satin stitch is created. This is used chiefly for monograms, edge finishes, and cut-work embroidery.

Cams or disks are used to create more complicated designs, scallops, block shapes, arrowheads, tree shapes, saw-toothed edges, diamonds—all variations of the satin stitch.

Even more unusual stitches are possible with another device which controls movement of the material as it is fed into the machine. By gentle back and forth feeding, while the needle swings from side to side, other decorative stitches are made possible: featherstitches, leaves, Greek designs, scrolls, etc. The effect is a machine embroidery as effective as hand embroidery but much easier and speedier to make. Machines which take the automatic disks and control the feed are known as "fully automatic." Such machines can make buttonholes automatically without even turning the fabric, blind stitch, hemstitch, make eyelets, and do a score of other chores.

This type of machine embroidery is ideal for decorating sheets, pillowcases, linens, place mats, towels, curtains, layettes, children's dresses, bonnets, toys, etc.

*The sewing machine head* can usually be purchased as a portable model which comes in a portable carrying case. Such machines can generally be mounted in sewing desks or console cabinets, as required. The Elna is made only as a portable machine.

The furniture of your sewing machine is a valuable part of the complete unit and should be built with extra strength to carry so heavy a piece of machinery as a sewing machine. Check it for quality just as you would any piece of furniture. Doors should fit neatly. The cabinet should not wobble on its legs. Drawers should fit snugly and slide smoothly. Veneer and finish should be equal to that of any other good furniture.

Read the manufacturer's guarantee of performance. Your machine should be fully and clearly guaranteed against defects or poor performance. The guarantee should cover the machine furniture as well.

# 7. GENERAL INFORMATION FOR SEWING

THE information presented here is the kind that will later become routine to you. It is wise to read this part through so that these points will be highlighted for you.

Most of the time, two pieces of fabric are sewed together with right sides facing each other and wrong sides of the fabric on the outside. Directions usually say "right sides together." Usually a plain seam is used, that is, a line of stitching a certain distance from the raw edges, most often ½ inch to ⅝ inch. This seam is then pressed open. A gauge is used to make the line the same distance from the edge all the way down. See p. 24. To hold the fabric together while you are sewing, pin the edges together with a series of pins, with the heads near the edge. Mark the sewing line with chalk. A new machine will sew over pins because of its hinged presser foot but the pins must be placed perpendicular to the edge. It is a good idea to invest in such a foot if you do not have one. If you do not have a hinged foot, slow the machine as you come to the pins and pull them out. Putting pins in this way will eliminate basting and, indeed, hold your work more firmly than if you basted.

Get into the habit of backtacking at the beginning and end of your work. If your machine has a backtacker this is easy, for the machine will go backward as easily as forward. If not, start a short distance from the edge with the fabric facing the opposite direction from the way the seam is to be stitched; stitch to the edge, then, with the needle in the material, lift the presser foot, pivot the work around, lower the presser foot, and stitch the seam properly, going over the few stitches you have just made. At the end of the line of stitching, turn the work around, and go back over the last few stitches in the same way. There are certain times when you will want to tie your threads. This is how you do it. At the very end of the material, merely take the two threads, and tie them together in a square knot. Put the right thread over the left and under, then put the left thread over the right and under. Tighten. This is a strong knot that does not pull out. Where the threads have to be tied in the center of the fabric, rather than at the edge, give the under thread (on the wrong side) a jerk. This will form a loop from the other side because of the pressure exerted by the jerk on the thread; pull up this loop, thus getting both threads on the same side of the fabric and tie a square knot as described above. Another way is to thread a needle with the thread end on the right side, push the needle through to the wrong side and tie the ends.

Press as you go along. See pp. 13-14, 264-266. This is one of the secrets of good work, and remember, if you feel you are losing time from the sewing, that you are probably saving time because of the greater ease and facility with which you will be able to sew the pressed seams.

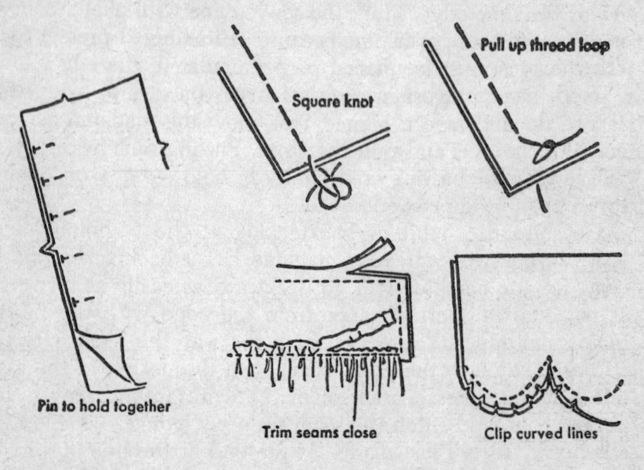

When turning enclosed seams, as in collars, cuffs, facings, etc., trim the seams close (⅛ or ¼ inch) to avoid unnecessary and ugly bulk. Trim especially close at corners for really smooth lines. Curved lines, for example at the waistline, neck edge, armhole, scalloped trims, etc., are clipped with little triangular cuts that extend right to the seam line, naturally only as close as is possible without actually cutting the stitching. Directions usually say "trim seam and clip curves."

When the directions tell you to edgestitch, that means you are to sew as close to the edge as you can in a very straight line. Learn to watch the edge of the presser foot and to use this as a guide. Do not watch the needle, for that is confusing and can make you a little dizzy.

Don't neglect any markings on the pattern. Patterns are made to fit together perfectly. If you do not sew on the indicated lines, one piece will not fit another. If you are careless and sew the shoulder seams ½ inch from the edge when the pattern calls for ⅝ inch, the collar will be very queer looking when you are through, for the ends will not meet properly at the center of the blouse.

Do not remove pattern pieces from fabric until you are ready to use them. Otherwise, the similarity in shape of some pieces may be very confusing.

Don't attempt to do any sewing until you have really learned how to use the machine. This is the first big job. Don't neglect it. Practice religiously until you can control the speed of the machine and can sew a line that is really straight.

The inside of your work should look almost as good as the outside. You wouldn't sweep the dust under the carpet. Remember that the principle is the same.

Watch grain lines of the fabric. Lengthwise lines, in general, run in a straight line through the center of your body perpendicular to the floor. Crosswise lines are parallel to the floor. A garment with grain cut carelessly can never look professional and the chances are that it will shift its position as you wear it and be very uncomfortable.

# 8. *PRACTICE STITCHING AND PROJECTS*

To DEVELOP skill and confidence, practice will be necessary.

1. Thread the machine enough times to be able to do it routinely. Make sure the thread is between the tension disks, not in back or in front. Develop the habit of raising the take-up lever to the highest point. See that thread enters needle from grooved side.

2. Practice winding bobbins and inserting them in bobbin case correctly. Pull up bobbin thread and lay both threads back under presser foot. Is small wheel inside balance wheel tight? Is screw attaching presser foot to machine tight? Is there any thread from spool wound around spool pin? Is needle set in right?

3. Try a piece of practice material before stitching at all times. Is tension correct? Stitches should look alike on both sides. Check with the instructions in your machine manual. Is stitch size correct?

4. To learn to stitch straight with ease, practice without thread first. Use paper with straight lines, traced circles, mazes, wavy or scalloped lines, crossed loops as flower petals, and any other intricate designs. Use double thicknesses of paper.

5. Work with machine threaded on designs traced on inexpensive material. Start with enough thread between the toes of the presser foot so that needle will not become unthreaded. Watch the edge of the presser foot as a guide, not the needle. Stop with needle at the highest point, pull work straight back, and cut thread with thread cutter, located be-

hind presser foot. Push threads back before continuing. Learn to backtack at the beginning and the end of seams. Never

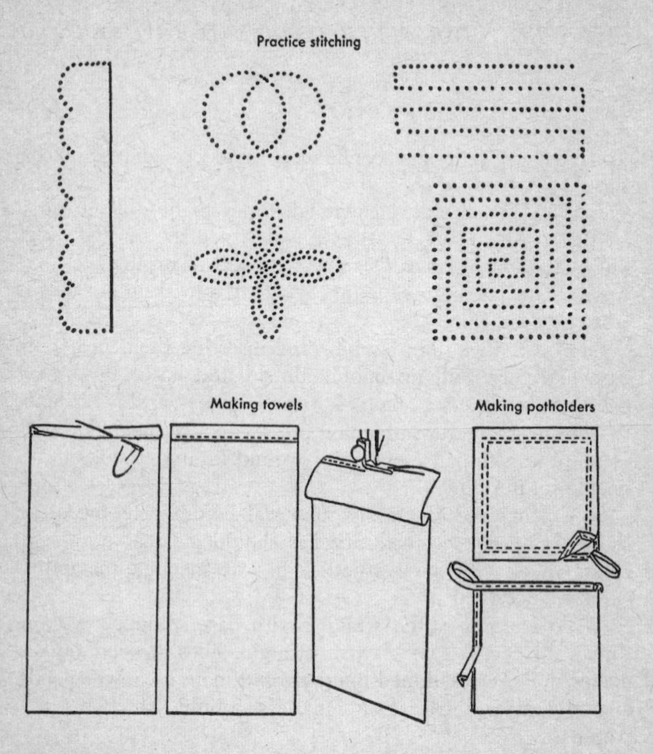


turn balance wheel the wrong way. Do not allow garment to hang unsupported.

Here are directions for some simple objects to make so that your practicing will be constructive. If you have any difficulty, use the index of this book and read full directions for the process that bothers you.

*Towels*: Buy 2½ yards of toweling and cut into 30-inch lengths for three towels. Make narrow hems on both cut edges. On one towel, baste and hem by hand. On the second, baste and edgestitch near fold. On the third, use the machine hemmer. This will give you practice with several methods.

*Potholder*: Put two small washcloths right sides together, and stitch around ½ inch from edge, using a ½-inch gauge, on three sides. Trim corners and turn inside out. Make a loop by taking a four-inch piece of tape and basting it to corner with edges ½ inch inside. Turn in raw edges of potholder ½ inch and baste, catching in loop. Stitch ½ inch from edge on all four sides and do a second line of stitching inside first using the width of the toe of the presser foot as a guide.

A second method is to put the two cloths wrong sides together and baste bias binding all the way around, making the loop out of the binding. Have binding a little narrower on stitching side to catch in under side and then stitch. You may also use the machine binder to bind the edges.

*Pincushion*: Cut out two four-inch circles or squares. Turn in edges ¼ inch all around and baste. Baste a seven-inch strip of elastic on to wrong side of one piece with ½ inch of elastic extending inside edge on two opposite sides. Place second piece of material on top, wrong side down, and stitch all around near edge on three sides. Fill with cotton wadding, baste raw edges together, and stitch across.

*Place mat*: Use suitable material—gingham, linen, basket weave, etc.—and cut into piece 12 x 18. Turn edges under to wrong side ¼ inch and baste wide rickrack or fringe to wrong side covering raw edge. The trim extends on the right side. Stitch all around.

*Scarf*: Use brightly colored silk and handroll edges on a rectangle 40 x 19. Or, roll the long edges and fringe the short ones. To do this, draw out a crosswise thread ½ inch from the edge, and overcast through drawn thread line up into material; or machine stitch, near drawn thread. Pull out all threads below to make fringe.

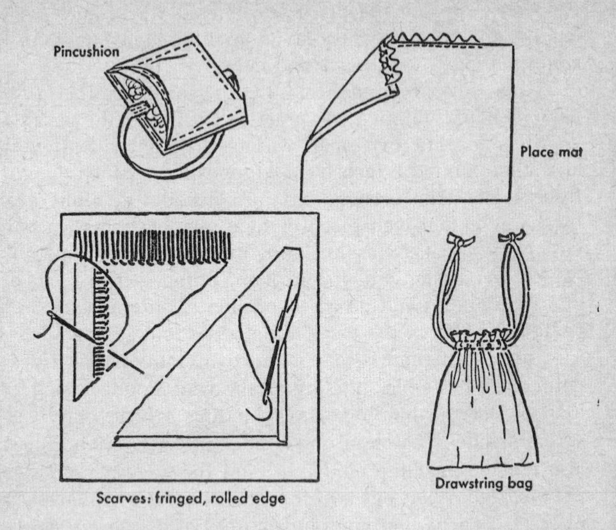


*Small drawstring bag*: Cut out piece 12 x 28 and lining piece 12 x 26. Fold in half crosswise, right sides together, and stitch ½ inch from edge up two long sides on both pieces. Turn right side out and put lining in bag, wrong sides together. Pin together at side seams and bottom, and baste lining to bag at top to hold in place. Turn down ½ inch on top, baste, then turn down two inches, baste and stitch. Clip one stitch of seam on top hem on both sides and stitch two lines above and below opening ½ inch apart. Cut two strips of ribbon or tape 30 inches long. Insert one with bodkin or safety pin through one side and draw all the way through, pulling out on same side. Do the same with the other on the other side. Knot ribbon edges or fasten with decorative stitches, and pull to draw.

*Aprons*: 1. Use large scarf or cut out 28-inch square and handroll edges. Sew two tapes to two opposite corners for ties.

Cut a triangle off third corner and handroll resulting straight edge. Attach a tape to ends of cut corner to make a loop that will go around the neck comfortably.

2. For a novelty tea apron use four identical colored or printed 12-inch square handkerchiefs. Join two in a French seam or a stitched fell seam (see p. 109). Gather top by hand or machine. Fold third handkerchief in half right sides together. Turn back corners on top thickness to meet at center bottom fold, and baste together. Then baste this edge to gathered edge, right sides together, pulling up gathers to fit, and stitch. Fold fourth handkerchief on diagonal and cut.

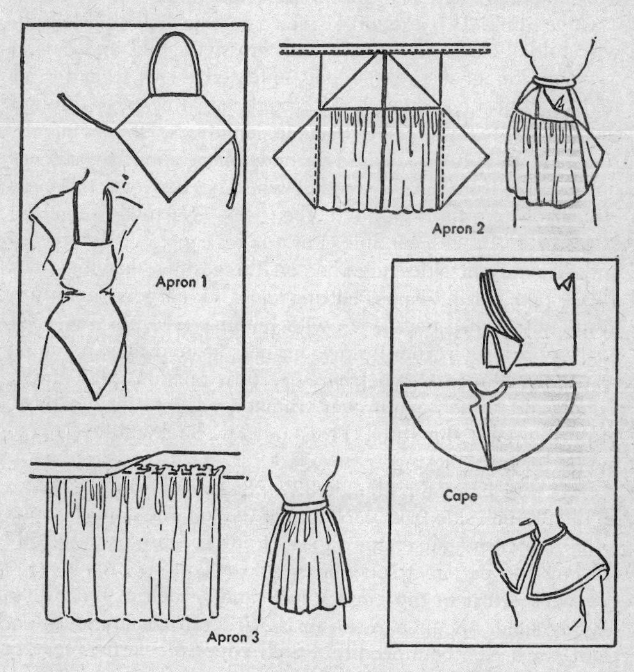

Join cut edges to sides in a stitched fell seam. The effect will be circular on the bottom and the two turned back edges on the top will make pockets. Finish top edge with 1 1/3 yards matching grosgrain ribbon, one-inch wide, stitching ribbon over apron top so that center of ribbon is in center of apron. Free edges will make ties.

3. Use one yard of 35-inch material. Selvages are on sides. Bottom is narrowly hemmed by hand or with hemmer. Gather top by machine with longest stitch. Pull gathers up so that apron fits comfortably, and fasten. Finish off top with 1 1/3 yards ribbon. Ribbon is attached to wrong side and turned over and slip stitched to position on right side.

*Cape*: Fold 1¼ yards of 41-inch fabric in half in a lengthwise fold. Fold in half again with crosswise fold and cut an arc (quarter of a circle) along unfolded edges from top of fold to opposite corner. Cut through one thickness through second or crosswise fold down to lengthwise fold. Cut out small arc at bottom, where two folds meet, about two inches up and out from corner, so that when opened out, the cape will fit comfortably around the neck. Narrowly hem all edges or finish with binding. For a lined cape, cut two pieces and seam, right sides together on three sides, leaving neck edge open. Trim seams, cutting close at corners, and turn inside out. Finish neck edge with binding (see pp. 136-138) or trim off ½ inch from inside thickness around neck, opening seams for ½ inch down from top, turn outside edge under ¼ inch and ¼ inch again over trimmed edge to inside. Baste to position and slip stitch. Press and sew hook-and-eye opening on for front closing.

*Half slip:* Draw a rectangle 32 x 28. Measure in five inches on the 28-inch side from each end of the top and connect point to bottom corners to shape slip. Cut out and use as pattern to cut out two petticoat sections of silk or cotton. French seam the sides. Turn in top edge ¼ inch and ½ inch again. Stitch, leaving small opening to run in elastic. Run in narrow elastic to fit waist line comfortably. Stitch edges of elastic together and finish hem opening by hand. Turn up bottom hem to desired length or finish with embroidered edging.

*Dress:* Use a tube of jersey because of its softness and draping qualities. Buy 1½ yards for average height figure. Cut in half lengthwise. Put two pieces together, fold in half lengthwise and cut out neck as for cape above, about two inches out and down from fold. Open out fold, and on one piece cut slit down about four inches. See if this goes over your head easily, and bind entire edge with bias binding. Use commercial binding or cut your own from scraps if you can. Mark down nine inches on sides from top and three inches below that. Cut from nine-inch mark in three inches and down on a diagonal to three-inch mark. Join this slashed edge in a seam on wrong side, gathering in larger edge. (See pp. 107-112.) Sew down two long sides with fabric right sides together. Finish off armhole edges with binding, try on with belt, and mark hem. Finish hem. If desired, mark waistline with chalk and sew in elastic thread to hold fullness in place.

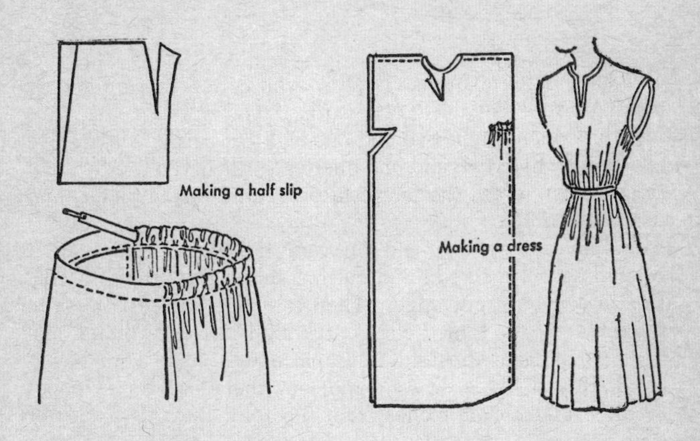


*Dirndl skirt:* Since you are probably very anxious to begin, here are directions for a simple garment that you can make

MAKING A DIRNDL SKIRT

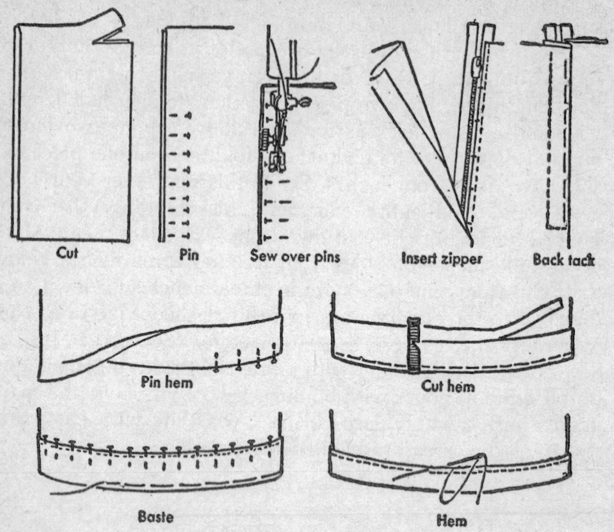


without a pattern. Buy a closely woven cotton fabric for your first try. You will need two yards if you are less than five feet three inches tall; two and one-eighth yards if you are five feet four or five; two and one-quarter yards if you are five feet six or seven. Wash the fabric to prevent shrinkage later, and press it smooth.

Spread the material out on your table and straighten it by pulling out a thread and cutting across the drawn thread. Do this on both cut edges. Then fold one cut edge over to the other. At the folded edge cut straight across two and one-half inches from the fold. This piece will make your waistband. If you like a wider band, cut the piece three inches or three and a half inches from the fold. Put this aside for later use.

Now take the rest of the material and turn it so that the right sides of the fabric are touching each other and the wrong sides are facing you. Pin the sides together with pins perpendicular to the edge leaving a seven-inch space open on one side for a zipper. Use a gauge and insert pins ⅝ inch from edge of skirt to give an accurate seam line. Stitch at the machine on the pinned seam line, beginning and ending by backtacking. Go to the ironing board and press the seams open.

The next step is to insert the zipper. Buy a seven-inch skirt placket zipper that matches your material. Baste the seam along the opening you have left just as though you were going to close it up. Press the seam open, making a sharply creased edge, and pull out the basting. Crease back edge ⅛ inch outside first crease and re-press. Now pin the back edge of the skirt at the crease very close to the metal of the zipper. Baste with small close stitches. The zipper should be closed facing to the right side, the tab should be at top of opening. Use a cording or zipper foot to stitch very close to the metal. Pin the front edge of the opening over the zipper on the same side on which you have just stitched. The stitching should come to the fold. Baste straight down on the front side of the zipper, making sure that you have caught the tape and the material. Stitch very close to your basting, and across the bottom, making sure to backtack. Remove the pins and basting.

To gather the skirt, push the stitch-regulator lever all the way down (or turn the knob all the way to the right) to give you a very large stitch. Before you start to gather, mark a line ⅝ inch from the top edge of the skirt all the way around with tailor's chalk. Now, along this line, start stitching from the side seam to the middle of the front. When you cut the thread, leave a tail hanging of four to five inches. Now start again from the middle of the front where you stopped stitching and continue across to the other side seam. Repeat from the side seam to the middle of the back and then from this point to the side seam from which you started. Start again, and ¼ inch above the first gathering line; repeat the whole process, as before, in four sections.

Take out the waistband piece which you have set aside. Measure your waistline and cut off a piece from one short end so that band measures three inches more than your waist. Stitch two short ends, right sides together, trim seams, and turn right side out. Press sharp crease at top. Mark point three inches from end with a pin or chalk. Fold band in half crosswise to marked point and mark halfway point. Mark halfway point of each section so that you have four parts marked off, plus the three inches.

With the waistband on the wrong side of the skirt, pin through one thickness of the band so that the three-inch mark at the end is at the front edge of the zipper, the halfway mark at the side seam, and each of the other two marks at the center, where you have ended your gathering sections. Now pull up gathers in each section to fit waistband. Wind the threads around a pin to hold securely, then pin the band and skirt together and baste. Stitch ⅝ inch from edge, working carefully when you come to the pins. Turn band up, turn raw edge under ¼ inch, and baste over stitching on the right side of the skirt. Stitch very close to the fold, keeping the edge of the presser foot along the fold. Watch this, not the needle, as you stitch. Press and fasten the band with snaps or hooks and eyes carefully sewed on (see pp. 173, 175). Pull out all bastings and gathering lines if you wish.

Your last job is the hem. Try on the skirt and have someone mark it for you with a skirt marker or with a yardstick and pins. Turn the hem up all around on the marked line, putting your pins perpendicular to the bottom edge. Be sure you have pinned a careful smooth line and baste close to the bottom edge. Remove the pins and press. Even out the hem by measuring two inches all around from the bottom up to your pin line, using a gauge and mark with tailor's chalk. Cut off all around on this line. Now turn in the top edge of the hem ¼ inch and edgestitch. You do not need a hem binding on a washable cotton. Pin the stitched edge to the skirt, taking tiny little tucks all going in the same direction where there is too much fullness. Baste, remove the pins, and press.

Then hem, making your stitches practically invisible on the right side by catching only a thread or two of the material.

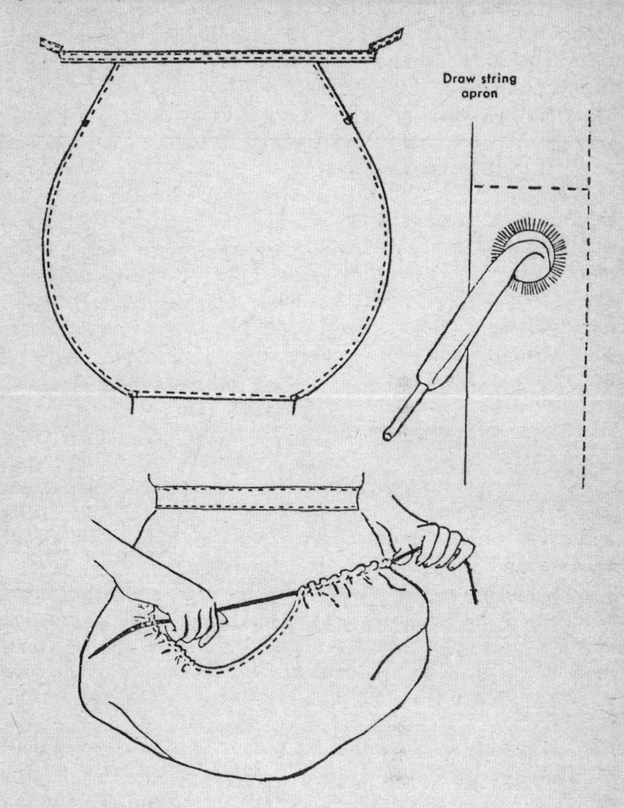


Here are four more practice projects that will give you useful additions to your working wardrobe.

A *square-bib apron* is a real cover-all and a three-way

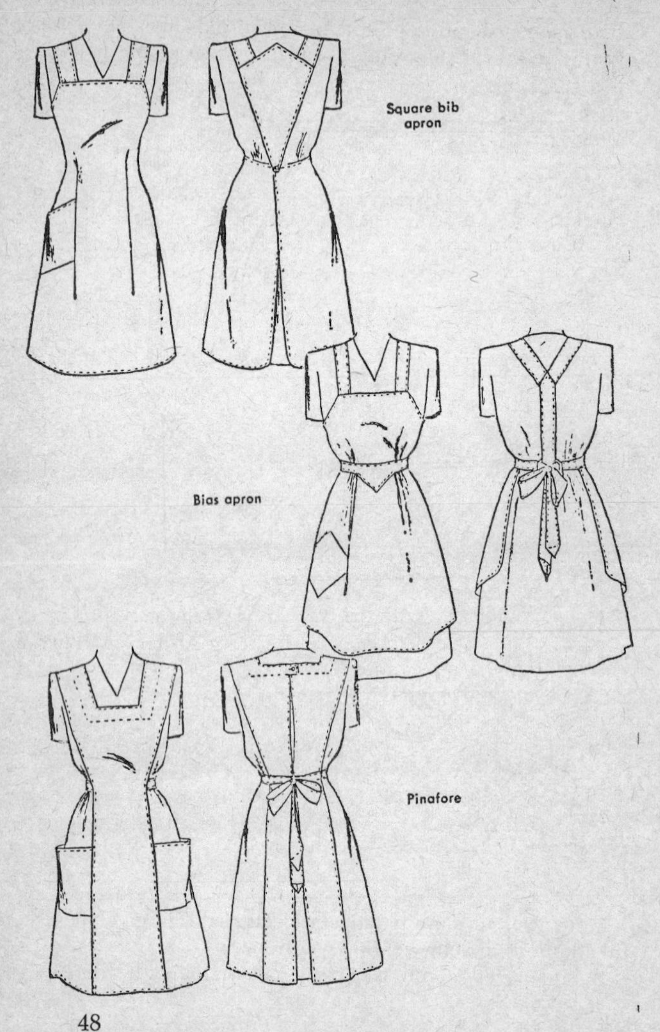
Square bib
apron
Bias apron
Pinafore

time-saver. It is easy to make, to put on and to iron. Cut crosswise of the goods, it has the bib and skirt in one piece. Shoulder straps can be pulled far apart so you needn't rumple your hair when you slip the apron on. The V-shaped waist piece and the skirt fasten over one easy-to-reach button in the back.

A *bias apron* is ideal for informal service, church suppers, etc. It should be made of a dainty print or a smart plaid. The whole project requires only a yard and a half of material—one yard for the apron body and an extra half yard for the pocket, straps and band.

Gathers to nip in the waist and a band with ties, applied over the gathers, give shape. A single band holds shoulder straps together in the back so they can't slide. The sash runs through two loops and ties at center back.

A streamlined *pinafore* is ideal for the woman who hasn't time to iron ruffles. The opening down the back requires only two fastenings, a button at the neck and a tie at the waist. This avoids the usual row of buttons that are awkward to fasten and may scratch furniture. Ample pockets in the gathered part of the skirt are particularly useful.

A double-duty *"basket apron"* folds up into a large pocket when you pull the drawstring. This is a serviceable round-the-house apron. When you pull the drawstrings you have a basket for carrying clothespins, garden pickings, eggs, or a mess of odds and ends. This apron should be made of sturdy cotton, with strong drawstrings that slip easily through the edge of the casings. Strong strings or heavy fishline may be used for this purpose. (See p. 47.)

# 9. *SELECTING A FABRIC*

THE fabric picture is not the simple, uncomplicated thing it used to be, for many fabrics are finished to masquerade as others, and new synthetics require special care. Fabrics are made from fibers from natural or synthetic (man-made) sources, spun into yarn, made into cloth in a variety of ways, and finished to give various effects and special qualities. The best known fibers and the ones you are most likely to use in your home sewing are the following:

*Cotton*: a vegetable fiber that grows around the seed of the cotton plant.

*Linen:* a vegetable fiber, possibly the oldest known fiber, that is obtained from the stem of the flax plant.

*Wool*: an animal fiber obtained from the fleece of the sheep.

*Silk:* an animal fiber spun by the silkworm as it makes its cocoon.

*Rayon:* a synthetic fiber, manufactured by three different processes, from wood pulp and chemicals.

*Nylon:* a synthetic manufactured from coal, air, water and other substances.

*Plastic:* a synthetic manufactured from cellulose, acid, and camphor.

*Glass fiber*: a synthetic made by heating glass tubes, which have been chemically treated, and pulling the resulting product into thread. You will be most likely to use this fiber for curtains, and possibly coat linings.

These fibers, after being cleaned and prepared, are spun into yarn, and then made into cloth. The following is a brief resumé of the different ways of cloth making.

1. Weaving: This is the most common way of making cloth.

There are several basic weaves and all the others are variations. If you examine cloth closely, you will be able to tell the kind of weave used.

–*Plain weave:* crosswise threads go over one lengthwise thread and under the next, in alternating rows.

–*Basket weave:* a variation of plain weave, in that two (or more) crosswise threads go over two (or more) lengthwise threads, and then under two (or more). Monk's cloth is an example of this weave.

–*Twill weave:* crosswise threads go over two lengthwise threads and then under two. On the next row, the crosswise thread goes under one, over two, then under two; and on the next row, under two, over two. The resulting effect is a diagonal one, as seen in cheviot and serge.

–*Herringbone* or chevron weave: a variation of the twill weave in that the diagonal goes down, then up, to give a characteristic chevron-like effect.

–*Satin weave:* the crosswise threads go over one lengthwise thread and then under several others to give the shiny effect that you see in dress and lingerie satins.

–*Crepe weave:* plain weave done with highly twisted threads or combination of plain and satin weaves to give an all-over pebbly surface.

–*Gauze weave:* crosswise threads go through paired and twisted lengthwise thread to give an open mesh effect. Leno is another name given to this type of weave and its best known example is marquisette, used for curtains.

–*Pile weave:* Loops are made on the cloth in the weaving and these are cut, as in velvet, or left uncut, as in terry cloth.

–*Figured weave:* a combination of plain, twill and satin weaves, where patterns are woven into the cloth. The Jacquard loom is used for this weave, as seen in damask and brocade.

–*Double weave:* done with two or more crosswise and two or more lengthwise threads to get reversible cloth with different color or design on each side.

–*Lappet weave:* plain or gauze weave in which a design

is embroidered during the weaving process, as in dotted swiss.

2. Knitting: This is a method of making cloth by connecting and interlocking loops. It gives great elasticity, is noncrushable, is easily laundered, and, if done by machine, is inexpensive.

3. Felting: This is a very old process for making cloth. Wool is treated with heat, pressure and moisture until felt of desired thickness and firmness is produced. Fine felt hats are made from fur.

4. Braiding: for certain flat or tubular fabrics.

5. Twisting: as in lace making.

6. Knotting: as in making nets.

Cloth is finished in a variety of ways, many of which are listed below:

—*Bleaching* to whiten.

—*Dyeing* for color.

—*Printing* for color and design.

—*Embossing* between rollers for a raised design.

—*Napping* with wires to pull up the short ends of the fibers for a fluffy, soft effect. The nap is then cut evenly.

—*Sueding* between emery-covered rollers.

—*Glazing* for a high sheen.

—*Mercerizing* to improve luster and add strength and elasticity. This is done by treating chemically with alkali.

—*Sizing* with starch to make fabric seem more firmly woven.

—*Weighting* with metallic salts, sugar, china clay, to give body and firmness to cloth.

—*Calendering* between heated rollers to give a glazed or watered surface.

—*Beetling* to bring out luster of linen by pounding with wooden hammers.

—*Tarnish proofing.*

—*Mothproofing.*

—*Waterproofing* or finishing to be water repellent.

—*Fireproofing.*

—*Mildewproofing.*

—Finishing for crush resistance.

–Finishing to prevent fading from the action of gas.

–Coating with milium, a metal applied to reflect heat, thus conserving warmth.

Frequently, it is important to be able to distinguish between different fibers. Some simple identification tests are discussed below.

1. If a sample of the fabric is burned, these are the results:

–*Cotton* flares up, burns quickly, smells like burned wood or paper, leaves a light, feathery ash.

–*Linen* burns like cotton.

–*Rayon (viscose* and *cuprammonium)* flares up, burns quickly, smells like burned paper, leaves almost no ash.

–*Rayon (acetate)* seems to melt and drip, the edges curl and pucker, smells like burned sugar with acrid odor.

–*Wool* burns slowly, smells like burning hair or feathers, stops burning if flame is removed, leaves crisp, beadlike ash.

–*Silk* burns slowly with a smoldering flame, leaves a crisp, black ball, smells like burning wool, but less intense.

–*Nylon* smells like burning sealing wax, melts as it burns, leaves a light brown, round hard bead.

2. If a thread is broken, the different fibers react differently.

–*Cotton:* the ends curl up, look dull and fuzzy.

–*Linen:* the thread snaps and the ends are hard and uneven.

–*Rayon:* the thread breaks easily and ends look like bundles of wires.

–*Wool:* the thread pulls apart and ends are kinky and springy.

–*Silk:* ends are smooth, straight, and lustrous.

–*Nylon:* ends are fuzzy.

3. Sometimes it is difficult to distinguish between cotton and linen. If oil is dropped on samples of cotton and linen cloth, the linen will develop a translucent spot, easily seen when held up to the light, while the cotton will remain opaque. Another distinguishing test for these two fibers is to see how fast they absorb a drop of water. Cotton holds the drop for a moment, then the water spreads slowly and un-

evenly. The water is immediately absorbed very evenly in the linen sample. Two samples of equal weight, when dropped into a dish of water, will show a difference, because linen absorbs so rapidly that it will sink to the bottom almost immediately.

4. Alkali will destroy animal fibers, so vegetable and animal fibers can be differentiated by treating a sample with ammonia, washing soda, lye, or Clorox. If the cloth has both kinds of fibers, the animal fiber will disintegrate and the vegetable part will be left.

In buying and handling material, there are certain terms used which the consumer should know. Some of the more common ones are listed below:

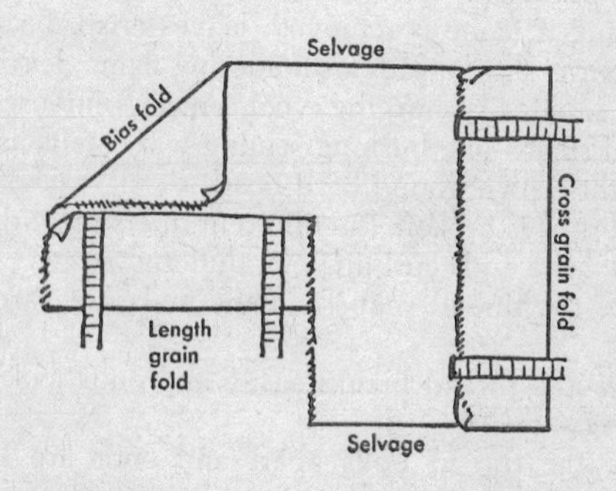


*Selvage* refers to the self-finished edge that will not ravel.

*Warp* refers to the lengthwise threads in the cloth. The warp threads are always parallel to the selvage. The warp threads are often the strongest threads in the fabric.

*Filling threads* are the crosswise threads that are woven over and under the warp. They run from selvage to selvage. They are also called the weft, the pick, the woof.

*Thread count* refers to the number of warp and filling

threads in one square inch of the fabric. It is an indication of quality, but not necessarily of strength.

*Yarn-dyed* means that the yarns were dyed before they were made into cloth.

*Piece-dyed* means that the cloth was dyed after it was woven.

*Seconds* or *irregulars* refer to fabric or garments with slight defects. Often these are oil spots, broken selvages, slight misweaves that do not affect wear.

*Carding* is preparing fibers for spinning into yarn by cleaning and straightening them with brushes.

*Combing* is a cleaning and straightening process that makes fibers smoother and more lustrous than just carding.

*Ply* refers to the number of threads twisted together to make yarn for making cloth. Two-ply means two threads; three-ply has three threads.

*Wale* is a rib or ridge as seen in corduroy or piqué.

*Tensile strength* refers to the amount of strain the fabric can stand without tearing.

*Abrasion resistance* refers to the amount of friction the fabric can stand without fraying or tearing.

*Slippage resistance* refers to resistance to slipping at the seams during wear, caused by slipping of warp threads across weft.

*Spun rayon* is rayon woven from very short yarns.

*Butcher linen* is spun rayon, not linen at all.

*Worsted* is hard and durable woolen fabric, made with long highly twisted fibers, laid completely parallel to each other.

*Virgin wool* is pure wool never used before, as it comes from the animal.

*Pulled wool* is wool removed with chemicals from the body of the dead animal.

*Reprocessed wool* is wool that has been woven into material once before but has never been worn.

*Re-used wool* or *reworked wool* is made from old garments that have been worn.

In buying fabric, examine samples as carefully as possible.

Study labels, and where you do not see a label, ask for one anyway. Sometimes it has fallen off the bolt. Crush the cloth in your hand, hold it up to the light, grasp it gently with both hands and pull it to test slippage. Look for evidence of shrinkage control on labels.

"Pre-shrunk" or "shrinkproof" on a label may mean nothing at all. The "Sanforized" label guarantees shrinkage of not more than 1%, an amount that will not affect the fit of the garment. A label should give a maximum shrinkage guarantee. In general, loosely woven materials shrink more than firmly woven ones.

Colorfastness is very important to the fabric shopper. The term "colorfast" alone is better than no guarantee at all, but it is more reassuring if it says colorfast to sunlight, or to washing, or to perspiration. Dyes guaranteed not to fade under one condition may under others. If there is no information available, try out a sample by washing, boiling, and exposing to strong sunlight. Be sure to buy washable notions for washable garments. Vat dyes are best for cottons.

Two-ply and three-ply yarns are stronger than singles, and give evidence of better quality. So do combed yarns. For durability, avoid novelty weaves and stick to plain or twill weaving. Yarn-dyed fabrics hold color better than piece-dyed ones. Look for balanced thread count, one with same or almost the same number of yarns in each direction; for example, an 80 square percale. This means 80 warp and 80 filling threads in one square inch. With silks, look for label "pure silk," or "pure dye silk."

If you buy a washable fabric that has not been pre-shrunk, shrink it yourself by placing the folded material in cool or lukewarm water for several hours. Dry it and press. Allow an extra ¼ yard for shrinkage when buying. For a wool fabric that has not been sponged, to pre-shrink it, allow an extra ⅛ of a yard, and roll it in a wet sheet. Allow it to stay overnight, then hang it carefully and allow it to dry. Press if necessary.

# 10. *SELECTING A STYLE*

## *Dressing to Suit Your Figure Type*

THERE is no "secret" to dressing well. If you will analyze your figure carefully, you will learn to select pattern lines that emphasize your good points—and that minimize your bad ones.

Women who have ideal or "average" figures can wear almost any line or style. But most of us are not that fortunate. You will probably find that you fall into one of the four basic figure classifications—or that you have one or more of the minor figure problems studied below. You may also find that you do not come under just *one* figure type or have just *one* problem. For example, you could be *short* with a *short neck* and *full bust.* You would have to look under the suggestions for the *short figure* and the *full bust figure* and under the suggestions for the *short neck.* On the other hand, you may be *tall* with a *flat chest* and *wide shoulders.* You would then look under the suggestions for the *tall figure* and under the suggestions for the *flat chest* and *wide shoulders.*

If you will combine the lines and style features suggested for your figure type with those suggested for your minor figure problems, you will find the styles that are flattering and right for *you.*

## WHAT TO DO ABOUT COMMON FIGURE PROBLEMS

**◄ SHORT OR PLUMP NECK?**
The V-neckline will be the most flattering. Use only simple finishing details at the neckline. Try your hair in an upswept style—it will add to your neck length.

**LONG THIN NECK? ►**
Choose high necklines, perhaps softened with ruffles, a choker necklace or a collar in a contrasting color. Hair should be long to detract from neck length.

**◄ NARROW SHOULDERS?**
Build up your shoulders with pads. Avoid the raglan or dolman sleeve. Wide lapels, puffed sleeves, short capes, pinafore effect, bright colored yokes and neckwear, and double breasted jackets are all good.

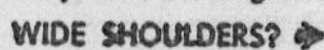

**WIDE SHOULDERS? ►**
Never use broadened, padded shoulders. Raglan and dolman sleeves, halter necklines and narrow lapels are good. Vertical lines in neckwear or trimming will draw the eye away from shoulder width.

**◄ LARGE WAISTLINE?**
Try to achieve an unbroken line from shoulder to hem with panel fronts, full length trimmings and coat-type dresses. Avoid accenting the waist with wide or contrasting belts.

**LARGE ABDOMEN? ►**
Avoid tight fitting clothes, double breasted styles and narrow skirts. Skirts with front drapery or fullness are good.

**◄ THIN OR HEAVY ARMS?**
Avoid extremes in sleeves—too tight or too loose. Instead, choose natural, soft effects.

**FLAT CHEST? ►**
Avoid tight fitting blouses. Wear shirred bodices, vestees, ruffles, jabots and fabrics with crispness and "body."

## BASIC PRINCIPLES FOR THE FOUR FIGURE TYPES

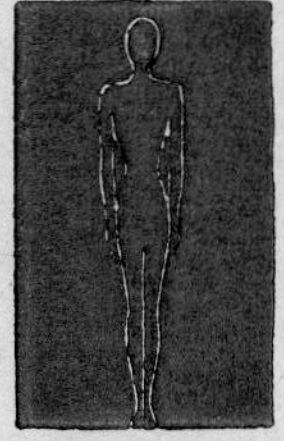

### ARE YOU TALL?

If you are over 5' 7", you fall into this classification. Avoid the up-and-down lines that add to your height. Instead, make an asset of your height by wearing the bold dramatic clothes that no other type can carry. Never try to appear shorter by "stooping over."

1. Dramatic peplums cut height.

2. Wide belts and interesting details through the torso are good.

3. Double breasted suits are flattering.

1. Long torso effects equalize leg length.

2. Skirts should be slightly flared —never tight.

3. Jackets should be fairly long.

1. Waistlines extending below the belt are slenderizing.

2. Two-piece dresses with a soft look are good.

3. Coats may be straight or full cut —either three quarter or full length.

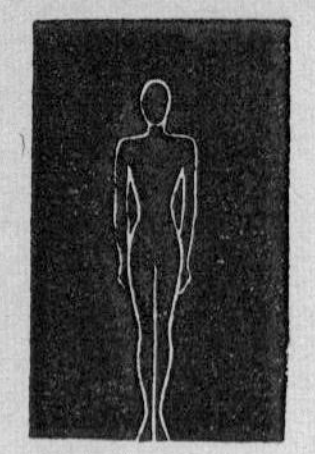

### ARE YOU SHORT?

You are "short" if you are 5' 3" or less. You will want to wear lines that carry the eye up and down, giving a longer overall effect. Choose softness in line and detail. Avoid bold prints, dramatic or mannish clothes which tend to over burden your figure.

1. Short boleros and high-cut waistlines are good.

2. Princess lines—unbelted or with a very narrow belt.

3. Try pinafore effects with lowered waistlines.

**All Short Figures**

1. Button-down-the-front dresses give a long, smooth line.

2. Pockets should be high placed.

3. Unbelted, full length sport coats add height.

**Short, Full Figure**

1. Wear gored or tucked skirts with matching lines in bodice.

2. Fullness in bodice just below bust is flattering.

3. Try variations of the princess style and contrasting front panels.

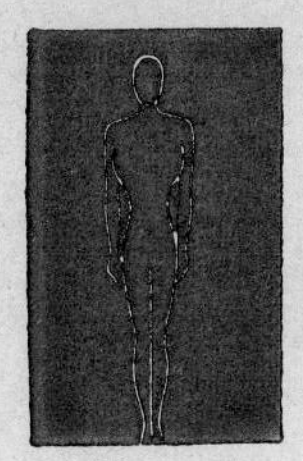

## ARE YOU LARGE AT THE TOP?

If you are "top heavy," you will want to wear lines that emphasize your slimmer hips and draw the eye away from your bust. Never wear tight fitting clothes—do not try to wear clothes with "fussy" details.

1. Fancy low-cut necklines are good.

2. Try tapered fullness at the shoulder.

3. Boxy jackets with slim skirts are good.

1. Wear a simple untrimmed bodice with interesting skirt details.

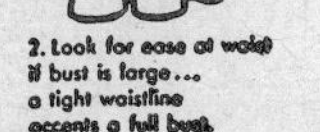

2. Look for ease at waist if bust is large... a tight waistline accents a full bust.

3. Straight boxy, collarless sports coats are excellent.

1. Wear V-shaped vestees or dickies, with flattering ease in bodice.

2. Surplus style bodices are flattering.

3. Coat dresses or redingotes achieve a slim line.

# SELECTING A STYLE

## ARE YOU LARGER OVER THE HIPS?

This is your figure type if your hips measure 12 or more inches larger than your waist. You should wear lines that draw attention to the *upper part of your figure.* Be careful to wear skirts that are not too tight fitting as they will emphasize your hips.

**Average with full hips:**

1. Tapered lines from waist to shoulder on dresses and suits are good.

2. Contrasting darker skirts make hips appear slimmer.

3. Try dresses with front fullness, plain back.

**All full-hipped figures:**

1. Contrasting yokes and sleeves draw the eye away from hips.

2. Keep skirt flared even in "straight skirt" seasons.

3. Wear boxy, straight or tuxedo front coats.

**Plump, with full hips:**

1. Wear interesting shoulder details.

2. Fly front or buttoned front dresses are slimming.

3. Contrasting vestees or blouses to draw attention to upper part of figure are flattering.

# 11. *PATTERNS AND THEIR ADJUSTMENT*

## *How to Select the Correct Pattern Size*

When you buy your pattern, *don't* ask for the size you wear in a ready-made dress. You may find that you will need an entirely different size in a pattern. So that you will get "made-to-order" fit easily and quickly, follow the instructions below in choosing your pattern size.

1. Take your measurements or have the salesgirl take them for you. (See next page.)

2. Check your own measurements against the scale on next page. These are the standard measurements found in any pattern catalog at your favorite store.

3. It is usually best to buy the pattern size nearest your bust measurement and then make the other necessary adjustments.

*Exceptions to this are: A.* Your hips are unusually large in proportion to bust measurement. In this case, buy according to hip measurement and adjust top section to your measurements. (Consult pattern instruction sheet for directions.)

*B.* The pattern has a complicated skirt section. Order the pattern size nearest to your hip measurement because it will be simpler to adjust the blouse than the skirt in this case. (Consult pattern instruction sheet for directions.)

*Note:* If the difference between your hip and bust measurements is so great that the above method seems inadvisable, order two size patterns. It will then be fairly simple to make the necessary adjustment at the waistline.

### *How to Measure for Patterns*

1. *Bust:* Measure bust round largest part. Hold tape easily; do not pull too tight. Do not let it slip down in back.
2. *Waist:* Measure natural waistline. Hold tape easily, do not pull too tight.
3. *Hips:* Measure hips about seven inches below natural waistline. Tape may be drawn fairly tight.
4. *Sleeves:* Measure length of arm from armpit to wrist. Do not pull tape too tight.

### *Scale of Measurements for Women's and Misses' Patterns*

| Size | 10 | 12 | 14 | 16 | 18 | 20 | 40 | 42 | 44 | 46 |
|---|---|---|---|---|---|---|---|---|---|---|
| Bust | 28 | 30 | 32 | 34 | 36 | 38 | 40 | 42 | 44 | 46 |
| Waist | 24 | 25 | 26½ | 28 | 30 | 32 | 34 | 36 | 38 | 40 |
| Hips | 31 | 33 | 35 | 37 | 39 | 41 | 43 | 45 | 47½ | 50 |
| Sleeve length (underarm) | 16¼ | 16½ | 17 | 17½ | 18 | 18 | 17¾ | 17¾ | 17½ | 17½ |

There are two types of patterns to choose from: printed, which have all guide line directions printed on the pattern, and perforated, which have little holes, or perforations, usually in three sizes. Before you choose a pattern, consider first your ability to sew. If you are a beginner, do not start with a garment that has difficult lines and a great many details. Choose a style suitable for your knowledge, skill, and needs. Buy a skirt pattern by the size of your waist, and a blouse or dress pattern by the size of your bust. The usual measurements for women's sizes are shown in the chart above.

Buying according to bust measurement is very important, for it is much easier to alter the waist and hips than it is to change the bust. If your bust is 33, most often a 16 pattern, which is cut for a 34 bust, will be your best choice. Commercial patterns are cut a size smaller than ready-to-wear garments.

All your measurements should be taken very carefully, and written down. Do not hold the tape too tightly.

### *Measurements Needed to Check the Pattern*

1. *Bust:* Measure fullest part of bust, keeping tape parallel to the floor. Measure both front and back between side seams.

2. *Chest width:* At a point six inches down from shoulder seam at neck line, measure from armhole seam to armhole seam.

3. *Back neck seam:* Measure along back neck line, from shoulder seam to shoulder seam. Stand tape on edge to measure a good curve.

4. *Upper back width:* Measure straight across back from top of one armhole seam to the other.

5. *Width across shoulder blades:* At a point seven inches down from shoulder seam at neck line, measure from armhole seam to armhole seam.

6. *Blouse length, center front:* Measure from base of neck straight down to waistline.

7. *Blouse length, center back:* Measure from collarbone at back of neck to waistline.

8. *Blouse length, over bust:* Measure from middle of shoulder seam, over bust, straight down to waistline. Keep tape parallel to center front.

9. *Blouse length, over shoulder blades:* Measure from middle of shoulder seam, over shoulder blades, to waistline. Keep tape parallel to center back.

10. *Armhole depth:* Tie a cord around your chest, level with bottom of armhole. Measure from shoulder seam at neck line straight down to this cord. If one shoulder is higher than the other, measure the high one.

11. *Shoulder height:* Measure from shoulder seam at top of armhole, down the back to the cord tied around your chest.

**MEASUREMENTS NEEDED TO CHECK THE PATTERN**

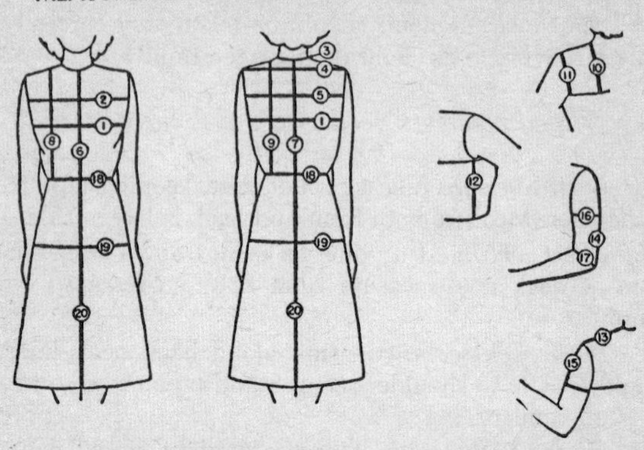

12. *Underarm length:* From the cord tied around your chest, measure from armhole down to waistline. Or measure the underarm seam length if you are wearing a dress.

13. *Shoulder length:* Measure from base of neck to top of armhole line.

14. *Sleeve length:* Measure from top of armhole, down over the elbow with arm bent, to wristbone. Also measure distance from elbow to wristbone.

15. *Sleeve-cap length:* Tie a cord around your arm, level with the bottom of the armhole. Measure from top of armhole seam to this cord.

16. *Upper arm (or sleeve width):* Measure around fullest part of upper arm. This is usually at bottom of armhole. Also record distance of this measurement from the top of the armhole seam.

17. *Elbow:* Measure around elbow, with arm bent.

18. *Waistline:* Measure snugly where you want the belt to be. Take both front and back measurements between side seams.

19. *Hips:* Measure at widest part of hips or thigh, whichever is larger, keeping tape parallel to the floor. Record distance of this measurement from the waistline.

20. *Skirt length:* Measure from the waistline to bottom of the skirt or desired distance from the floor—at center front, center back, and sides.

Check the style version you are going to make on the outside of the envelope, then take out the guide sheet, and find what pieces you will need for this version. Take them out and get ready to alter the pattern to fit you. It's a rare person who will be perfectly fitted without some changes. The whole problem in fitting is to adjust material to the rounded lines of the body. Since you cannot slash into the fabric, you must alter the paper pattern.

To measure the pattern, pin in all darts, tucks, pleats, etc. Pin the front and back bodice pieces together at the side seam, one over the other, flat. Do the same with the skirt pieces, and pin them together at the waistline. Be careful to note seam allowances, and special margins on some patterns. Do not include them in your measuring. Measure the pattern from center front to center back along the waist seam line, through the fullest part of the bust, at the hips seven inches below the waist, and at all other measurements on the chart above. Compare these with your own measurements, but remember that you are measuring only half the pattern. In addition, you must have additional allowances for ease, usually three inches for the bust and hips, one inch for the waist, ½ inch at elbow and front and back waist length. Note what adjustments you must make. Example:

| | Your measurements | Pattern measurements | Necessary change |
|---|---|---|---|
| Waist...... | 27 inches | 14½ inches (29 inches) | Take off 1 inch |
| Bust......... | 34 inches | 18½ inches (37 inches) | No change |
| Hips ...... | 38 inches | 20 inches (40 inches) | Add 1 inch |

Your waist is 27 inches and you need 1 inch for ease. The figure in the parentheses (29 inches), is the actual measurement after you have doubled the half figure. You must, therefore, make the pattern one inch smaller in the waist. Thirty-four-inch bust plus three inches for ease is 37 inches, therefore, there is no change. Thirty-eight-inch hips plus three inches allowance for ease is 41 inches. Therefore, you must add one inch.

All the more common alterations are illustrated in the following pictures. There are a few very important points to bear in mind.

1. In lengthening and shortening, always make fold or slash perpendicular to the grain lines of the pattern (shown by the arrow or perforation) or to the lengthwise grain line.

2. In allowing for increases or decreases in width, always have folds or slashes parallel to center front and back lines.

3. If one piece is changed, alter all pieces which must be attached to it, so that the pattern will still fit together perfectly when you are finished.

*To shorten waist:* Make a tuck between waist and bust.

*To shorten skirt:* Make a tuck between hip and knee.

*To lengthen waist:* Slash pattern between waist and bust. Insert tissue paper, pinning at edges.

*To lengthen skirt:* Slash pattern between hip and knee. Insert tissue paper, pinning at edges.

*To shorten sleeve:* Make tucks between shoulder and elbow and between elbow and wrist.

*To lengthen sleeve:* Slash pattern and insert tissue paper, pinning at edges, between shoulder and elbow and between elbow and wrist.

*To widen shoulders:*

a. Make a spreading lengthwise slash from shoulder to waist. This includes alterations for bust and chest.

b. Make a right-angled slash from shoulder to armscye (armhole) to include alteration for chest.

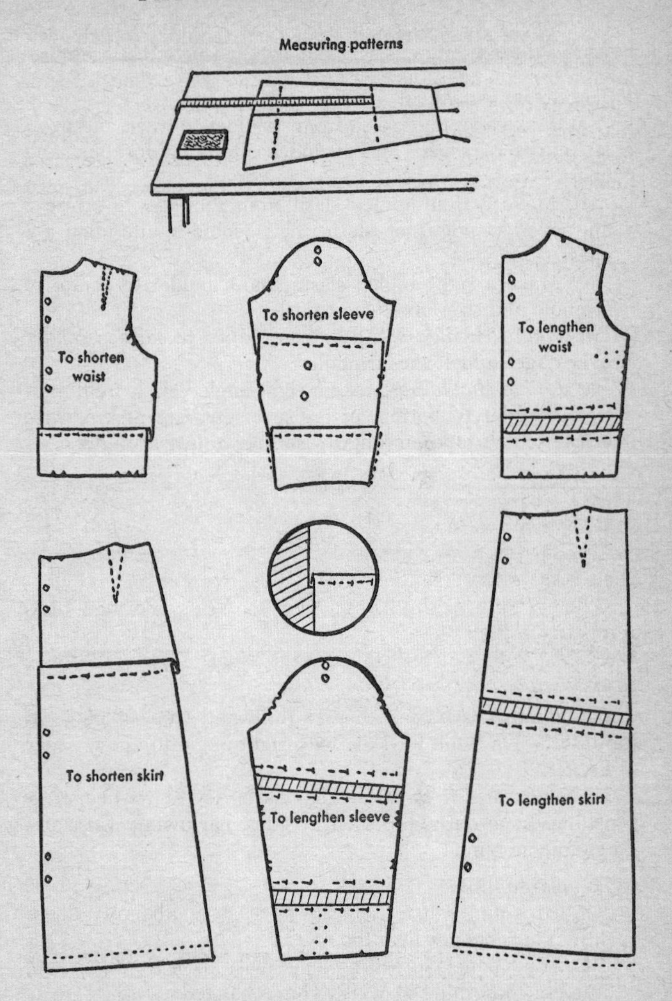
Measuring patterns
To shorten waist
To shorten sleeve
To lengthen waist
To shorten skirt
To lengthen sleeve
To lengthen skirt

c. Make a right-angled slash from shoulder to center of armhole (for shoulder alteration only).

*To narrow shoulders:*

a. Make a straight slash from shoulder to waist and overlap edges of slash. This includes alteration for bust and chest.

b. Make a right-angled slash from shoulder to armscye and overlap edges of slash. This includes alteration for chest.

c. Make a right-angled slash from shoulder to center of armhole and overlap edge of slash.

*For square shoulders:* Add tissue paper to raise shoulder at arm edge, and lower armhole.

*For sloping shoulders:* Make a right-angled slash from middle of shoulder to bottom of armscye. Overlap at crosswise line, use scotch tape on lengthwise line, adjust shoulder.

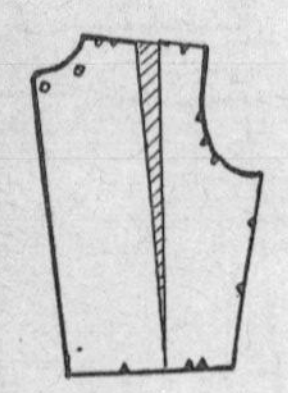

**Left: To widen shoulders**

**Right: To narrow shoulders**

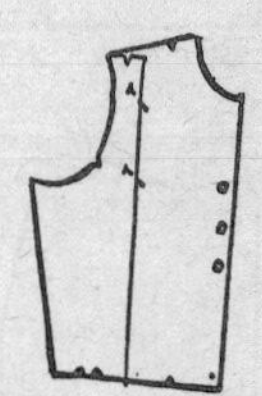

*To enlarge waist:* Slash bodice front and back making tissue inserts. Do same for skirt with right angle to allow paper to lie flat.

*To narrow waist:* If pattern has darts, sew darts deeper at waistline. If no darts, taper off at sides, narrowing waist and skirt same amount.

*To enlarge hips:*

a. Hips and waist: Lengthwise slash all the way down skirt. This changes hem too.

b. Hips alone: Spreading lengthwise slash from hem up, tapering to nothing at waist. Hem changed.

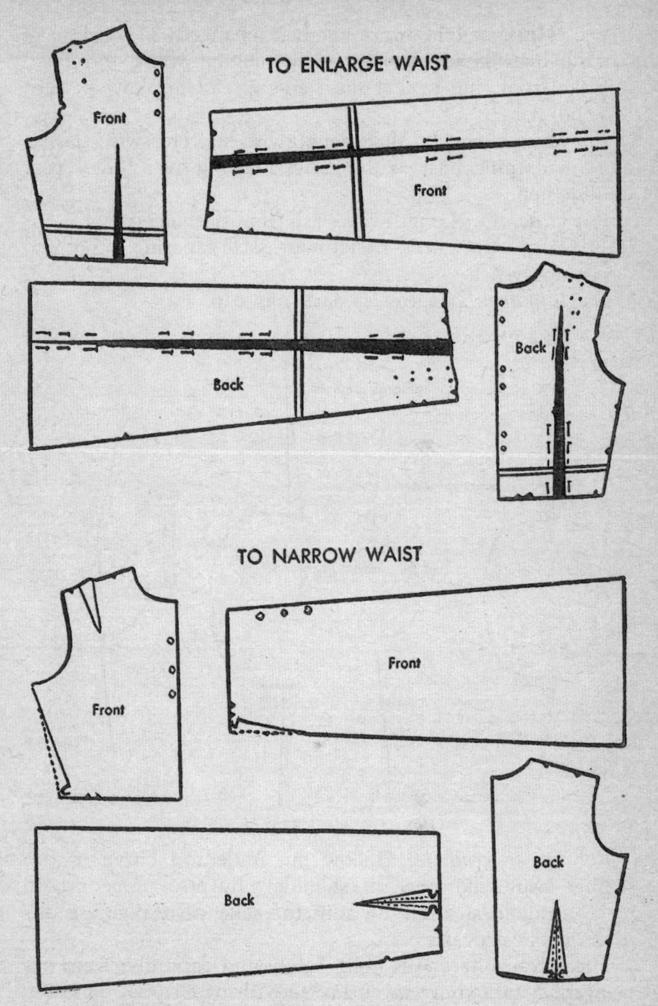
TO ENLARGE WAIST
Front
Front
Back
Back
TO NARROW WAIST
Front
Front
Back
Back

c. Hips, neither waist nor hem changed: Make a slash wide over hips, tapering to nothing at waist and hem. Slash from side to first slash and spread to allow pattern to fall flat.

*For large stomach:* Make lengthwise and crosswise slashes as for enlarging bust, with slashes meeting over fullest part of abdomen.

*For large arm:* Lengthwise slash from sleeve cap.

*For large upper arm:* Lengthwise slash tapering to nothing at cap and wrist.

*For thin arm:* Lengthwise dart from cap.

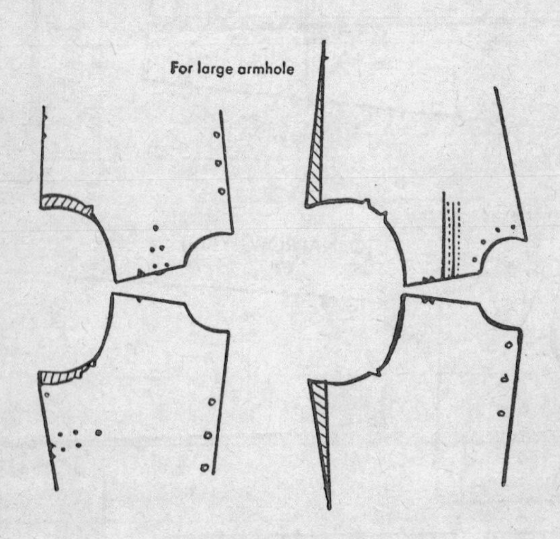


*For larger armhole:* Hollow out underarm curve or use smaller seam allowance at shoulder. Reverse procedure to make armhole smaller. Be sure to make corresponding adjustments in sleeves.

Make your alterations deliberately and carefully. Keep remeasuring with your tape measure with pattern flat on table.

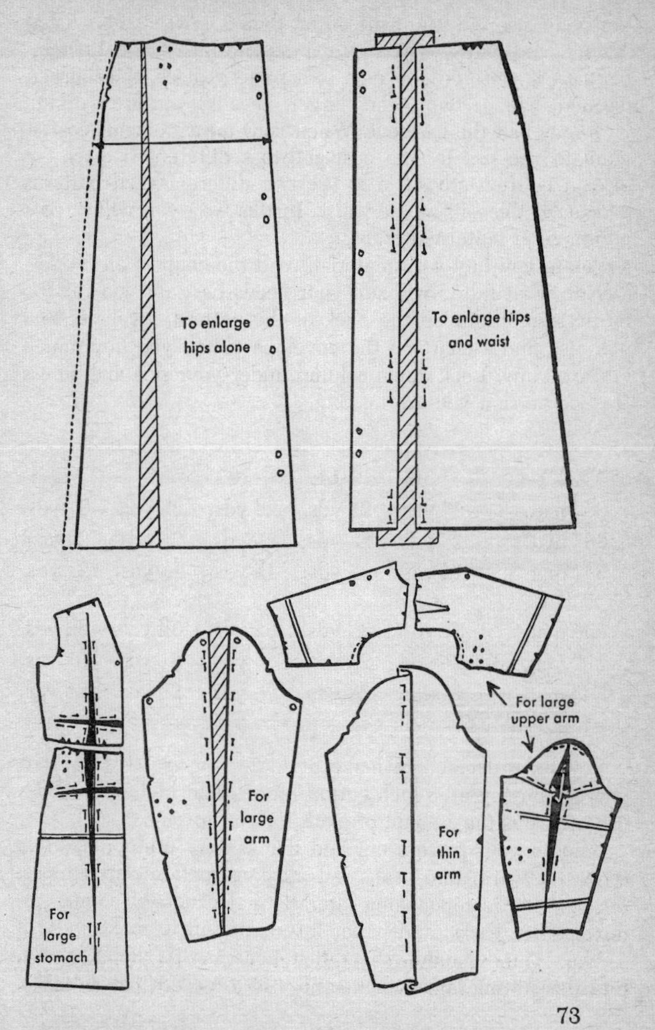
To enlarge hips alone
To enlarge hips and waist
For large stomach
For large arm
For thin arm
For large upper arm

You may also try your pattern on, but this is not very satisfactory, and will give you only a general idea of fit. Remember that if you add one inch to a pattern piece, the finished garment will be two inches larger, because you are working with only half the garment. When your measurements correspond to one size for the bust and to a different size for the hips, it is often advisable to use two different-sized patterns and make them fit at the waist. In this way you will have a minimum of pattern alteration.

Before you buy your material, read the chapter on fabrics. Decide what fabric will suit your needs best and look at the fabric suggestions on the back of the pattern envelope. You will also find a chart on the envelope to tell you how much fabric to buy. Look down column under your size and across to style version you are making.

| STYLE 1 | 12 | 14 | 16 | 18 | 20 |
|---|---|---|---|---|---|
| 35″ mat. | 2¼ yds. | 2¼ yds. | 2½ yds. | 2¾ yds. | 3 yds. |
| 39″ mat. | 2 yds. | 2 yds. | 2¼ yds. | 2½ yds. | 2¾ yds. |
| 54″ mat. | 1½ yds. | 1½ yds. | 1¾ yds. | 1¾ yds. | 2 yds. |
| STYLE 2 | | | | | |
| 35″ mat. | 3 yds. | 3 yds. | 3¼ yds. | 3¼ yds. | 3½ yds. |
| 39″ mat. | 2¾ yds. | 2¾ yds. | 3 yds. | 3 yds. | 3¼ yds. |
| 54″ mat. | 2¼ yds. | 2¼ yds. | 2¼ yds. | 2¼ yds. | 2¾ yds. |

You have decided to make Style 2. You are size 16, and you are buying a 35-inch cotton fabric. The underscored figure indicates the amount of cloth for you to buy.

Smooth your pattern out and if it is very crumpled, press it with a warm iron. Take out all construction darts, tucks, etc., pinned in for making alterations. Do not, of course, remove darts, tucks, and paper inserts put in to make pattern fit you. On the guide sheet that comes with your pattern, find the cutting layout that applies to you. You will find this

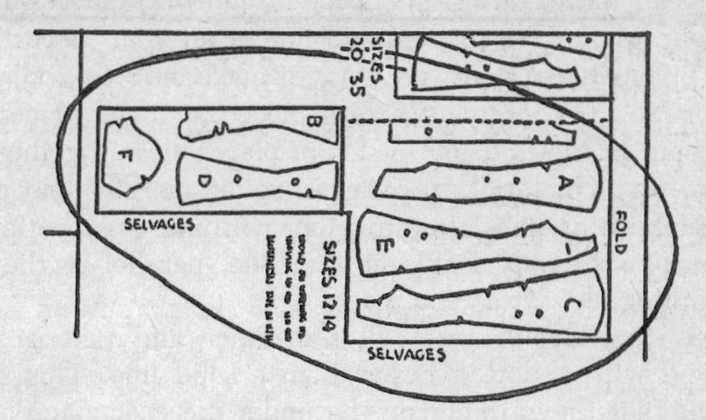


Circle the layout for identification

in a similar way to that in which you found out the amount of material to be bought: by style version, your size, and the width of your material. Circle it so you can find it again easily. Straighten your material by pulling a crosswise thread and cutting across from selvage to selvage. Press to remove wrinkles and lay cloth on table making the kind of fold indicated in the circled layout.

Before you start to pin, there are certain points which you must have clearly in mind. Perfect grain lines are the secret of professional looking clothes that hang right and fit right. Fabric has three grains, lengthwise, crosswise, and bias. The lengthwise or straight of the goods will, as a general rule, hang straight from top to bottom on your figure. In placing pattern on cloth, the grain lines must be measured so that they are perfectly accurate. The lengthwise grain line is indicated on your pattern with an arrow or series of perforations. To get it right, do the following:

Place pattern on the fabric so that the arrow seems parallel to the selvage. Put a pin at one end of the arrow, and measure with a ruler the distance from this end of the arrow to the selvage. Measure the other side, adjust and pin. Remeasure to be sure. DO NOT GUESS. With very short arrows, lengthen the line with a ruler.

Put all pieces on in this fashion, following the order given in your layout. Pin in the grain line of all your pieces before you put in the rest of the pins, to make sure that all pieces fit on fabric properly. Where a piece has to be placed on a fold, pin in the fold line first. Pin pieces close together so as not to waste material. In patterns having margins that get cut off, pin cutting lines close together with margins overlapping. Place pins directly inside cutting line, parallel to the edge, smoothing out flat as you work.

On your layout, you will sometimes find pattern pieces printed with a dotted rather than a solid line. This usually means that they are cut on the under piece of material with something else cut out of the upper thickness. Or it may mean that the piece has to be cut twice or on a fold. Use your common sense and you will easily be able to decide what to do.

When cutting, use shears and cut with long straight strokes, not short choppy ones. When you come to a notch, cut it out,

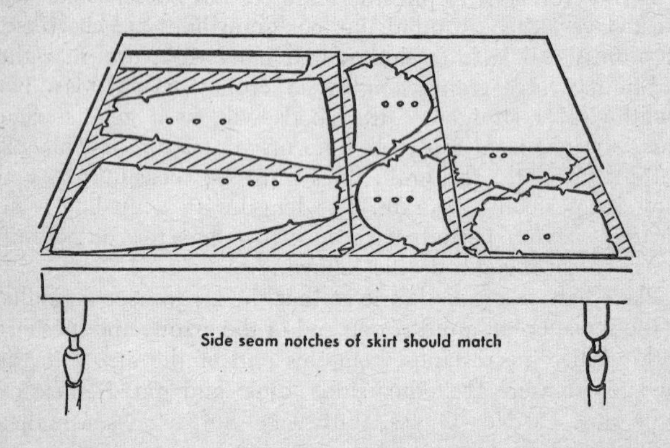

Side seam notches of skirt should match

not in, so that you do not weaken the seam at that point. Notches will help you put your pieces together later on. Do not remove the pattern after the piece is cut. Always keep your work flat on the table as you cut, with one hand holding down the fabric close to where you are cutting.

Certain materials have to be cut very carefully. Where a fabric has a design running all in one direction, all pattern pieces must face the same way, or you will end up with some parts of the print upside down. For such materials, the pattern pieces are placed on single thicknesses of material and cut twice. The same principle applies to napped fabrics like corduroy and velvet, and to plaids. The chart which tells you how much fabric to buy will usually tell you how much extra you need, by saying "fabrics with nap." One-half yard is the usual extra allowance needed, but sometimes it is more. Be sure to match plaids at sides, center seams, and sleeves. With large prints, match the design at center seams. See the special cutting notes, which follow this chapter.

Study your pattern guide carefully and thoroughly. Be sure to note any special cutting instructions. Do not cut in haste, for once you have cut, you cannot undo your work.

One more point. When cutting out fabrics that fray readily, it is advisable to cut an extra ¼ inch over the seam allowance of the pattern for finishing the seams later. It is also a good idea to cut an extra ¼ inch or ½ inch on the seam allowance where the zipper will later be inserted.

# 12. *CUTTING AND MARKING THE WORK*

When fabrics are napped, or have a definite up and down design, the pattern must be placed on the fabric and cut with all pieces facing in the same direction. If you do not do this, you will find that your finished velveteen dress seems lighter in some parts, and considerably darker in others, or that your new print is upside down in the back. A fabric that has a diagonal weave, such as gabardine, must be treated as though it had an up and down design. Thus, you may not fold material crosswise and cut out both skirt halves at once as usual. You must cut one on single fabric thickness, and then the second similarly but with the pattern on the reverse side. You may make lengthwise folds, however, without danger.

Where you are using a print of any considerable size, decide how you want the print motifs spaced on your finished garment. Don't cut without a little planning. Space prints so that joinings at seam will be graceful.

With stripes, plaids, and border designs, you must make up your mind to slightly unlearn some of what you have just learned, namely: to be careful to put pattern pieces on the fabric, watching that the markings indicating straight of goods are accurate. Sometimes, in order to match stripes, we must put pieces on crosswise grain. For example: with border prints, the designs are usually printed along the selvage, and therefore pieces which will have a border of this design are placed on the crosswise. If the border design is of such a nature that it need not follow a straight edge, then the pattern pieces may be cut on proper grain.

With plaids, it is necessary to study the plaid enough to see if there is an up and down to the design, or a right and left. With a right and left motif, be sure that the pattern is centered on a center line of the design. This is a crosswise line. With an up and down design, the pattern is placed on a lengthwise line that is central to the design. In some cases, in order to get the design right, pieces that would ordinarily be placed on a fold must be cut with a seam allowance and seamed together. See that matching notches, as at side seams, at sleeve and armhole, etc., are placed on same color or size stripe in the design. Darkest or heaviest stripes should face towards the bottom of the garment, and are most pleasing when they fall directly across the shoulder. Very often the design cannot be matched the whole distance of a skirt seam, or around the entire sleeve curve, and the matching of a small portion is sufficient.

It is necessary to buy extra fabric in order to be able to match designs. Some material must be wasted in this process. As little as ¼ yard, or as much as one yard, is necessary, depending on the kind of design. Sometimes it is said that you should buy a length equal to the size of the complete design without repetition, for each two places that must be matched.

Before you remove the pattern from the fabric, you must mark all guide lines. The most satisfactory way is with tailor tacks, because they mark all sides of the cloth at one time. To make a tailor tack, use a long double thread (heavy thread or darning cotton is the best) without a knot, and take a tiny stitch in the center of a perforation, leaving a piece of thread about ½ inch to ¾ inch hanging. To complete the tack,

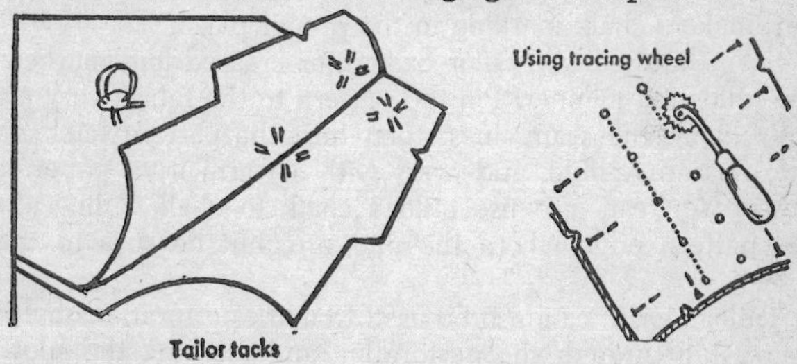

Tailor tacks

take another tiny stitch, leaving a good sized loop and another piece of thread. If there are several perforations in a row, save time by going from one to the other, leaving a good sized piece of thread between. Later cut these threads through the center between the loops. If the pattern is printed, use a hole punch or simply scratch a hole with a pin, so that you do not catch the paper when making the tacks. Tailor tack all marks for darts, tucks, pleats, and matching points. Tailor baste seam lines, gathering lines, pocket outlines, etc. To tailor baste, use a double thread, make lines of even basting, but leave loops instead of flat stitches on right side. Cut through the thread loops to remove the pattern from the material.

Now remove the pattern. The tailor tacks will come right through the holes. It is advisable to use threads of several different colors in tailor tacking and basting so that you will be able to distinguish the different markings later. Make a note of the color that is used for each purpose. Always mark the center front and back lines in skirt and bodice pieces.

After the pattern is removed, spread the two sections of material apart carefully and clip through the center of the threads. Thread markings will be visible on all four sides.

A tracing wheel will mark lines accurately and quickly but it can be used only on certain fabrics, like cotton and linen and silk. Use tracing paper with wheel.

The notches you have cut out will enable you to put matching pieces together properly. If you have neglected to cut any out, make a chalk marking in the proper place.

Seam lines can be tailor basted, or creased and marked in the following manner. Pin the pattern to the fabric very carefully along the seam lines, then turn the pattern back until the pins are visible, and press with a warm iron, paper side down. You can also use tailor's chalk to chalk a line along the pattern edge where the pins are, but be sure to use a ruler.

Tailor's chalk can also be used to mark perforations by putting a pin through the perforation and marking the spot on both sides with the chalk. Or, one piece of chalk may be placed on the under side of the perforation, and the top side marked with a second piece fairly heavily so that pressure will cause the under piece of chalk to leave its imprint also. Still another method is to use chalked thread. Thread a needle, run thread over tailor's chalk and put needle through perforation. Small chalk dot will be left on all pieces. Renew chalk frequently.

Marking accurate, true guide lines can not be overemphasized if you are striving for perfection. No time spent in marking your work is wasted.

After all guide lines are in, make a line of uneven basting on the center front and the center back. Have the long stitches on the right side of the garment. A line of running stitches or machine stitches ¼ inch from the edge of the armhole and the neckline and around the waist of the skirt will prevent stretching.

To pin baste, place pins (no more than four inches apart, and closer on curved seams) perpendicular to the edge of the material, with the heads facing out so that they may be easily removed as you come to them. Machines with hinged feet will sew over pins placed this way, and an experienced person can eliminate basting with thread. When you put pins in for fitting, be sure to pin them parallel to the edge.

You may baste in several ways when putting your work together. Dressmaker's basting is best on long seams because it is easily done and holds the material firmly. Diagonal basting is good for fabrics that slip easily, and slip stitch or alteration basting is used for matching plaids or when basting alterations made on the right side of the garment. (See pp. 9, 10 for complete directions and illustrations.)

For seams that will get a lot of strain in fitting, it is a good idea to use machine basting, because of its strength. Use the longest stitch (push the stitch regulator all the way down) to make it easy to rip later.

And speaking of ripping, this is how you do it. Break one stitch with a pin or fine scissors, scratch the loose thread with

# 13. *FITTING*

No MATTER how well a dress is made, it will lose all its value if it does not fit its wearer properly. The first step in fitting is choice of a pattern of correct size, and one that is suitable in style for the wearer. The next step is proper alteration of the pattern to fit individual measurements. Ways of adjusting the pattern for different problems are described from pp. 63 to 77. Even careful choice of a pattern and accurate alteration do not completely eliminate fitting, for fit on paper does not mean that fabric will drape "just so" or conform to body lines perfectly.

There is definitely such a thing as fitting too much, being too critical, and forgetting that certain fullness may be part of the design. Don't fit yourself when you are in a tense mood, ready to pick on anything and everything. Approach fittings in a relaxed frame of mind and don't change things on the spur of the moment. Be methodical; move slowly. Be sure that the garment is well pressed before you try it on. If you have pressed as you sewed, there is little additional pressing necessary when it is time to fit the garment on.

It is important to analyze the reasons for whatever difficulties you find, such as wrinkles, pulling of fabric, bulges, etc. When you know what is causing the trouble, think about how to remedy it. Only when you are sure of yourself should you make a change. Make a careful note of what to do to change your next pattern to avoid a similar fitting problem. In general, it is a good idea to work from the shoulders down, because the weight of the garment hangs from the top. Look for each of the following details.

*Shoulder line* must be straight, smooth and becoming. It must not be too high or too low, nor must it extend out too far.

*The waistline* must be an even straight line following the natural waist curve. Too high a waistline is very uncomfortable for the wearer. Too low a waistline is unbecoming. The waist should be snug without being tight.

*The center front* and center back lines are perpendicular to the floor and conform to the center lines of the body.

*The bustline* appears smooth and has an easy fit. Gathers will fall in a straight line over the bust towards the waist, but will not slant towards the underarm seam.

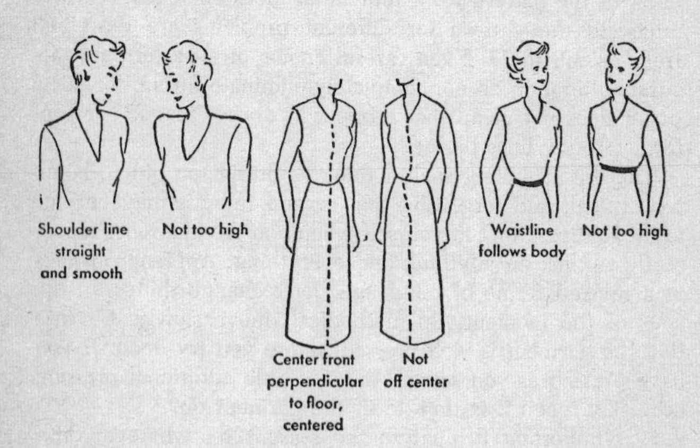


*The side seams* hang straight down to the floor. The hips have a smooth and easy fit, never snug.

*The sleeve* hangs straight without twisting, no pulling up when the arm is bent.

*The hem* is straight and even. It is a good idea to let a dress hang for a while before putting up the hem. This is especially true of a garment cut on the bias.

When fitting, pin all openings together as they will be in the finished garment. Wear the dress over a proper foundation garment and with proper shoes. Don't wriggle around and don't stand stiff as a ramrod. Keep your body relaxed and in a natural position.

It is often easier to fit the bodice of a dress and the skirt separately, then join them together later. However, the new way of fitting garments is to finish the entire front, then the entire back, join them at the shoulders, and fit the sides on the body. The sleeves, at this point, are not yet in. Fit over the shoulder pads, for they can make a great deal of difference. Pin the side seams from waist to armscye, to get a smooth effect over the midriff and an easy fit over the bust. Then pin side seams from waist to several inches below the fullest part of the hips.

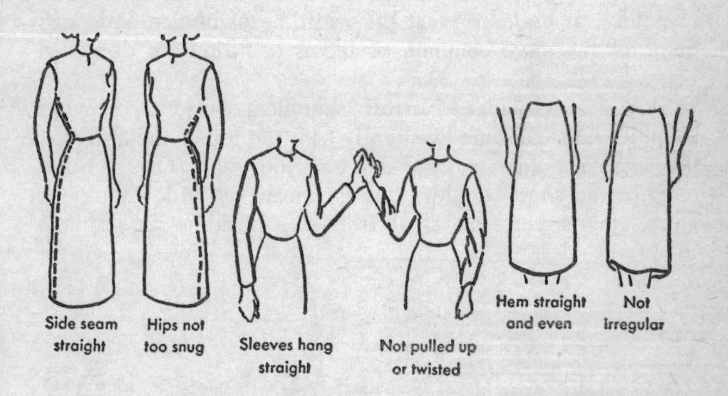


Remove the dress by leaving the pins on one side of the seam, that is, by pulling the pin out just far enough to release one side of the seam. Later the seam will be stitched using the same seam allowance on both sides. The seam allowance of the last pin below the hips will indicate the size of the seam down to the hem line. Turn the garment inside out and pin both edges together with the pins perpendicular to the edge, heads on the outside. Let the pins mark the stitching line for you, by having the space between the place where the pin goes into the material and the place where it comes out again very small. The stitching line goes right through the middle of this space.

The side seams are then stitched, the zipper inserted or placket applied, sleeves stitched into the armhole, the belt made. The garment is just about completed when you have the second fitting. There should be no further change necessary if you have followed all the rules. The hem line is marked at this time, with attention paid to the demands of fashion, modified by your own special needs and the principles of good proportion.

Darts, tucks, and gathering can all be utilized to shape garments and take up fullness. Use several small darts rather than one large one. Darts can be used at shoulders, around necklines, at underarms, at the waistline of bodice and skirt. Some of the more common problems of fitting are discussed below:

*Shoulder problems:* Narrow shoulders cause too long a shoulder line. To remedy, slightly trim the top of the armhole, use larger shoulder pads, or dart shoulder seam. On the other hand, a too short shoulder line is caused by wide shoulders. Here, unless you can steal from the neckline or armhole

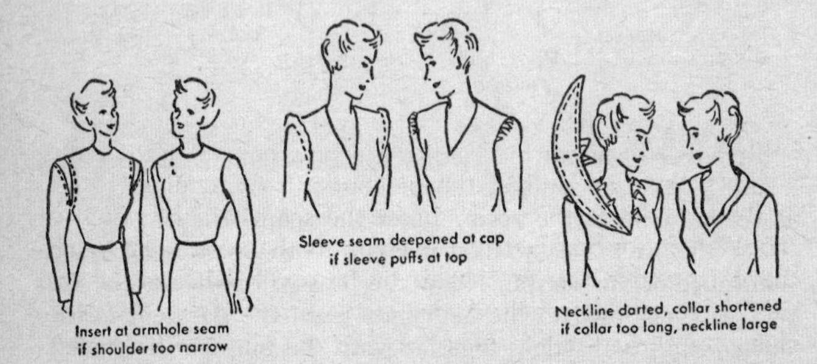

Insert at armhole seam if shoulder too narrow

Sleeve seam deepened at cap if sleeve puffs at top

Neckline darted, collar shortened if collar too long, neckline large

seams, you must insert a piecing at the armhole or in the middle of the seam. This, of course, should be worked out to give a decorative effect.

*Too square shoulders* cause wrinkles from the shoulder tip to the center seams (A). To correct: rip the seam, lift it at the neck edge and slope it towards the tip (B). Letting out the shoulder seam at the armhole is another possible method (C).

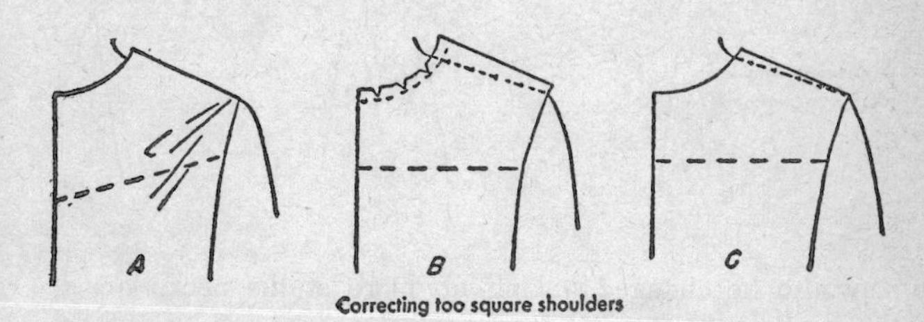

Correcting too square shoulders

*Neckline problems:* If the base of the neck is large or the shoulders slope excessively, there may be folds from the sides of the neck (A) towards the armhole. A change of shoulder pads sometimes helps. The shoulder seam may be let out at the base of the neck or it may be deepened near the armhole (B).

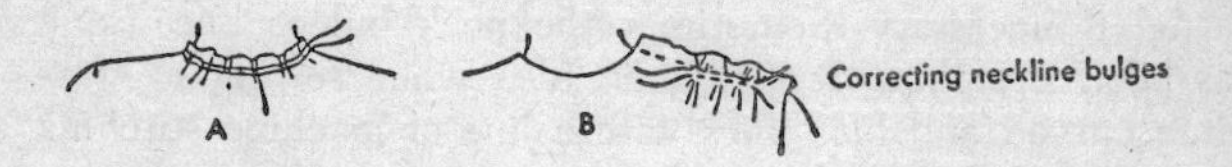

Correcting neckline bulges

When there are wrinkles at the back of the neck, the back of the dress may be too tight, the neckline too high, or the shoulders fat or rounded (A). To correct: shorten and narrow the darts and tucks, or change the armhole seam by taking smaller seam allowance in the seam of the dress, but not changing the seam of the sleeve (B). The shoulder seam

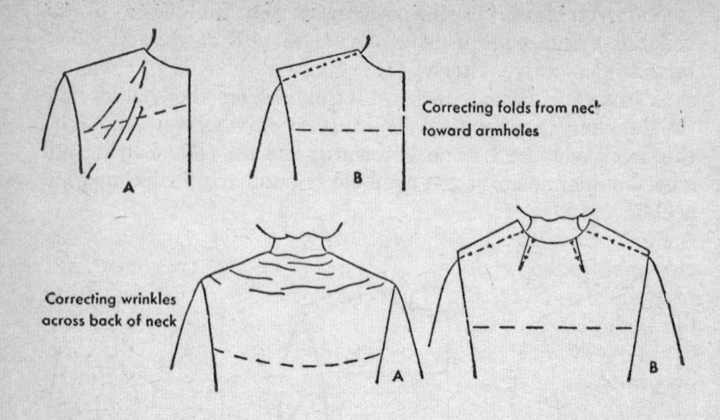


may also be changed, taking up more at the neck, less at the armhole.

If the garment is too wide at the chest, the neckline may bulge in the front. To remedy: gather the neckline (A), or rip the shoulder seams, smooth the extra fullness up and out into darts, tucks, gathers (B). Then refit the shoulders. The neckline may also bulge in the back if the neck is too large or the wearer is very round-shouldered. Slight fullness is eased in (see p. 35); more is taken up into darts, tucks, and shirring (B). The back shoulder seam can be raised and darted if necessary. Sometimes the neck bulges because it has been stretched. It is a good idea when sewing to stay-stitch curved and bias lines with a line of machine stitching to prevent such stretching.

A thin neck and narrow shoulders may cause the neckline to be wide and low. The shoulder seams must then be deepened, the neckline darted, or the entire front lifted after the underarm and shoulder seams are ripped. A large neck or poor posture can cause too tight or too high a neckline. To correct: the neckline must be clipped into and the neck cut down, or the front shoulder seam may be let out.

*Collar problems:* The neckline seam may show because the collar is too long. The collar must be restitched to fit. Too long a collar or too large a neckline may cause the collar to stand away from the neck. Make the collar smaller or dart the neckline to make it smaller. If the collar rolls too high, the dress neckline is probably not as low as it should be, and must be trimmed down. Or, a larger seam for the collar and neckline may be stitched.

*Bust problems:* The most important thing is to get the crosswise grain accurate and parallel to the floor, with no diagonal wrinkles (A). If there is drawing across the bust, the bodice is probably too narrow, the bust very large, the figure overly erect, or the grain pulled out of line. If the bust does not fit, it is usually best to get a new pattern. To correct: let out the underarm seam to widen, or, if there is not a large

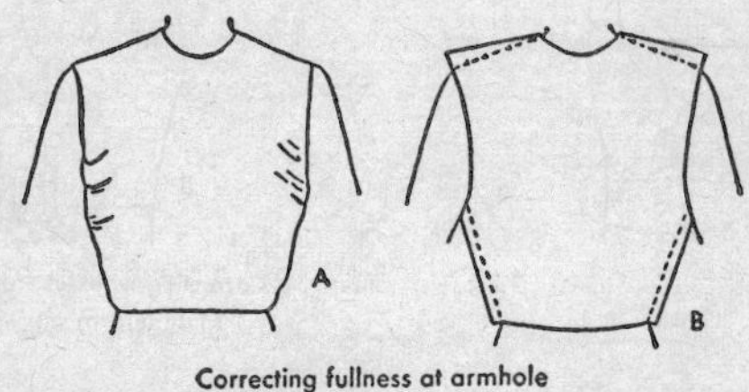

Correcting fullness at armhole

enough seam, piece it (B). Changing the size and position of the underarm darts, or adding darts, may also be helpful. However, the bust measurements are basic to the pattern, and affect all other measurements.

Overly erect figures and prominent busts may cause wrinkles from the bust to the waistline at the underarm seam. The seam is let out on the front bodice shoulder to give more length over the bust, and the underarm seam, also only on the front bodice, is let out.

If the blouse sags below the bust in the front, it is due to a flat chest or round shoulders. The shoulder seams are ripped and the front bodice is raised. If there is sagging below the shoulder blades in the back, the figure is probably overerect or sway-back. Here the shoulder seams are ripped and the back raised.

*Armscye and sleeve problems:* Be very careful in cutting out the armscye, for a very tiny cut can completely change its size. If the underarm seam of a bodice sags below the armpit (A), the armhole is too large or the shoulders slant too much. The shoulder pad may be changed, the underarm seam deepened (B), or the shoulder seam deepened at the armhole.

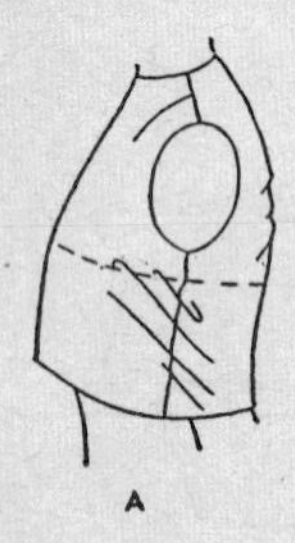


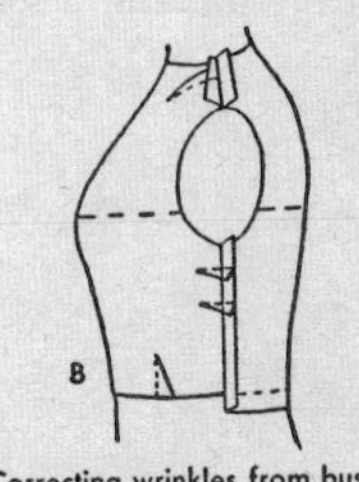


Correcting wrinkles from bust to underarm waistline

If the sleeve puffs up at the top, the fullness of the sleeve cap is not well distributed, and must be adjusted. Or the cap may be too wide or high and the sleeve seam (not the armhole seam) must be deepened at the points of puffiness.

A slightly loose sleeve may have underarm seam taken in. A very loose sleeve, however, must be recut. If the sleeve twists, it may be in the wrong armhole and must be changed. Or, the grain may be incorrect, the elbow too tight, the shoulder bone too prominent, or the sleeve cap too full at either the front or back. Recut; shift poorly placed fullness; or let out elbow darts or underarm seam at the elbow.

Square shoulders, large arm muscles, or too short a sleeve cap, may cause wrinkles from the top of the sleeve to the underarm. The lower edge of the sleeve may stick out. To fix: rip out the armhole seam, and raise the sleeve in the armhole by hollowing out the sleeve until the crosswise grain of goods is straight at armhole level. A very slight difficulty of this type may be taken care of by letting out the top of the sleeve cap.

If the sleeve draws across the arm near the level of the armpit, the sleeve cap is too narrow, the armhole seam too wide, or perhaps too high, or the upper arm is too large.

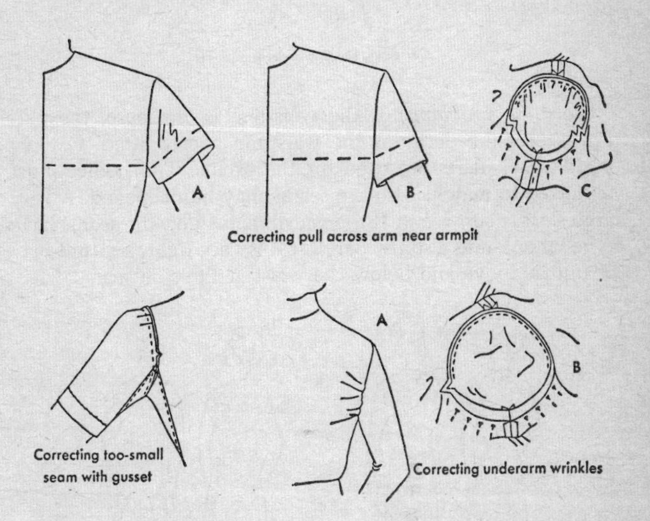


Correcting pull across arm near armpit

Correcting too-small seam with gusset

Correcting underarm wrinkles

The seams on the sides of the armhole must be let out, the sleeve raised and the top recut to get extra width. If the underarm seam is too small to be let out, a gusset may have to be inserted. (See p. 250.)

Underarm wrinkles are caused by too narrow a blouse, tightness at the underarm seams and in the armhole, or a roll of flesh at the underarm and across the back (A). The underarm seam must be released to give more room across the bust (B).

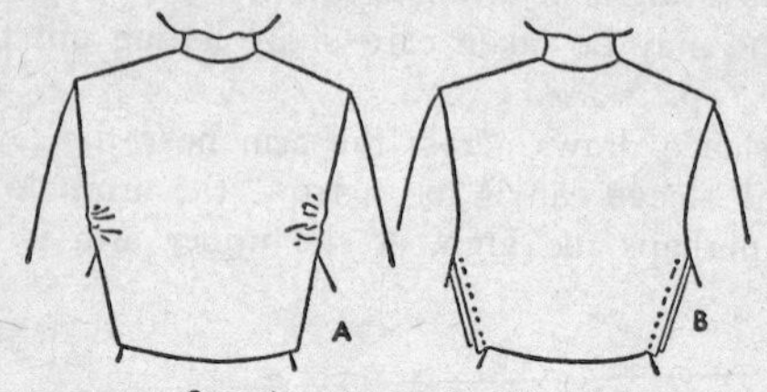


Correcting sagging underarm seam

*Waistline problems:* If the waistline is too loose, the pattern is probably large or the waistline poorly fitted. Gathers or side back darts are used for the excess. The bodice must be darted to match. Also the seams may be deepened. A very large skirt is best recut. If the waistline is tight, the seams have to be let out, and also the darts. If it is very tight, a gusset may be put in above and below the waist at the side seams.

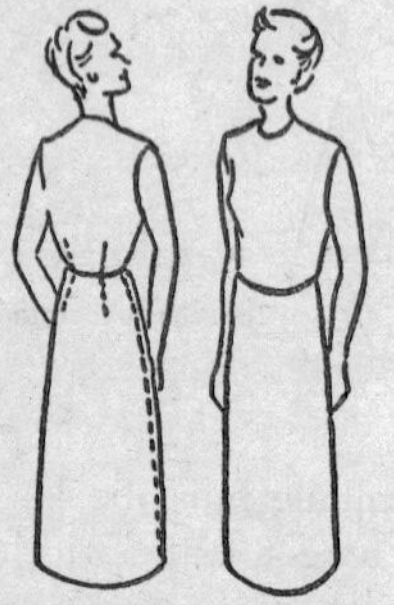

Deepen seam, gather or dart if waistline is too loose

Release side seam, raise waistline if skirt cups in seat

If the lower skirt hem pokes out in the front, the cause is, believe it or not, that the blouse is too short (A). Raise the back of skirt to even out the grain lines, then redo the waistline seam (B). A short blouse will also cause the waistline to be too high. Often it is necessary to change the yoke seams (whenever there is a yoke) or to insert a set-in belt or other piecing.

*Skirt problems:* Crooked or puckered side seams (A) are due to poor sewing, crooked stitching, or tight tension. The seams must be restitched carefully (B).

If the skirt draws at the hips or rides up (C), the skirt is too small, and the seams must be let out. The skirt may also be raised at the waistline, fitted to the bodice, and the excess material removed (D).

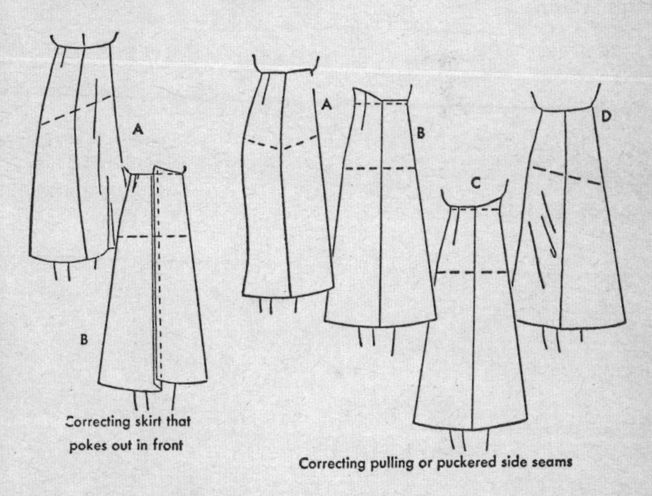


Correcting skirt that pokes out in front

Correcting pulling or puckered side seams

When the back of the skirt is too long between the waist and the hips, the grain is dropped and the side seams of the skirt swing forward. To correct: the skirt is raised at the back waistline and the excess fullness darted. In a one-piece dress, without a waist seam, the garment must be raised at the shoulders.

If the skirt cups in at the seat, the skirt is too narrow, and the side seams must be released. Also raise the waistline. Cupping of seat of the skirt may be due to the fabric weave. This will happen more frequently with such fabrics as jersey and loosely woven woolens. To prevent this type of cupping, stitch a back panel of taffeta to the inside seams at the back of the skirt.

If pleats slant, instead of hanging down straight, check to see whether the waistline seam needs lifting at the top of the pleats, or whether the skirt is too narrow in the seat.

Crosswise fold across the back means that the skirt is tight at the hips or that the figure is sway-back. Raise the skirt at the waist.

# 14. *MAKING A SKIRT*

If you have tried the practice projects, and especially the dirndl skirt, you are certainly ready to work with a skirt pattern. Measure your waist, holding the tape snug, but not tight, around your waist. Buy a pattern for your size waist for a four-gore (section) skirt with a waistband. On the back of the envelope, check the amount of material you will need, buying more for a napped material or a one-way print.

Take out your pattern pieces: front, back, waistband. Pin the front and back pieces together on the side seams, matching notches. See directions, pp. 74-77. Measure from the center back seam to the center front seam on the waist seam line marked on the pattern. Keep the tape flat. The measurement, multiplied by two, should be the same as your waistline, plus about ¼ inch for ease. Measure seven inches below waist for hip measurement and compare with your own measurement, also taken seven inches below the waist. You need an additional three inches here for ease. If the measurements differ, you will have to alter the pattern. Check alterations for waist and hips. Measure length of skirt pattern from waist to hem line, and compare with your own length. To shorten the pattern so you do not waste material, or to lengthen, see p. 68.

If you have changed the waist of the skirt, you must also change the waistband. Pin the band on to the front and back pieces, matching notches. Pin in a tuck, or slash and insert tissue paper, at points corresponding to waist alterations.

Straighten the fabric by pulling out a crosswise thread and cutting across on the drawn thread. Take pins out of pattern except for pins used for alterations. Look at your pattern primer or guide to find the picture of the layout of the pattern that applies to you, your size and fabric width. Circle it. Probably it looks like this:

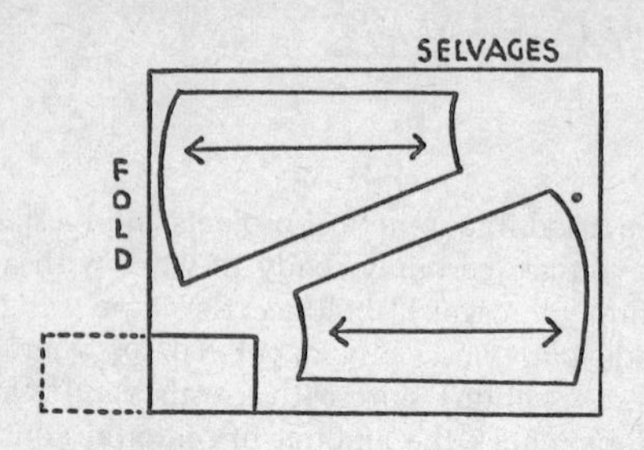


Make the proper fold, with the wrong side out, having selvages meet exactly. Place the front piece on the fabric so that the bottom edge is at the fabric fold or edge. Don't waste material. Insert a pin at one end of the perforations or the arrow marking the straight of the goods. Measure from the selvage to this line. Adjust the pattern to get the same measurement on the other end and pin. (See pp. 67, 75.) Pin around the outside of the pattern, pins three to four inches apart. Smooth the pattern flat. Pin inside margin line if you have a pattern with a margin. Pin on the other skirt piece in the same manner. Remember that pieces must be put on in the same direction if you have a napped fabric, such as corduroy. Pin on the waistband last. You will need only one thickness of fabric for this, so do not pin through both thicknesses of the material. The pattern may show the band pinned on the fold. This means to cut out the skirt pieces, then open out the material, and place the band onto the single thickness.

To cut, use shears, and cut with straight long strokes. Cut notches out when you come to them. Avoid a choppy, jagged cutting line. On the side seam from notch up, cut the seam ¼ inch to ½ inch wider, to give an ample allowance for the zipper.

the edge. (See pp. 33, 74-76.) Pin in center back seam in same way, then stitch these seams on the machine. Watch your seam allowances. They must be accurate. Press the seams open.

Now pin front and back, right sides together, on side seams, leaving left side open from notch up for the zipper. Stitch with longest stitch on the machine. That means you must adjust the stitch regulator. Try on the skirt. Turn back the seam allowances for the zipper one over the other as though the skirt were finished. Examine yourself critically. Check chapter on fitting (p. 83), and make necessary waist, hip, and side-seam adjustments. When the skirt is fitted to your satisfaction, restitch the side seams with proper stitch. Machine basting is easily pulled out. (See ripping, p. 81.) Press the seams open.

Insert the zipper. (See instructions for dirndl skirt, pp. 45, 96, 97.) Stitch the waistband short ends, right sides together, trim seams, turn the band right side out, press. Attach one thickness to the wrong side of the skirt, at the seam line, matching all notches. Turn ¼ inch on raw edge of the band under, baste onto the right side of skirt over the stitching. Edgestitch. Finish with hooks and eyes (p. 173), or a buttonhole (pp. 176-179). For a bound buttonhole (p. 178), you must put in the buttonhole before attaching waistband.

Finish the seams (p. 107) by pinking or with one of the other finishes. Finishing the seam by overedging with the zigzag machine will prevent raveling.

Finally do bottom hem (see instructions, pp. 113-117). If your skirt is not cotton, you will have to make one change. Do not turn in the edge of the hem ¼ inch and edgestitch. Instead, apply seam binding to the right side of the raw edge, easing in the hem to fit the straight binding. Put the binding on close to the edge and stitch a straight line. Then hem the binding to the skirt with tiny stitches that do not show on the right side. If you have chosen a skirt with a great deal of fullness at the bottom, gather the edge to be applied to the binding so that you will have a smooth finish. (To gather, see pp. 11, 130.) A final pressing will enable you to wear your skirt.

# 15. *MAKING A BLOUSE*

If you have been following along in this book, and trying the suggested projects, you have learned, by now, something of how to use a pattern. Working with the three pieces in the skirt pattern is different from working with a more complicated pattern, so let's try one of the latter variety. Measure the fullest part of your bust, your waist, your hips, and buy a pattern for a button-down-the-front sports blouse with a collar and sleeves. Check the back of the envelope for the yardage needed. Circle the layout on your pattern guide sheet. As already discussed, pin pattern front to back at side seams, and measure with a tape. Compare waist, hip, shoulder, bust, armhole, sleeve length measurements with your own, and make all necessary pattern alterations. One important point: pin in all darts and tucks before measuring and measure only from center front to center back. Do not include facings in your measurements.

Unpin pattern pieces, straighten the material, and, checking with the pattern layout, pin all pieces on to the fabric. Cut. There will probably be some pieces that you do not need. That is because several styles may be made from the same pattern. Make necessary tailor tacks and marks for buttonholes, pockets, darts and tucks, fold line for facing, etc.

Start by pinning in darts and tucks. Read directions on pp. 118-122 first. Stitch darts and tucks by machine, being very careful to eliminate dart bubbles by stitching to a point and along the edge of the fold for a few stitches when ending off the dart. If there is a pocket, construct it according to directions for patch pockets (pp. 146-147), and baste it on to the left front of the blouse, on pocket markings. Stitch very carefully in a completely functional, or in a decorative way (contrasting thread, several rows of stitching), and be sure to reinforce the top at each side where there is a lot of strain.

If you are going to make bound buttonholes (see p. 178), they must be done at this time, even though it seems funny to construct buttonholes before you have put in even one seam. Your buttons must be selected so you will know what size the buttonhole is to be. It is sensible to use bound buttonholes only if you have very good fabric, and especially if the blouse is not to be washed. Washing in soap and water may eventually wash a bound buttonhole out. Check p. 178 for construction details in making bound buttonholes. If you are making a worked buttonhole, wait until blouse is almost finished before doing buttonholes.

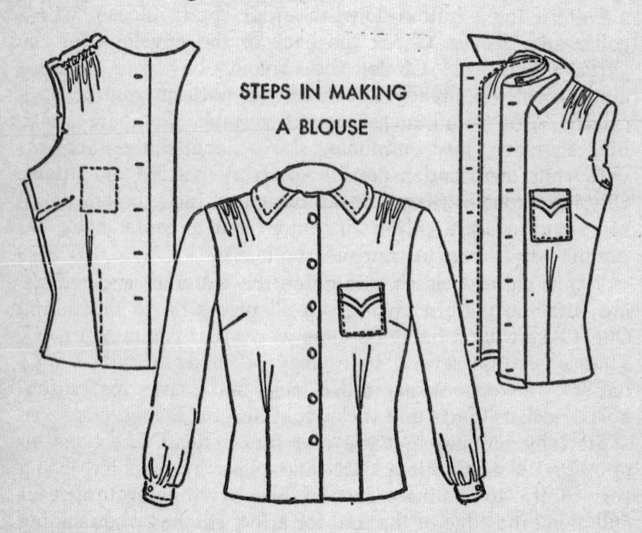


Join the shoulder seams, right sides together. It may be necessary for you to ease (p. 36), or gather (pp. 11, 130), one side of the shoulder to the other before you stitch by machine.

Fold back the front facings on the marked fold line, pin in the side seams and try on for the first fitting. Read notes on bust, sleeve, armhole problems (pp. 89-92), and examine yourself critically. Repin side seams to fit correctly. Make any necessary changes, although the chances are that your only changes will be made in the pinned side seams. When you are satisfied, change the pins which were put in parallel to the edge for fitting, to the perpendicular position for stitching and stitch the side seams. Press all seams open as soon as they are sewed.

Finish the neckline, facings and bottom hem next. Stitch around the collar seam line on three sides (not on the notched edge) and trim the seam all around. Turn collar to the right side; press. Baste the collar onto the right side of the blouse, matching the center lines of the collar and the back of the blouse, and also matching notches. Fold front facing on the indicated fold line to the front of the blouse over the collar. The top will be caught in the neckline seam, the bottom in the hem. Turn in the raw edge of the rest of the facing ¼ inch and stitch close to the turned edge. Finish as described under "non-convertible" collars (p. 156). Stitch across the bottom of the facing on the seam line on both sides, from the fold to the facing edge. Trim neckline seam and seam at bottom of facing. Turn to wrong side. Hem the bias or collar self-finish at the neckline. Catch the facing at the shoulder seams. Press the finished neckline. Turn up the bottom hem, the amount being indicated by the seam you have just stitched on the bottom of the blouse.

At this point you may put in the worked buttonholes (see p. 177), if you have not made the bound ones. Sewing stores will put in buttonholes for you at a small charge. If you are convinced that you are going to be a sewer, you will find it a good investment to buy yourself a buttonholer. You may, of course, do worked buttonholes by hand, but this is very time-consuming and it is difficult to do an evenly sized and spaced series by hand. If you are patient and unusually neat, you can, however, get good results. Here, however, using a zigzag type of machine is a definite advantage because this type of machine will make quickly and neatly any length buttonhole, corded or plain, without attachments. Check pp. 176, 248 for sewing on buttons.

Stitch the underarm seam of the short sleeve, right sides together. Make and attach the cuff (see pp. 167-169). Check pp. 162-164 for setting in the sleeves. Insert sleeves into armholes and stitch. Press blouse and try on for final fit. As the last step, the seams are finished in some suitable way (see p. 112).

If you have a long sleeve, make a sleeve opening in one of the ways described and illustrated on pp. 162-165. Put in any elbow darts called for, stitch the underarm seam, press. Add the cuff or wristband, then set in the sleeve.

For any detail not mentioned in this chapter, see the pattern guide. While explanations are brief, they are usually complete and well illustrated. Use your imagination if you have any desire to decorate the blouse. See the chapters on decorative stitches and finishes, pp. 180-204.

# 16. *MAKING A DRESS*

You have now made a skirt, and also a blouse. Constructing a dress involves very few new problems. You may finish the bodice completely, then finish the skirt completely, and join them at the waistline to make a dress. In this case, your general order of assembly for the dress would be: pattern alterations, pinning pattern on to fabric, cutting, marking the work, bodice darts and tucks, bound buttonholes or fabric loop closings, bodice side, shoulder and center seams (left side left open below notch for zipper), collar and neckline, sleeves and cuffs, finishing details for bodice, skirt darts, seams (left side open above notch for zipper), pleats. Try on the bodice and skirt for first fitting. Make necessary corrections.

To attach bodice and skirt, drop bodice, right side out, into skirt, held wrong side out. With the two right sides together, match and pin bodice and skirt at centers and side seams. Seams have been pressed open, of course. Darts and tucks at waist usually face in towards each other, that is, towards the center. Baste the waistline seam carefully by hand or machine (longest stitch). Try dress on with the shoulder pads in place and zipper opening pinned closed. Dress was previously fitted at shoulders, neckline, bust, waist, and hips. Recheck these parts, and carefully check waistline position for looks and comfort (see pp. 84, 92, 93). Stitch waistline seam after all corrections are made.

Insert dress placket zipper, usually nine-inch or ten-inch (see pp. 45, 141-145). Allow the dress to hang in the closet for a day or two so that bias parts have a chance to sag. Finish the seams, then try on the dress and mark the hem (p. 46).

STEPS IN MAKING A DRESS

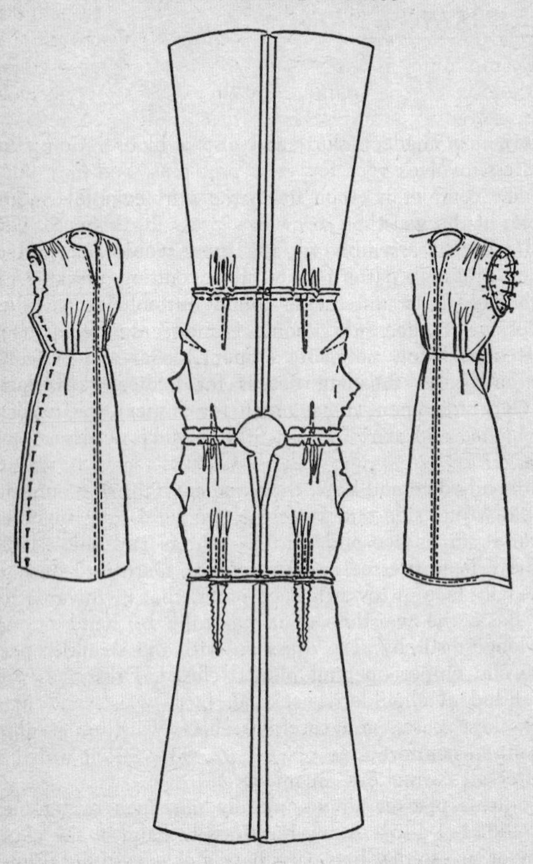

Unless your dress is cotton, you will probably want to finish the hem with seam binding. Mark the hem, turn up bottom at marked places with pins, placed perpendicular to the fold, and baste close to the fold. Press. Measure the desired hem depth from the fold with a gauge all around and cut off the excess. Seam binding is applied and stitched to the raw edge. Where there is a lot of fullness in the hem, it is a good idea to run in a row of gathering and gather the hem edge to fit the straight binding. Finally, hem free edge of binding to skirt.

The newer way to assemble garments is to make the entire front, then the entire back, join them at the shoulders, fit and finish the sides. This order was used in the preceding chapter in making a blouse. The general order, after cutting and marking, would be: darts and tucks, bodice front center seams, if any; skirt front seams, bodice and skirt fronts joined at waistline and seamed; bodice back center seams; skirt back center seams; bodice and skirt backs joined at waistline and seamed; front and back joined at shoulder seam; neckline, including collar and facings finished; shoulder pads pinned in. The garment is then tried on for a fitting and the side seams are pinned in to fit. After any corrections are made, side seams are stitched leaving an opening for the zipper or placket. Make the sleeve, apply the cuff, set the sleeve into the armhole. Insert the zipper or placket. Try on for a fitting and mark the hem. Finish the last details, finish the seams, turn up the hem. Make the belt and belt carriers.

Work carefully. Make yourself a promise that you are not going to rip. That means studying what you have to do. Check your pattern guide sheet. Use the index of this book over and over again, and check instructions and illustrations. Don't get so that you don't see the forest for the trees. Each detail has to be done separately, but always know, before you begin, what the relationship of the particular detail is to the whole. Certain problems, such as bound buttonholes, fabric loop closings, monograms, should be worked out on practice fabric first. These are the details that can most quickly label your

# 17. SEAMS AND SEAM FINISHES

SEAMS are the lines of stitching which hold two pieces of fabric together. In general, we try to make seams as inconspicuous as possible, and in most cases, as strong as possible. The type of seam we use depends on the strength and the appearance we want to give. In some cases the seam may be used as part of the decoration, or for a functional purpose.

*Plain seams* are simplest and are used most often. Put two pieces of material, right sides together, and stitch on wrong side at required seam allowance, usually ½ inch to ⅝ inch from edge. Open and press flat. Edges may be pinked.

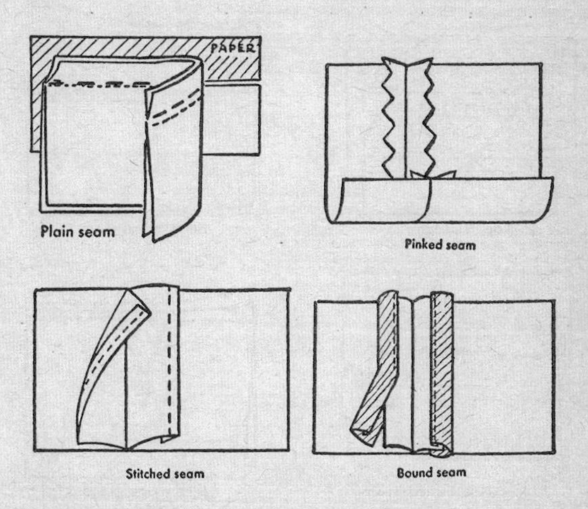


Plain seam

Pinked seam

Stitched seam

Bound seam

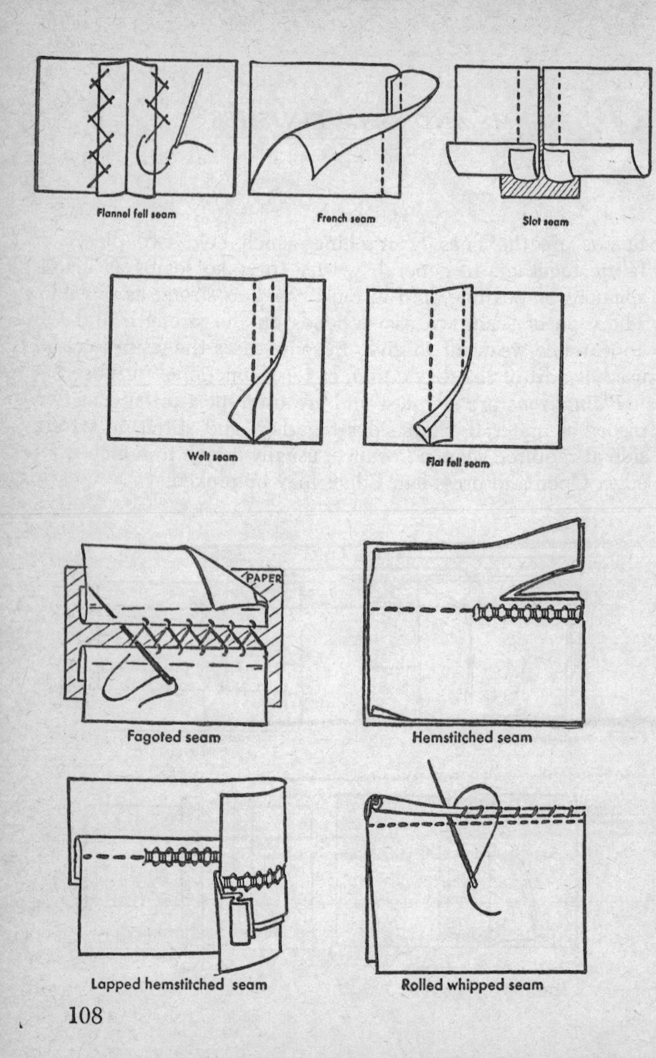


Flannel fell seam

French seam

Slot seam

Welt seam

Flat fell seam

Fagoted seam

Hemstitched seam

Lapped hemstitched seam

Rolled whipped seam

*Stitched plain seam* is made in the same way as a plain seam and then stitched again on the right side ⅛ inch from seam line on one or both sides for a tailored effect.

*Flat fell seam* is used when you need a flat finish, as in shirts and pajamas. Make a plain seam, trim one edge to ⅛ inch, turn in other edge ¼ inch. Baste to position over trimmed edge and edgestitch. This is usually done on the right side.

*Hemfelled seam* is made like flat fell except that seam is hemmed, rather than edgestitched, for a softer effect.

*Flannel fell seam* is used on heavier fabric, like wool. Make a plain seam, trim one edge to ⅛ inch, and fold other part over without turning in raw edge. Catch stitch.

*Welt seam* is used for flat finish on heavy material. Make a plain seam on wrong side, trim one edge, fold the other over it without turning in the raw edge, and stitch on outside. For double welt, stitch a second line close to original seam stitching.

*Slot seam* is a decorative seam, sometimes to show another color or design underneath. Turn both seam edges under on sewing line, lap them over a strip of material, with edges meeting or not as desired, and stitch the proper distance from the fold on both sides.

*French seam* is used for sheer materials and underclothes. Make a plain seam on right side (with wrong sides together), ¼ inch outside the seam allowance. Trim edges to ⅛ inch, turn to wrong side and stitch on seam allowance to make this seam within a seam. Do not allow any frayed edge to show.

*Upholsterer's seam* is made like a French seam except that you start on the wrong side and the finished seam shows on the right side. The effect is like that of cording and is often used for slip covers.

*False French seam* is made with a plain seam on wrong side. Turn edges under ¼ inch and sew together with running stitch or by machine.

*French fell* is made with a plain seam and one thickness is then trimmed to ⅛ inch. Fold other edge over cut edge, turn in ¼ inch, and hem to machine stitching.

*Fagoted seam* has a space between fabric edges. Decide how far apart edges are to be, turn edges back one-half the width of the finished open space, baste them to a slip of paper, and fagot (see pp. 197,198). Very decorative.

*Hemstitched seam* is basted as for plain seam, and pressed to one side. Have seam hemstitched and trim seam allowance close to hemstitching. A line of machine stitching can be done ⅛ inch from stitching on wrong side. Decorative.

*Lapped seam* will look like a fell seam when finished. Turn one piece of material under on the seam allowance. Baste the folded edge on to the right side of the other piece, at the seam allowance. Edgestitch. *Tucked seam* is similar to lapped seam except that the final stitching is done not at the edge, but at a distance from the fold. The effect is like that of a tuck.

*Lapped hemstitched seam* is done by lapping seams, as explained under lapped seam. Hemstitch over the basting, trim away seam on wrong side.

*Machine picoted seam* is like hemstitched seam, but the hemstitching is cut through the center to picot.

*Rolled whipped seam.* Make a plain seam, trim the allowance to half, roll edges tightly a little at a time, putting needle under roll, not through it.

*Strap seam* is used for decoration. Plain seam is made and pressed open. On the right side, baste a strip of material with edges turned in, and edgestitch both sides. Braid and other trimmings may also be used.

*Corded seam* uses cord which has been basted inside a bias strip (see pp. 54, 184, 185). Place bias covered cord on the right side of one piece of material with basting directly on seam line, cut edges towards edge of fabric. Baste and place second piece of fabric, right sides facing, edges together, in position as for plain seam. Baste and stitch on seam line, using cording foot.

*Piped seam.* Fold bias strip (see pp. 54, 139) in half and place on the right side of fabric with fold ⅛ inch inside seam line. Baste and place other piece right side down on top; baste

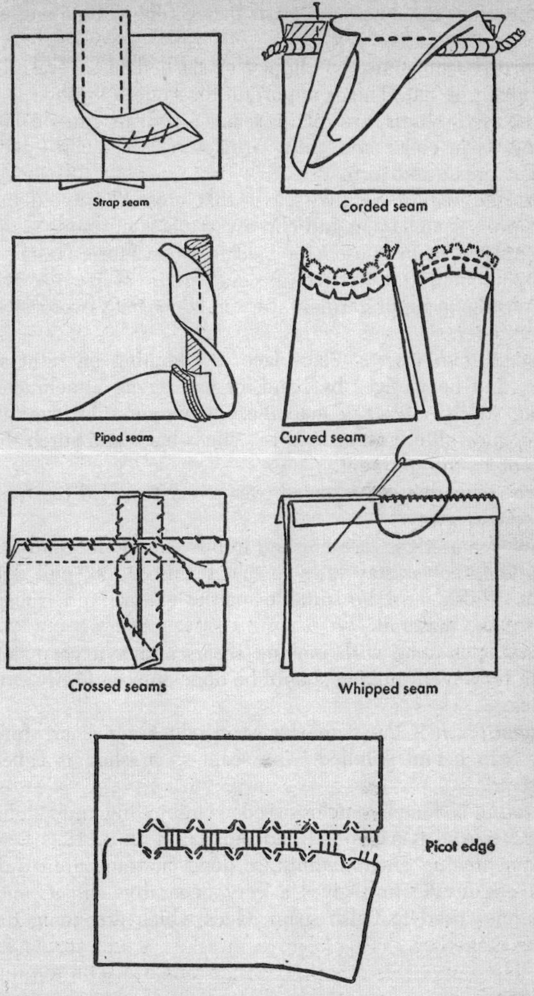
Strap seam

Corded seam

Piped seam

Curved seam

Crossed seams

Whipped seam

Picot edgé

and stitch. Trim seam, press so that piping falls along edge of seam. Decorative.

*Curved seam* must be clipped or slashed in several places to make it lie flat. This is important for smooth finish.

*Enclosed seams* are plain seams used in double thicknesses, as in collar and cuffs. Trim very close, clip edges to lie flat, press, and turn.

*Crossed seams* are two seams that cross. To avoid bulkiness, press seams open and clip away edges of under seam.

*Whipped seam* is used for piecing when fabric is not wide enough to cut full pattern. Be sure grain of piecing is the same as the grain of garment, turn in edges, and overcast with tiny stitches.

*Seams with inserts.* Place lace or trimming on right side, baste, and hem edges by hand, or use zigzag attachment or zigzag stitch on zigzag machine. On wrong side, cut fabric away, and roll edges, or turn the edges back and stitch them, but not to the garment.

*Bias seam* should be sewed over paper to avoid tightening. Tear paper away.

Raw seam edges are finished to prevent fraying and raveling and to act as stay lines so that seams do not pull out of shape. Finish must be suitable for the texture and transparency of the material.

*Pinking* is done with pinking shears and is a very simple finish. However, pinking should be done only on firmly woven fabrics.

*Clean finish* is the name for seam edges which are turned back ⅛ inch and stitched. The seam so finished is called a silk seam.

*Binding* is done by enclosing edges in binding and stitching.

*Overcasting* is explained and illustrated on p. 12.

*Hemstitching* and *picoting* are done on transparent fabric seam edges. Picoting gives a very decorative effect, and is sometimes used to finish seam edges which are going to be fagoted together.

# 18. *HEMS*

A HEM is a twice turned edge. Its width is the same all along the hem.

Unless it is used for decorative purposes, a hem should be inconspicuous. The steps in making a hem are: (1) Measure. (2) Pin. (3) Pin or baste close to fold on outside. (4) Measure and trim inside. (5) Press with damp cloth. (6) Finish with loose, invisible stitches. Slip stitching (see p. 13) is recommended for light cottons, light or medium weight rayons, firmly woven silks. Seam binding is recommended for heavy materials and materials which ravel. Catch stitching (see p. 13) is recommended for heavy fabrics.

To turn up a hem at the bottom of a skirt or dress, see p. 114.

*Plain hem* is made by turning in edge ¼ inch and stitching close to the fold. Baste stitched edge to position and slip stitch. With very heavy materials, sometimes only a single fold is made and the edge is catch stitched. Seam binding is also used on heavier materials. Gather edge first, sew binding on to right side at the edge and slip stitch.

A *narrow hem* is often used on sheer materials. Turn in edge ⅛ inch, turn again ¼ inch and hem. Or the second fold may be machine stitched on certain informal kinds of clothes, on towels and sheets. The foot hemmer attachment makes a narrow hem.

*Wide machine stitched hem* is made like a plain hem but stitched to position by machine. Used often for pillowcases and sheets.

*Rolled hem* is used for handkerchiefs and dainty lingerie.

Stitch close to edge, roll edge over enough to cover stitching, and slip stitch or whip (overhand).

*Turned picot edge* is good in transparent fabrics. Measure the hem, hemstitch the edge and cut through center for picot. Turn over ⅛ inch and slip stitch.

*Lingerie hem* is used for collars, ruffles and undergarments.

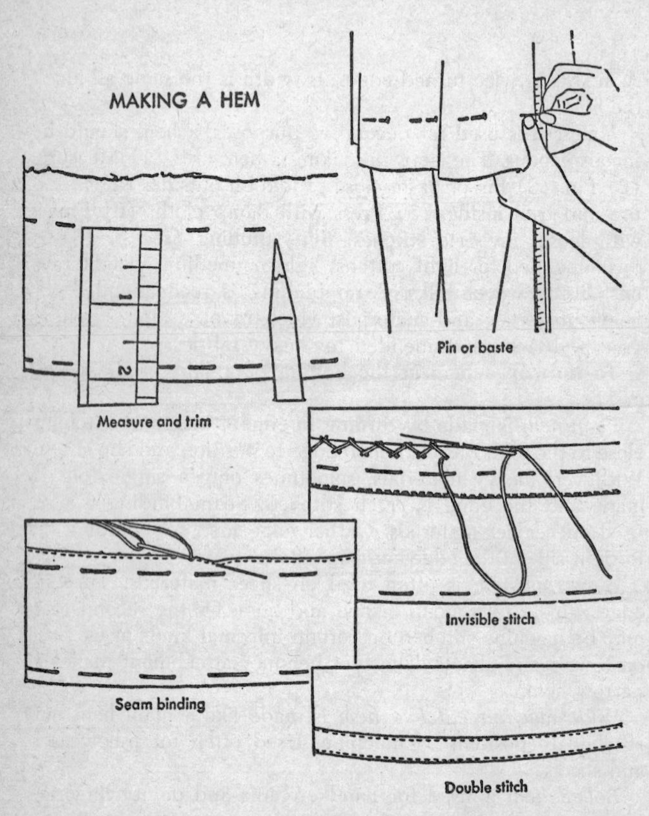

Turn in narrow hem on wrong side and baste. Take two firm tight overhand stitches one on top of the other, slip needle under hem concealing thread for ¼ inch, and repeat. Effect is like tiny scallops.

*Shell hem* is made like lingerie hem, but puffs are wider, and a few tiny running stitches are made between puffs. Or the puffs may be made with a simple overcast stitch.

*Napery or damask hem* is used on linens. Make a narrow hem, crease very sharply with your fingernail and fold hem

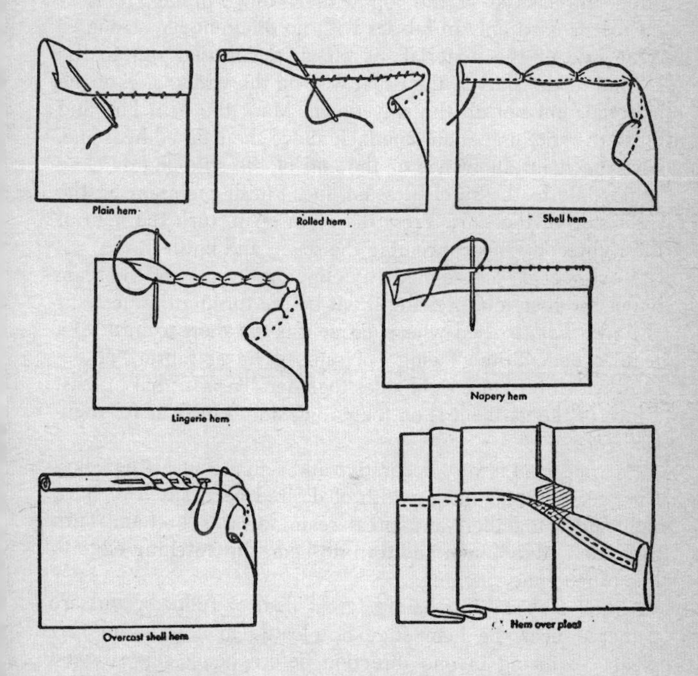

back to right side so that the fold of first turning and the new fold are directly in line. Make tiny overhanding stitches.

*Multiple stitched* or *stitched band hem* is done on sportswear with heavy fabric. Make hem depth of ¼ inch to ¾ inch and stitch near the fold as many times as desired, usually three to five. For heavy fabrics, omit first turn and overcast raw edges.

*A reversed hem* is a hem that is finished on the right side of the garment, contrary to the usual practice of turning a hem to the wrong side. It has a decorative function and is often emphasized at the top with cording, piping, or rick-rack. It is used only in fabrics with no difference in wrong or right side of the material. Stitch all seams that run to the bottom of the skirt in the usual way on the wrong side of the material, but not all the way down. Mark the hem line and finish the stitching about one inch above the marked hem line. Clip the seam allowance at the end of the stitching as close as possible to the stitched seam line. Finish the seam on the right side of the skirt. Press the seam open, turn the hem to the right side, thus concealing the seam, and finish it.

*Hem over a pleat* is made by clipping the part of the seam under the hem and pressing it flat before turning the hem.

*Faced hem* is used where garment is too short to turn up a regular hem. Stitch facing (of same grain as fabric) of desired width for hem, right sides together. Turn so that at least ½ inch of the garment is on the wrong side. Finish as for regular hem.

*Applied hem* is very decorative and is in a contrasting color. Cut piece on bias twice width of desired hem, stitch to skirt, right sides together, and press seam towards bottom. Turn in bottom edge ¼ inch and turn up hem, slip stitching edge to line of machine stitching.

*Circular skirt hems* have a great deal of fullness, and are gathered near the hem edge or pleated in a series of tiny pleats all facing in one direction before being slip stitched to position. Seam binding may be applied after gathering.

*Shaped hem*, for example a scalloped hem, is often highlighted with a decorative stitch such as feather stitching.

*Embroidered edging* at hem may be applied as follows: For tucked effect, stitch edging to skirt, wrong sides together. Press seam up. Stitch one tuck in fabric. Stitch close to fold of tuck over seam. Make another tuck if desired. For bias trim finish, stitch edging to skirt, wrong sides together. With bias right side down, stitch to skirt below seam, turn bias up, press, and slip stitch to position over seam.

*Hem with mitred corner:* Crease hems sharply, pin dart from corner to point where hems meet. Cut ⅛ inch outside pins, turn raw edges in ⅛ inch, and overhand them together. Then finish hem.

# 19. *DARTS*

DARTS are triangular arrangements which take up excess fullness in clothes and make them fit better. They are necessary because the body is not flat nor straight, but curved. Darts are usually made on wrong side of garment, and appear on right side only as a decorative effect, as in waistline darts in very slim skirts. The most usual places for darts are at the waistline tapering up to the bust, from the side seam of the bodice tapering in towards the bust, from the shoulder down, and at the neckline in back.

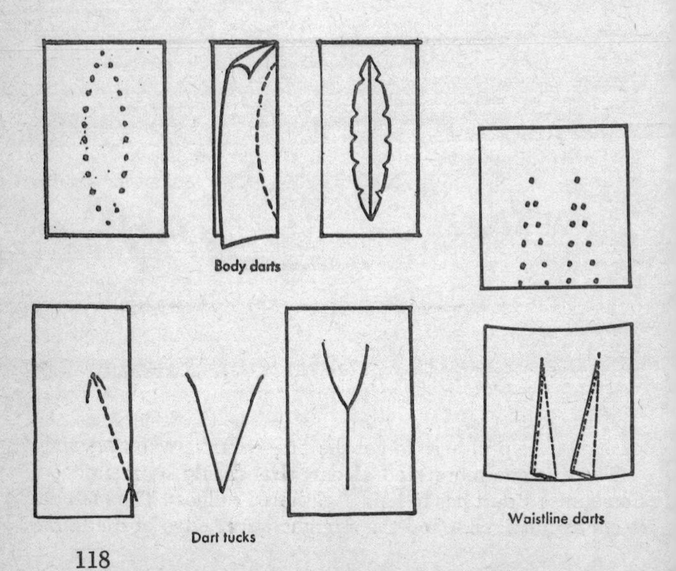

Patterns are marked, at the places where darts are to be made, with a series of perforations or printed dots. Mark the spots with tailor tacks, remove the pattern and fold the material between the tailor tacks. Put a pin into the center of the upper tack and through to the center of the under one. The tailor tacks should fall one on top of the other. If they don't, readjust the fold you have made till it is perfect, and secure the pin. Baste from one tailor tack to the next, starting from the point. Now stitch the dart at the machine, but start at the wide end and taper to the point. When you are a stitch or two before the point, start to sew very slowly. It is best to turn the balance wheel by hand here and to take three or four stitches in a straight line directly along the fold. Back-tack carefully or tie the thread ends with a secure knot. You will get a more professional effect if, when you place your material under the presser foot preparatory to stitching, you make sure that the line of basting from the wide end to the point is in a perfectly straight line parallel to the side of the presser foot. Do not allow this line to slant.

Some darts are wide in the middle and taper at both ends. They are called body darts, and are stitched in the same way as the simple darts just described. These darts, at the waist-line, are often clipped or notched to relieve strain.

A dart tuck is a dart that is stitched along part of its length. This gives a softer effect.

When a dart is very wide, or when it is made in heavy material, it is often slashed open and down as close to the point as is safe. It is pressed after slashing, the excess material is trimmed off to seam width, and the edges are overcast to prevent raveling.

When darts are finished, press them towards the center line or down away from the armscye if they are underarm darts. The latter is to prevent bulkiness at the armhole. A tailor's cushion is helpful here to get the proper curve when pressing.

There is one more kind of dart that should be mentioned. Sometimes a dart has to hold a gathered fullness. The material is cut as for a seam and the straight upper edge of the fabric

# 20. *TUCKS*

Tucks, like darts, are made to take in excess fullness and to mold the fabric to the body lines. They are also used as decorations. The main difference between a tuck and a dart is that darts are stitched to a point, while tucks are stitched in a straight line. They may be stitched on the right or wrong side. To make really professional looking tucks, use the machine tucker which marks the width of each tuck and the spacing between. It is most important that this be accurate.

*Plain tuck* is made by folding the cloth and stitching the desired distance from the fold. Use a gauge to get it absolutely straight.

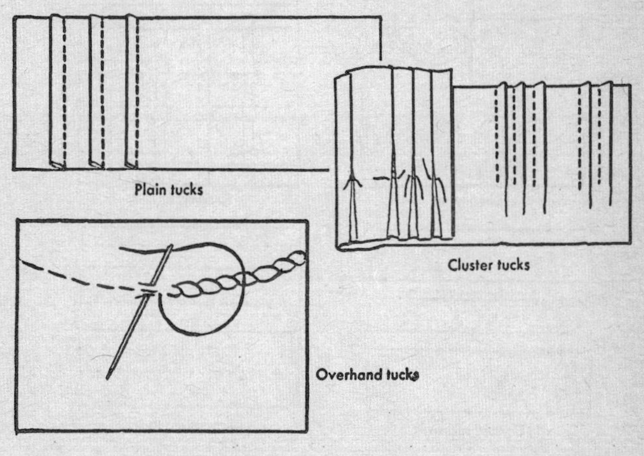

Plain tucks

Cluster tucks

Overhand tucks

*Pin tucks* are very tiny tucks that may be done by hand with tiny running stitches or by machine. They are very decorative on sheer fabrics.

*Hand-run tucks* are tucks done with very small running stitches, fine needle and thread.

*Overhand tucks* are very shallow tucks used for circular lines. Mark the line carefully, take up only a few threads of cloth and overhand over the marking. If desired, use contrasting thread or two lines of stitches, one worked from the right, the second from the left, to get a cross-stitched effect.

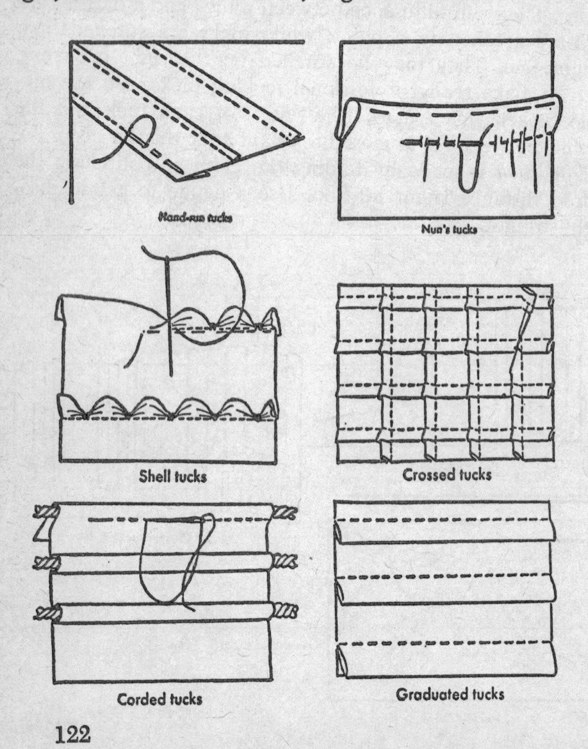

Hand-run tucks

Nun's tucks

Shell tucks

Crossed tucks

Corded tucks

Graduated tucks

*Nun's tucks* are tucks on flares. Crease the line and baste close to fold. Press, baste proper distance from fold, and stitch.

*Cluster* or *group tucks* are several tucks in a row. Watch spacing carefully and end off with backtacking or securely tied knot. Very often ended off in a slanting line.

*Shell tucks* are decorative and have a scalloped effect. Make tuck, and measure the shells, using a pencil dot marking. Shells are often ¼ inch deep and ½ inch long, although they may be finer or wider. At each dot, make two tight overhand stitches, then three or four running stitches and repeat overhanding at next dot. Or, pass needle under cloth between overhand stitches.

*Crossed tucks* are pretty for decorative effects. Make all horizontal tucks, press flat and carefully stitch vertical tucks.

*Corded tucks.* Encase cord in tuck and run by hand, or machine stitch with cording foot.

*Graduated tucks* are a series of tucks increasing or decreasing in size. Measure carefully and baste first to be sure effect is right before stitching.

# 21. PLEATS AND GODETS

Pleats are used for decorative effects and to add fullness. Pleated sections should be complete before being set into a garment. Mark the place for the pleats first with chalk or tailor's tacks very carefully. These markings are indicated on commercial patterns. Use plenty of pins and press often and well. It is a good idea when stay stitching slanting lines or triangles at the bottom of pleats (for reinforcement) first to trace on paper the desired design, and then stitch right over the paper. The effect will then be completely symmetrical and the paper may easily be torn away.

Pleats that go in one direction should be basted with diagonal basting. Pleats that meet at a center line should be slip stitched together to make sure that they do not slip apart. Dressmaking supply houses will steam special pleats into a garment if you desire.

*Plain pleat:* Fold through markings, press sharply, and bring to indicated line. Baste, press on inside, and stitch on the right side from top as far down as desired.

*Side or kick pleat:* Single pleats or plain pleats facing in one direction at side or center. Stitch fold an inch below top of pleat. Stay stitch a slanting line at top on right side.

*Knife pleats* are narrow plain pleats that go all around garment facing in one direction. They are made like plain pleats.

*Accordion pleats* are vertical overlapping pleats made only by machine or pattern. Put in hem first, use three times amount of material needed for hip size and do all seams except center back. Have the skirt pleated, then seam the center back. Several rows of shirring may be placed across the top if desired.

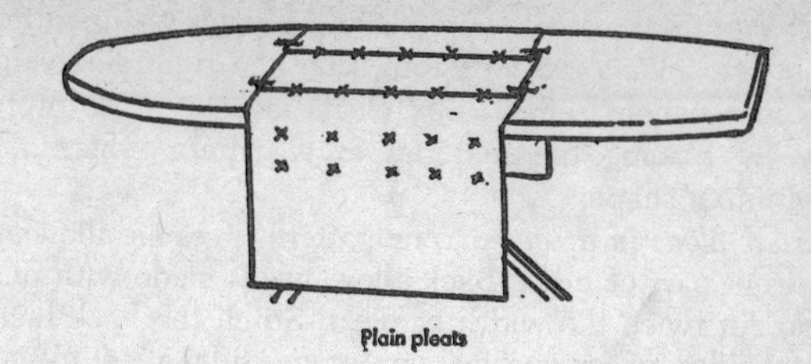

Plain pleats

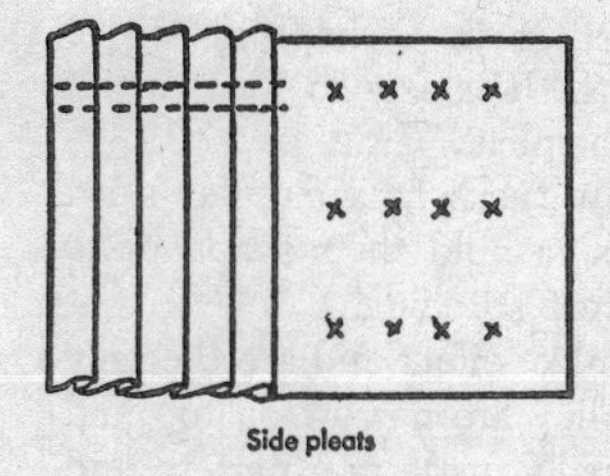

Side pleats

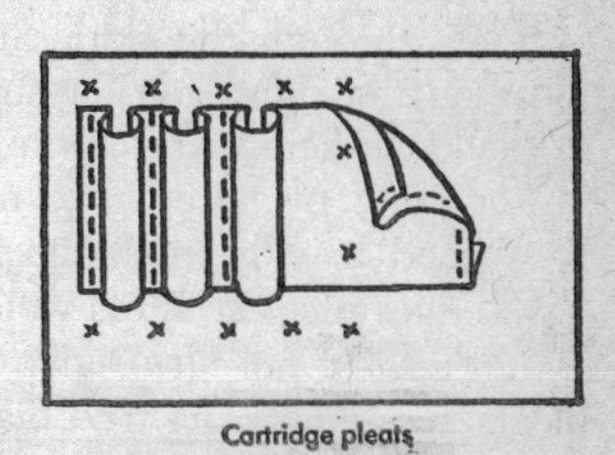

Cartridge pleats

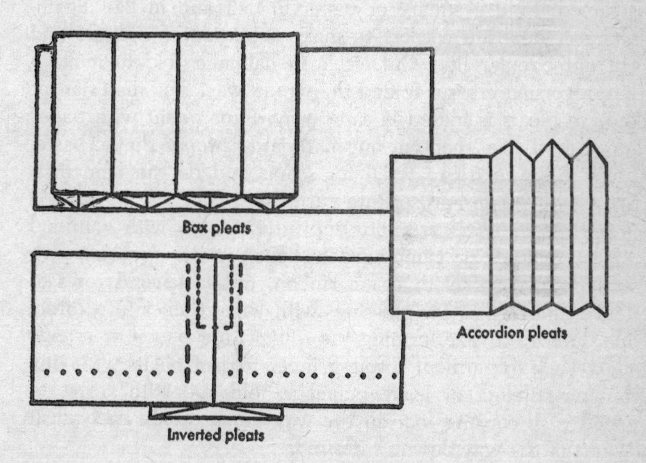

Box pleats

Accordion pleats

Inverted pleats

*Box pleat:* Make two plain pleats in opposite directions. Edges of two pleats are on wrong side and right side shows fullness in a paneled effect. Box pleats may be made professionally by placing the material in a pattern where it is steamed into a shape.

*Inverted pleat in a seam:* Your pattern gives an allowance for the front part of pleat. Back allowance is made with piece of fabric cut twice the width of pleat. Stitch the back facing fabric to sides of extensions on wrong side after pleat is pressed in place, and overcast or seam pleat to facing. Do not sew through the skirt. Stay stitch in V shape at top of pleat on the right side for strength. It is a good idea to put in the lower hem before forming the pleat.

*Radiating pleats* are like narrow tucks in a circular skirt. It is good to edgestitch the folds to hold their shape or to have edges picoted. Press well before stitching.

*Sunburst* or *fan pleats* give a fanlike effect and are the only pleats pressed on the true bias. They are narrow on top and wider at the bottom. They are usually made in a pattern and steamed. Fold a square of paper in half and in half again. Connect opposite corners to make a portion of a circle and cut out circular line. Cut circle in half and fold to make a fan, reversing creases folded the wrong way. The material for the fan pleats is folded in same way. Experiment with paper for desired size, then cut out material to proper shape, baste, press. Allow extra material for seams and do the hem first. Press with steam and set into garment.

*Cartridge pleats* are soft unpressed pleats with rounded edges applied as trimming on belts, waists, pockets. On straight piece of cloth or on ribbon, put in several rows of uneven basting as for gauging, with long stitches in a direct line. Pull up to size forming the rolls with a pencil or orange stick. Tack to garment through inner fold of pleats with tiny running stitches, or leave pencil in fold and stitch close to pencil with cording foot all the way down beside each pleat or part of the way down as desired.

Sunburst pleats

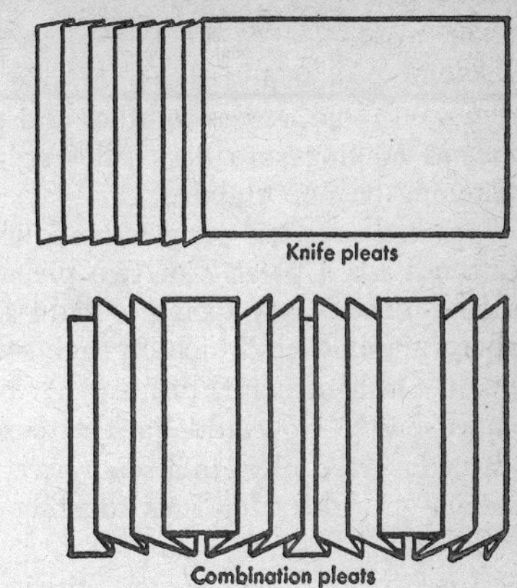
Knife pleats

Combination pleats

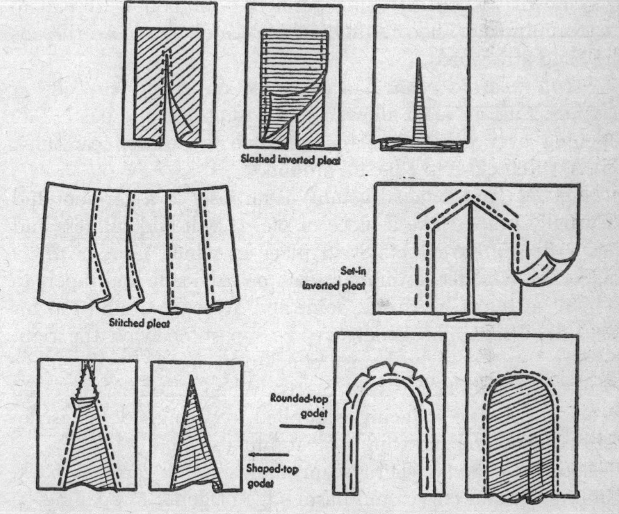
Slashed inverted pleat

Stitched pleat

Set-in inverted pleat

Rounded-top godet

Shaped-top godet

*Inverted pleat:* Like box pleat except that fullness is on the wrong side and the right side shows two pleats. Stitch down one fold, across to other and up, or stay stitch an angle at end making sure both sides are even. See suggestion for stitching on paper above.

*Slashed inverted pleat* is used where there is no fabric allowance for a pleat. Cut two pieces of fabric, each the size of the pleat; apply facing to right side of garment, and mark center line. Stitch ¼ inch on each side of center, tapering to a point. Slash to point, turn facing to wrong side, make pleat, press, baste. Now add back extension and continue exactly as for inverted pleat in a seam except that no stay stitching is shown on right side. Tack together with invisible stitches on right side.

*Stitched or stayed pleats.* Stitch down pleats flat as far as desired, then continue stitching along edge of pleat all the way down without catching garment. Cut bobbin thread to make unbroken line of stitching and catch the loose threads by hand afterwards.

*Set-in inverted pleat.* Cut away section of garment, clip at corners. Turn in seam allowance to wrong side and baste. Lay opening over pressed pleat and baste to position carefully. Press, stitch close to edge all around.

*A godet* (pronounced *goday*) is an inset in a garment and is usually shaped like a piece of pie. It will add fullness and has a decorative effect. Slash place at which inset is to be made, insert godet, forming a seam on each side that tapers to a point at top. Clip to the point and overcast around top for strength. Press. The godet may be top stitched on the right side and may also be hemstitched to garment. Small godets inserted in a collar are very pretty. When a godet is inserted in a seam, a stay or facing is applied to wrong side, as is described above for inserting a pleat into a seam.

*Round-top godet.* Turn seam allowance of garment back, clipping around curve, and baste edge of godet to opening on wrong side. Top stitch on right side.

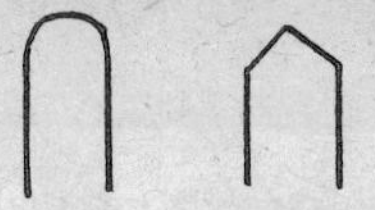

*Godet with shaped top.* As above but clip carefully to all corners.

*Applied godet.* Turn seam allowance of godet to the wrong side and baste flat. Apply godet to right side of garment in a lapped seam and stitch. To reinforce the top, cut a piece of fabric the same shape as the top of the godet and overcast or slip stitch it to the top on the wrong side.

# 22. GATHERS, RUFFLES, SHIRRING

GATHERS are made in soft fabrics where fullness must be taken up into a small space. They give necessary fullness and are also decorative. For heavier fabrics, pleats and tucks are used. Gathers and ruffles are best done on bias and crosswise threads.

*Hand gathers:* Use double thread and start with a knot. Make a row of small running stitches, pull them up to fit, and wind the thread around a pin till stitched. Two rows, ¼ inch apart, are better than one.

*Machine gathers* are done like hand gathers, but with longest machine stitch, seven to eight stitches per inch. Use slightly heavier bobbin thread, tie threads at one end, and pull bobbin thread at other end, to gather. Machine gathering foot will gather and stitch fullness.

*Shirring* is gathering done with three or more parallel lines of gathering. Elastic thread can be used in the bobbin for it shirrs as it stitches.

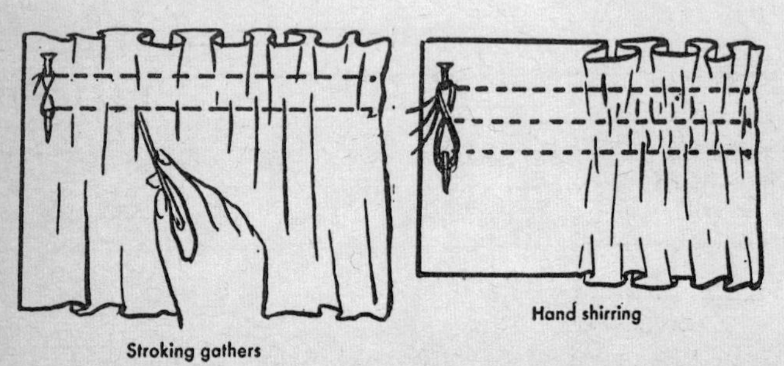

Hand shirring

Stroking gathers

*Stroking gathers:* Use needle or pin across folds to straighten material under gathering, and to space gathers evenly. Be careful with sharp pin points on delicate materials.

*Spacing gathers:* Divide gathering space into several equal portions and do the same for material to which gathered part is to be attached. For example, in attaching a gathered skirt

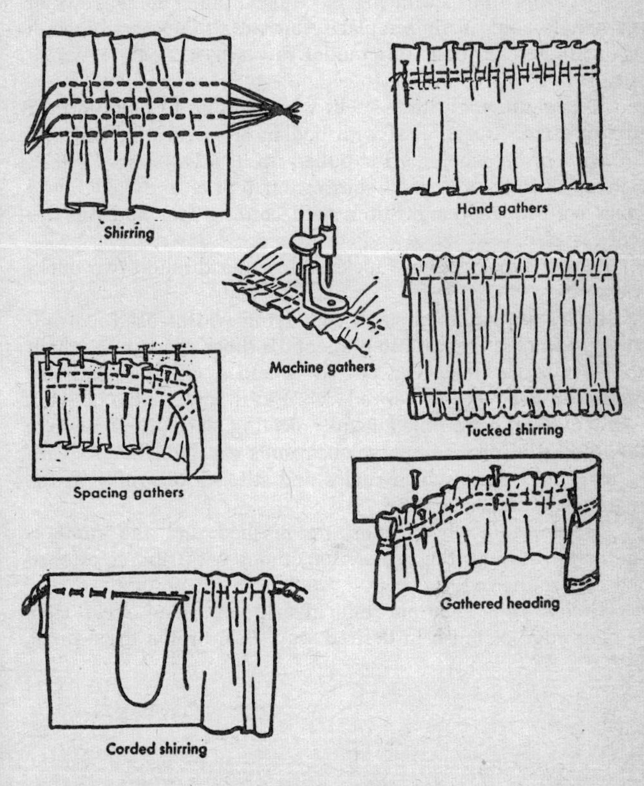

to a waistband, divide waistband into six equal parts, and mark with pin or chalk. Divide upper edge of skirt into six equal parts and mark. Run gathering lines in each section separately and attach band to skirt at the six marks with a pin. Pull up gathers in each section to fit waistband section. The gathering is thus evenly distributed. Straight edge is joined to gathered edge in a plain or lapped seam.

*Gathering stay* is a facing piece used under many rows of gathers to hold shirring in place. Cut out a piece wide enough for gathered portion, turn under raw edges, hem to wrong side.

*Corded shirring:* Stitch tucks wide enough to hold cord of desired size. Run in cord with bodkin or safety pin, and pull up cord to fit; when cord is pulled up, it gives shirred effect. Or, mark line for corded shirring on fabric, and fold fabric over cord on marking. Stitch with cording foot and pull up cord to size.

*Tucked shirring:* Baste tucks and gather through two thicknesses.

*Ruffles* are gathered strips of varying widths used as trimming. Fullness is most often about 1½ times space into which ruffle is to be sewn. Cut out strips and seam short ends together to get piece of desired size. Finish lower edge of ruffle with narrow hand-rolled hems, picoting, lace, binding, etc. With a little practice, marvelous results can be achieved with a machine ruffler, which ruffles and stitches the ruffle to the garment at the same time.

*Double ruffle:* Both ends are finished and the ruffle is gathered through the center, sometimes with ribbon stitched on over gathering.

*Circular ruffle:* Cut out ruffle in shape of a semi-circle. Hem longer edge or finish in desired way. Baste ruffle to garment,

right sides together, with ruffle held straight. Clip edge of ruffle to prevent pulling. (A circular flounce is similar but usually has less fullness.) Sew with a plain seam or top stitch on the right side.

*Applying ruffles:*

1. Bias binding: Baste ruffle to garment, wrong side of ruffle to right side of garment, ruffle facing down. Baste binding on seam line, right sides of binding and ruffle together, stitch all three thicknesses at one time. Turn binding up over seam and hem to position. Used to accent joining.

Bias binding may also be applied in this manner. Ruffle and garment are joined, right sides together. Bias is basted over ruffle and all three thicknesses are stitched. Bias is turned to wrong side and hemmed flat to the garment. Good for underwear.

2. Felled seam: Sew ruffle to fabric, wrong sides together, with plain material ¼ inch beyond ruffle (1). Turn ruffle down, press seam down, turn in edge of garment over seam, baste and stitch (2). Used for curtains, children's petticoats, etc.

3. French seam: The seam is stitched on the right side, and the allowance is cut to ⅛ inch. Turn to wrong side and stitch again. Good for applying ruffles to curtains or to collars and cuffs that are not faced and are of single thickness.

4. Tuck: Stitch a tuck ¾ inch from the edge of the garment. Attach ruffle ¼ inch from edge, wrong side of ruffle to right side of garment, press seam down. Bring tuck over to cover stitching and stitch close to the fold. Good for lingerie.

5. Self finish: Crease garment ¾ inch from edge, fold to right side. Attach ruffle ¼ inch above folded edge. Turn raw edge down, turn in edge ¼ inch and baste over stitching. Stitch or hand hem. Use for a faced collar, etc.

# 23. *HEADINGS AND CASINGS*

A HEADING is the part of the ruffle above the gathers. A gathered ruffle with a heading is very pretty at the neckline or as a decorative detail at the hem of an evening gown. A casing

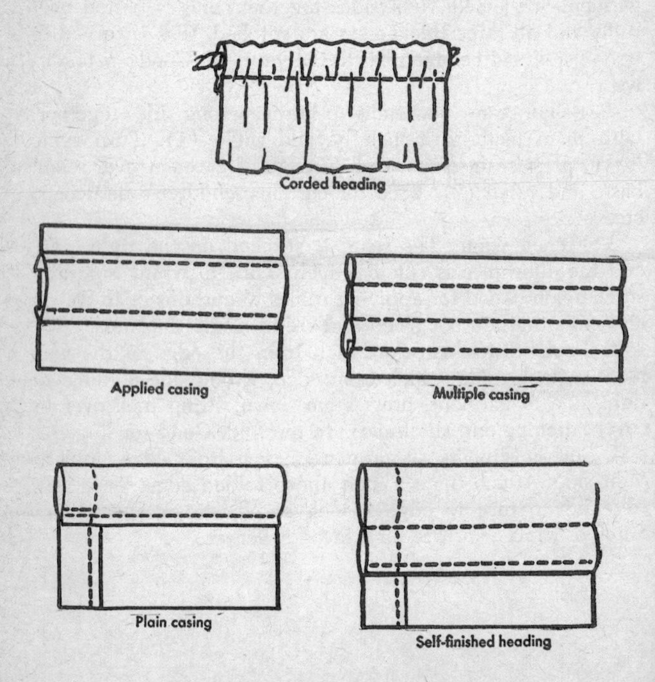
Corded heading

Applied casing

Multiple casing

Plain casing

Self-finished heading

is a hem with sides open through which to run elastic, cord, ribbon, etc.

*Self-finished heading:* Turn top edge down in a hem before gathering or stitching.

*Gathered heading:* Turn down raw edge in a hem and gather through both thicknesses.

*Straight heading with casing:* Turn down raw edge in a hem, and make two lines of stitching for the casing.

*Corded heading:* Turn down edge in a hem deep enough for the number of cords desired. Baste cord in place inside the hem and stitch on both sides with the cording foot. Then insert second cord underneath and stitch with cording foot. Continue until as many cords as desired are stitched in. This type of heading is very pretty on a bedroom lampshade.

*Plain casing:* Turn edge in a hem deep enough for desired purpose, baste and stitch. Hem will be ¼ inch to ½ inch for narrow elastic or ribbon.

*Applied casing:* Cut band wide enough, turn in raw edges on both sides, baste both sides to position, and edgestitch. Good when casing is not at top.

*Multiple casing:* Several casings under each other are formed with a very wide hem and the casings then stitched. Or, turn a narrower hem, stitch first casing, then apply as many casings as are needed below the hem, as described above.

# 24. *BINDINGS AND FACINGS*

RAW edges are often finished with bindings and facings for decorative and practical reasons. Facings are wider than bindings and are most often cut to the shape of the garment. To get a smooth finish, learn to clip around curves, trim seams close, slash to corners, and press very flat. With circular edges, ease binding or facing slightly when applying to outward or convex curve; hold taut to inward or concave curve.

Bindings and facings are often cut on the bias because of the great elasticity of this grain. To cut bias strips, fold cloth so that the selvage is perpendicular to itself. (See p. 137.) Press. Mark strips along fold the desired width with a gauge, and cut. To join short lengths together, place one piece on top of another with long cut edges perpendicular to each other. Stitch seam open, press flat, trim.

Binding sewed with zigzag stitch, either on a zigzag machine or using a zigzag attachment, will have a more decorative look and will follow the edge of the cloth more readily.

*Commercial binding,* #5, will fit into the regular machine binder, and, with a little practice, you will be able to apply bias binding with no basting. A machine binder with multiple slots will take other sizes of binding.

*Hand-felled binding:* Cut binding twice the width of the desired finish, plus seam allowance, and baste to garment edge, right sides together. Stitch on seam allowance and clip curved edges, trim seam, turn binding to inside and hem to line of machine stitching.

*Rolled felled or French binding* is made just like hand or flat felled binding finish except that double thickness of binding is used. Cut binding four times finished width plus seam allowance and proceed as above. The double thickness will give rolled effect. Do not try to press binding flat. Good for sheers.

*Imitation French binding* is made with double binding. Stitch right sides together, turn binding to wrong side and

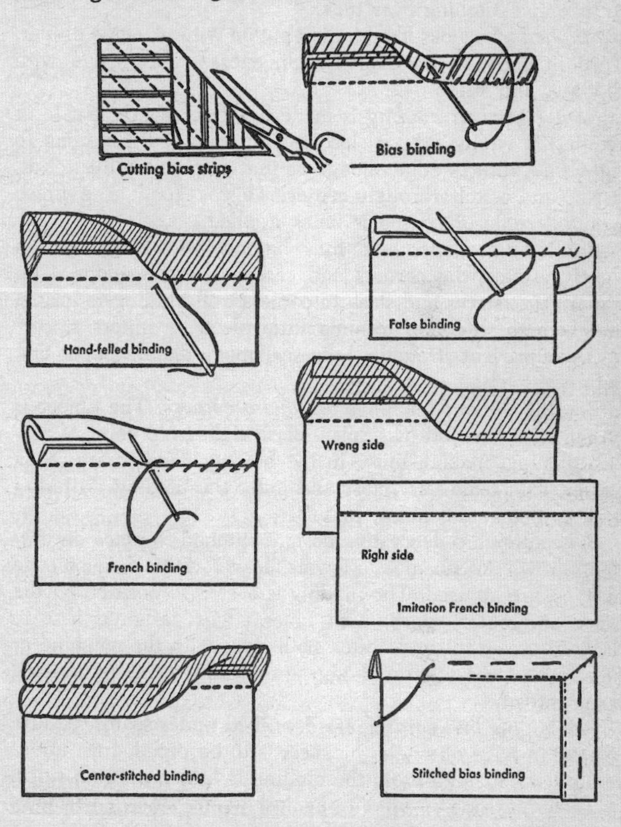

baste fold, turned in ¼ inch, just below original line of stitching. From right side, stitch on garment fabric, but not through binding, as close to binding as possible.

*False binding* is used when there is not enough material for cutting bindings. On the wrong side, baste and stitch a pin tuck, press towards edge, turn in edge ¼ inch, and hem to machine stitching over tuck.

*Stitched bias* looks like binding put on with machine binder. Turn in edges of binding ¼ inch, encase fabric edge with binding, and stitch.

*Center-stitched binding* is made by attaching right side of binding to wrong side of cloth in tiny seam. Turn binding to right side, turn in edge enough so that stitching will catch it, baste, and stitch through center. This is good as a finish where a ruffle or edging is being applied.

Binding a scalloped edge must be done with bias stretched tightly around the corners and eased around scallops. Clip around the curves and slash to corners, roll binding to inside, and hem to stitching, forming little pleats or miters at corners. To prevent stretching, pin scalloped edge on paper first before stitching.

*Binding cut-out openings or square corners.* The object is to get a very smooth flat finish. Slash right in to point of cut-out opening, making miter in the binding if necessary. At a corner, trim seam very close and miter the binding. Mitering is described under hems, p. 117.

*Bias motifs* are decorative designs stitched to place on outlines drawn in advance. Flowers, leaves, initials, geometric designs, are all used. The binding is basted to position on the inner and outer edges, with inner edges gathered first to draw in excess fullness. Stitch both sides with the machine or hand whip, or sew on with zigzag machine, using contrasting color thread.

*Bias piping and cording* are described under seams, p. 110. Where an edge of single thickness is to be piped, turn under raw edge ½ inch and fold the binding in ½ inch on both sides. Place wrong side of binding against wrong side of garment, with edge of binding extending over edge of cloth ⅛ to ¼ inch, and stitch to position from the right side. Slip stitch other edge to position.

*Continuous bias strip* is made where a very large quantity of binding is needed and it will save time to make it all at once. Fold material on a true bias, mark lines for cutting with tailor's chalk, using a gauge. Bring one end over to meet the other in a cylinder and pin edges together so that one side is above the other, exactly the width of one bias strip. Stitch seam and press open. Start cutting on the marked lines to get one long strip.

*Facings* are used where bindings or hems are impractical. Use the same fabric as the garment except where it is very heavy, and then use a lighter weight fabric. Facings for circular edges are cut along bias the same as for bindings, and applied in the same way, right sides together. When turning a facing to the wrong side, be sure that a small amount of the fabric of the garment is turned to the inside so that no seam will show.

*Fitted facings* are the same shape as the edge of the garment to be faced and are cut along the same grain. Commercial patterns give pieces for facings. Facing edgings, except edges to be joined to the garment in a seam, are usually turned in ¼ inch and edgestitched. With heavier fabrics, the edges may be left raw and catch stitched to position. Be sure to clip curves and corners, and try to attach inner edges of the facing to position in such a way that no stitches will be visible on the right side, for example, at seams.

*Facing a point,* as in a collar edge, is done by stitching the facing to the edge, right sides together, tapering to a very sharp point. Trim seam especially close at point. Turn, pushing out point with a pin.

*V-neck facing* is done by basting to place two overlapping strips. Pin in miter at corner, stitch, trim, press open. Stitch facing to edge, right sides together, trim seam, turn facing and slip stitch to position. Where facing is to be used as a trim, attach to the wrong side of garment and turn to the right side.

*Eye-slit opening* is faced, right sides together, with facing two inches wide and one inch longer than finished width of slit. Stitch an oval no wider than ⅛ inch at any point, and slash through the center to the corners; turn facing to wrong side, and finish raw edges by turning them in ¼ inch and making a running stitch all around. Tack corners.

*Tailored corner:* Mark seam line, cut diagonally into the corner to the seam line, fold back seam, press. To reinforce corner, cut a rectangular facing (or stay) and stitch diagonally to cut edge of the corner, right sides together; press, turn back stay, cut away any surplus. Turn in all edges ¼ inch and machine stitch or overcast by hand. Slip stitch to position. This is done to prevent a corner from tearing, as at a square neck.

# 25. *PLACKETS*

A PLACKET is a finished opening for hooks and eyes, snaps, buttons, zippers, etc., where necessary.

PLACKET OPENINGS

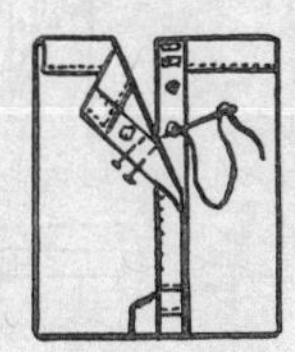
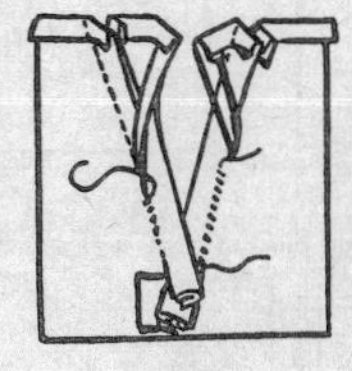
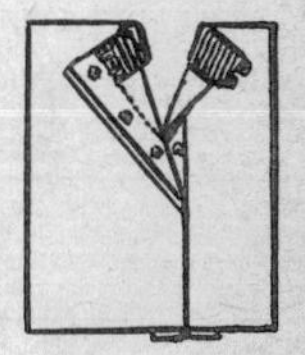

*Narrow hemmed placket:* Turn under narrow hem on each side of the opening. Fold the hem under on one side, forming a pleat, so that it laps over the other side. Reinforce lower end with diagonal backstitching. Used for infants' wear and underwear.

*Infants' placket:* Used for lightweight materials and very often in infants' clothes. Slash opening straight down and across at bottom, ¼ inch on each side of the long slash. Turn back raw edges the full width allowed for by cross slash and hem the edges by hand or machine. Lap edges by turning hem under on one side, and sew across lower end to reinforce. Often the stitches are fine running stitches or decorative feather stitching.

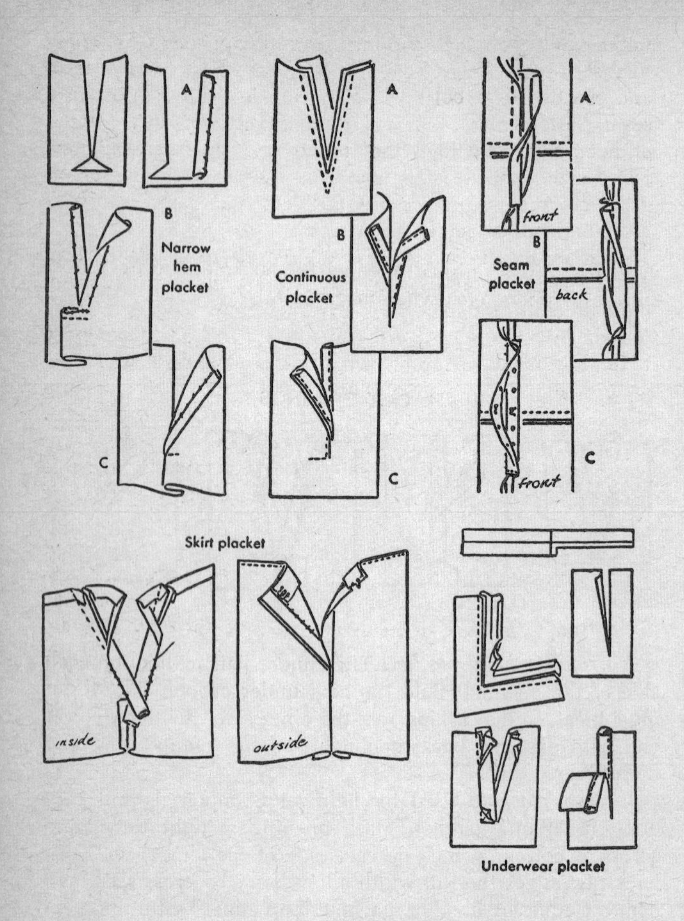


*Continuous bound placket:* Slash opening. Make facing two inches wide and twice as long as opening. Stitch to sides of opening, right sides together, stitching close at the point. Turn under raw edge ¼ inch and turn strip to wrong side, hemming to first stitching line. Fold top edge under to form overlap and stitch ends at bottom. When making this placket in a seam, slash seam allowance above and below opening. Instead of hemming, sometimes the turned free edges are stitched just inside first stitching line by machine. Used in undergarments, such as panties and half slips, and in clothes which are laundered often.

*Modified continuous placket* or *underwear placket:* Make as for continuous placket up to hemming down edges. Hem back edge to stitching as above. On front side, cut away placket to within ½ inch of bottom and ¼ inch of folded edge to remove bulk. Turn front strip all the way back on seam line, as for a facing, and hem by hand to garment. Since hemming will show on right side, placket is used for underwear mostly. However, in heavy materials, where removal of bulk is important, front edge can be slip stitched for almost invisible finish. Used in undergarments, children's clothes and sleeve openings. Less bulky than continuous bound placket.

*Seam placket:* Used for dress openings. Cut two bias strips one inch longer than opening and 1½ inches wide. Clip seam above and below opening. Sew strips on right sides together. Turn front strip back to inside flat, turn in raw edge and slip stitch to dress. Back piece forms an extension by turning raw edge in and slip stitching to seam line. Stitch strips together across top and bottom. Sew on snaps and hook and eye at waist.

*Skirt placket in two pieces.* With waistband: Cut two strips ¾ inch wide and one inch longer than opening. Open back seam flat by slashing back seam allowance, stitch strips to opening, right sides together. Turn to inside, hem to stitching or stitch just inside first line. Turn overlap (front) edge back and stitch to underlap across bottom. Waistband is usually added to skirt top over placket.

With inner belting: Finish placket as above except that overlap is turned on seam line, like a facing, all the way back, and strips are hemmed by hand to wrong side. Then make belt, as on p. 170, press and sew snaps into skirt placket. Belting hooks under placket to give firm smooth, usually higher, waistline. Do not catch belting and placket together.

*Zippers:* Baste opening as though you were closing it in a continuation of the seam. Press sharply and remove bastings. (Edges are turned back to inside.) Sew back edge on to right side of zipper close to metal. Stitch with cording foot. Front edge is pinned over zipper, completely covering it. Use one pin right under the other. Leave pins in, baste on front side of zipper, catching in tape. Stitch down and across at bottom for skirt; start across for dress, at top, then down and across at bottom.

Keep zipper closed when working. Back edge may be creased ⅛ inch outside seam line for greater ease in overlapping front. Bottom may be stitched diagonally, as well as straight across. Where seam allowance is not wide enough, stitch seam binding on to seam edges to extend them. If you can think that far ahead, it is a good idea to cut out an extra allowance at the zipper opening when cutting out garment.

In a slashed opening, as at the neck or the bottom of the sleeve, stitch facing pieces on to both sides of opening, right sides together; turn facings to wrong side and press before inserting zipper. Baste edges of the slash together with diagonal basting. Put zipper under basted edges, with center of metal directly under the basted edges. Baste on both sides of metal firmly and stitch with cording foot, down, across and up. Rip bastings.

Be sure to use right kind and size of zipper for your purpose.

Skirt zippers are seven inches and are open at the top.

Dress zippers are nine or ten inches and closed at both ends.

Tight fitting dresses may require a longer dress zipper, perhaps twelve inches. The top of the zipper should be about four inches above the waistline.

# 26. *POCKETS*

POCKETS are of two kinds: patch pockets, which are shaped pieces set on the outside of the garment, and set-in pockets, which are inserted into a slit, so that the bulk of the fabric is on the inside of the garment. Patch pockets are the simpler kind and are used for aprons, work clothes, and informal garments. The style chosen depends on the style of the garment and the individual taste of the wearer. Set-in pockets are usually made in more tailored clothes. General rules for pockets are: stitching on the outside must be straight for a good appearance, pairs must be carefully balanced, pocket must not be too high or too low, top corners must be carefully reinforced.

Pockets are sometimes finished off at the top ends with bar tacks. Make several vertical stitches, then work over them with

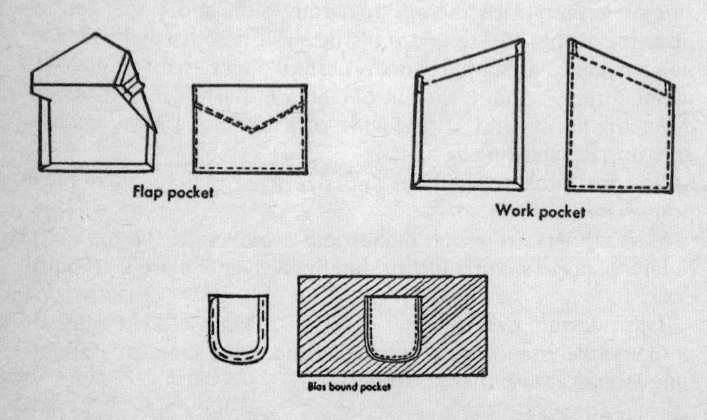

small overhand stitches that catch in garment material. Two smaller bar tacks may be placed horizontally on each end.

*Patch pockets:* The following are just a few of the many possible styles. It is a good idea to stitch a tape on the wrong side of the garment where the top of the pocket will be.

*Work pockets:* Turn in a hem on the pocket all around and baste. Baste and stitch pocket to garment. Or, turn in a hem on three sides, baste. Then turn down top hem and slip stitch to place. Baste and stitch pocket to garment.

*Lined patch pocket:* Cut two pocket pieces, turn in seam edges on each to wrong side, and baste; then baste two pieces together, wrong sides inside. Sew across top in a decorative manner by hand or machine, baste and stitch to garment.

Or, cut two pocket pieces, one smaller than the other by the depth of the hem. Stitch them across the top, right sides together, press the seam open. Bring the lining down so that bottom edges meet. The seam just made is no longer at the top. Stitch around on three sides, leaving a space of 1½ inches at the bottom to turn. Trim the seams, turn the pocket right side out, press. Turn in raw edges and slip stitch together. Baste and stitch pocket to garment.

*Flap pocket:* Turn under the edges of the pocket and the edges of the flap on three sides and baste. Sew right side of flap to wrong side of pocket across the top. Trim seam, turn flap over to right side, stitch flap down or use a decorative hand stitch around the edges. Baste and stitch the pocket to the garment.

Or, turn three sides of pocket under and baste. Cut out two flaps of desired shape, stitch them, right sides together, on three sides. Trim seams, turn flap right side out and press. Baste flap on to top of pocket, raw edges all meeting. Baste bias binding on top and stitch through all thicknesses. Turn bias to wrong side and slip stitch flat to position. Baste and stitch pocket to garment.

Or, turn three sides of pocket under and baste. Cut out two flaps, each double the width of the finished flap. Stitch on three sides, right sides together, trim seams, and turn right side out. Turn raw edges to inside and baste. Edgestitch all around. Fold flap in half and encase top of pocket in between. Baste and stitch flap to pocket, then stitch pocket to garment.

*Set-in pockets:*

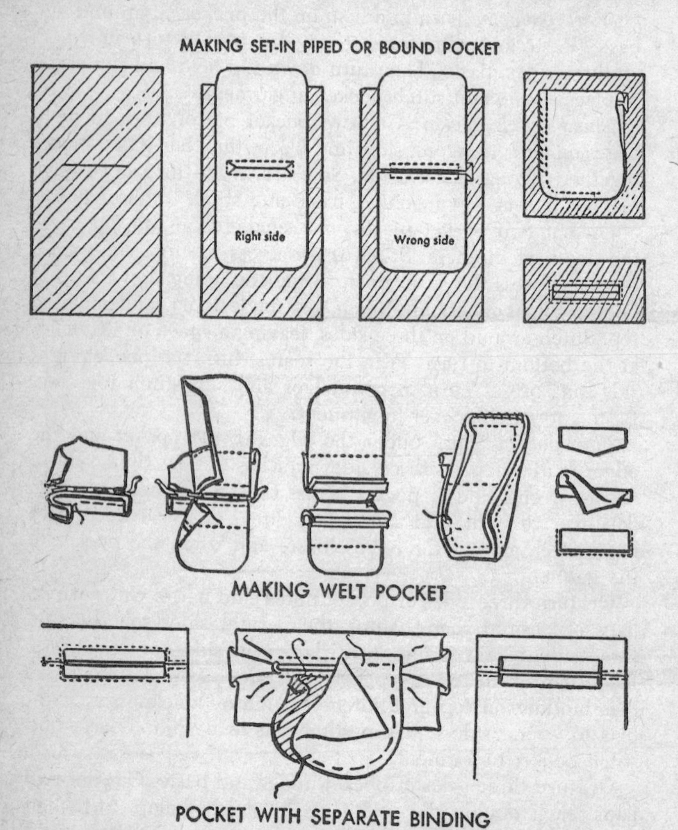

*Seam pocket:* Turn down top edge ¼ inch to wrong side and stitch. Fold along hem line to right side, stitch from top fold to bottom of hem, at the seam line on both sides. Trim top corners, turn hem to wrong side, stitch across top, if desired, and again at bottom of hem on right side. Turn in seam allowance all around, baste. Stitch pocket to garment.

*Bound patch pocket:* Baste binding on to edges of pocket, right sides together. Trim seams, turn binding to wrong side and baste. Binding may be slip stitched to the top of the pocket. Baste and stitch pocket to garment.

*Set-in piped or bound pocket:* Cut a piece for pocket, twice as long as finished pocket, plus one inch, and about ¾ to one inch longer than pocket opening. Fold in half crosswise, and place crease on marked line for opening, with strip open flat. Mark opening on pocket, baste in place and machine stitch a box exactly as long as the pocket opening, and ½ inch deep (¼ inch above and below crease). Slash through center to ¼ inch of ends, then diagonally to corners with small sharp scissors. Turn pocket to inside through slash. Make two little pleats from above and below so that edges meet in center of slash, and hold them together with a line of diagonal basting. Machine stitch a box around opening through the original stitching to catch binding in place permanently, or catch by hand with tiny invisible stitches from right side. On wrong side, turn pocket down, stitch all around through the little triangles formed by the slashing, but free of the garment, and overcast edges together. Sometimes the ends are finished with arrowheads (see p. 201). The finished pocket looks like a bound buttonhole (p. 178), gives a tailored look.

*Welt pocket:* The welt pocket also gives a tailored effect, especially with lightweight or medium-weight fabrics, and is made like the set-in pocket just discussed. While the piped pocket has two lips like a buttonhole, the welt pocket has just one. Make pocket like set-in bound pocket, as described above, but instead of forming two lips or pleats, fold the lower part up to meet the top of the opening exactly, and basted, together with diagonal basting. All other details are the same as above.

*Pocket with separate binding:* Cut binding about 2½ inches wide and one inch longer than the opening. Baste the binding in place over the marked place for the opening, stitch about ⅜ inch to ½ inch wide around mark for opening, slash through center of box and diagonally to corners. Turn binding to wrong side through slash, forming two pleats together that meet in the center. Diagonal baste the edges of these lips or pleats together. On right side, sew through original stitching for the box by hand or machine. Now cut two pocket pieces, one longer than the other about ½ inch. Stitch right side of longer one to upper edge of binding on the inside, and stitch right side of shorter one to lower edge of binding. Baste pocket pieces together to form a pouch, stitch around on three sides. Overcast edges together. Separate binding is used for contrasting decorative effect and can be repeated in buttonholes. Binding may be straight, rounded, or S-shaped for further decorative detail.

*Pocket with separate welt:* This type of pocket is used for heavy garments, as coats, and for wool skirts, jackets, and slacks. Cut welt piece 2½ inches wide and 1 inch longer than the opening. Fold it through the center crosswise, right sides out, and baste to the right side of the garment, the raw edges just below the place for the pocket opening. Cut two pocket pieces, one ½ inch longer than the other. Baste shorter piece, right side down, over the welt. Baste the longer piece wrong side down, above the welt. Stitch the length of the opening ¼ inch above and below the raw edges. Fold pouch pieces back on stitched line, slash through the center and diagonally to the ends of the stitching line. Turn pocket piece and welt ends through the slash to the wrong side. On the inside, stitch through the little triangles formed by the slash, and through the welt pieces; turn the upper piece down. Baste pouch together, stitch around, and overcast edges.

*Flap set-in pocket:* Cut out two flaps, stitch them, right sides together, on three sides. Trim the seams, turn right side out, press, and baste above the marked line for opening, raw edges down. Now proceed exactly as above for pocket with separate welt. To finish pocket, turn flap down.

*Pocket in a seam:* Stitch the seam, leaving an opening several inches shorter than the pocket. Stitch one pocket piece, right sides together to front opening, and other pocket piece to back opening, as far down as the bottom of the opening. Clip seam at bottom, turn pocket pieces to wrong side, and baste together to form a pouch. Stitch, free of garment, from top around pocket and up to seam opening. The top of the pocket is caught in the waistband of a skirt or in the waistline seam of a dress. This is a kind of secret pocket.

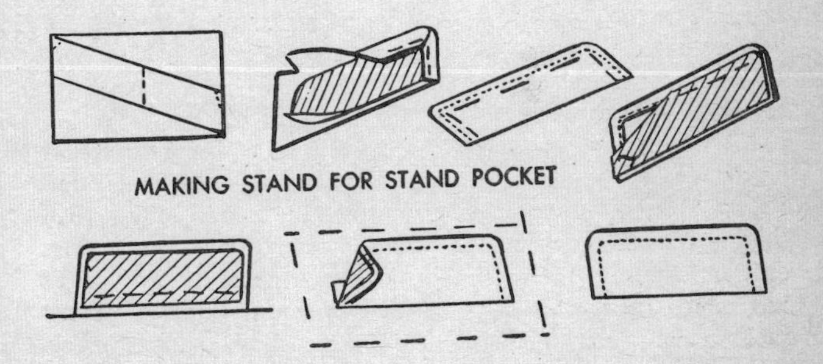
MAKING STAND FOR STAND POCKET

*Stand pocket:* This kind of pocket is good for clothes of masculine design. It is made like pocket with separate welt and flap pocket. The stand is different from the flap in that the flap faces down, while the stand is a straight piece facing up. Make the stand like the flap above. (For softer material, baste an interfacing on to the wrong side of one part of the stand, and turn edges of stand in ½ inch over interfacing. Stitch other stand piece on, right sides together; trim seams

# 27. *NECK OPENINGS*

THE neck opening depends on the style of the garment. You should choose styles that are becoming to you; for example, round necklines are unsuitable for stout, round faces, V-shaped lines are more flattering. (See pp. 58-62.)

*Round neckline:* Cut bias strip about two inches wide and the length of the opening plus one inch. Join the short ends in a ½-inch seam. Press seam open, turn in bottom edge ¼ inch, baste and stitch close to fold. Stitch bias to neckline at seam line, right sides together. Clip and trim seam. Turn to wrong side so that no seam shows on right side, slip stitch to position with practically invisible stitches on right side.

*Straight bound opening:* Mark, but do not cut, opening. Cut a straight piece about 2½ inches wide and two inches longer than length of opening. Turn under ¼ inch on two long sides and one short side; stitch. Baste piece to garment, right sides together, with center over marked line. Stitch ¼ inch from center on both sides, and straight across bottom. Cut through center to within ½ inch of bottom and diagonally to corners. Turn to wrong side and catch to position. Or, stitch a triangle, starting ¼ inch from center at top, and tapering to nothing at bottom. Slash to point, turn.

*Bound slash:* Slash opening and stitch on bias strip about one inch wide, right sides together. Trim seams, turn in raw edge of binding ¼ inch and stitch. Turn to wrong side. Hem to stitching.

*V neckline:* Pin 1½ inches bias on to both sides of V, right sides together. Miter point by overlapping two pieces and stitching a triangle. Trim seam and press open. Baste bias to opening. Stitch around V, pivoting at corner with needle down, presser foot up. Clip to point, trim seam, turn to wrong side. Turn edge of facing in ¼ inch and stitch near fold, then slip stitch to garment.

*Square neckline:* Pin bias pieces along both sides and bottom. Pin in miter at corners, stitch, trim seam, press open. Trim seam, turn facing to wrong side. Turn raw edge under ¼ inch, edgestitch, and slip stitch facing to position.

*Neck zipper:* Slash opening, turn back full seam allowance, clipping in seam at bottom to lie flat; press. Diagonal baste center folds together, and pin in zipper, with fold lines over center of metal, completely covering zipper. Baste on both sides and stitch with cording foot close to metal and across bottom. If seam allowance is not wide enough, add seam binding to edges before turning back; ½-inch seam will do.

Or, use a facing for lightweight fabrics. Cut out piece three inches wide and two inches longer than zipper. Turn in edges ¼ inch all around, slash for opening and turn back seam allowance as above. Baste folds close to metal on each side, wrong sides together. Then continue as above.

*Loop closing:* Slash opening. Sew loops on (see p. 174) between facings and garment. Sew facing on, right sides together, turn to wrong side.

*Placket opening:* Cut a facing piece 2½ inches wide, ½ inch longer than opening. Turn one long and one short edge in ¼ inch, stitch close to fold. Baste raw edge on to left side of opening, right side to wrong side of opening. Stitch. Turn to right side, baste over seam and stitch. Cut a facing piece one inch longer than opening and twice as wide as finished placket plus seam allowance. Turn in ¼ inch on long edges, crease lengthwise through center. Open, cut an angle on one side and straight across on other as in illustration. Turn this cut side in ¼ inch, clipping it at inside corner to lie flat. Recrease through center; insert right hand side of slash between edges, point down. Baste flat, stitch to point at top of angle, across and up other side. Close placket with basting, as it will look when finished, and stitch around point, catching in underlap. Buttonholes and buttons usually fasten a placket of this type.

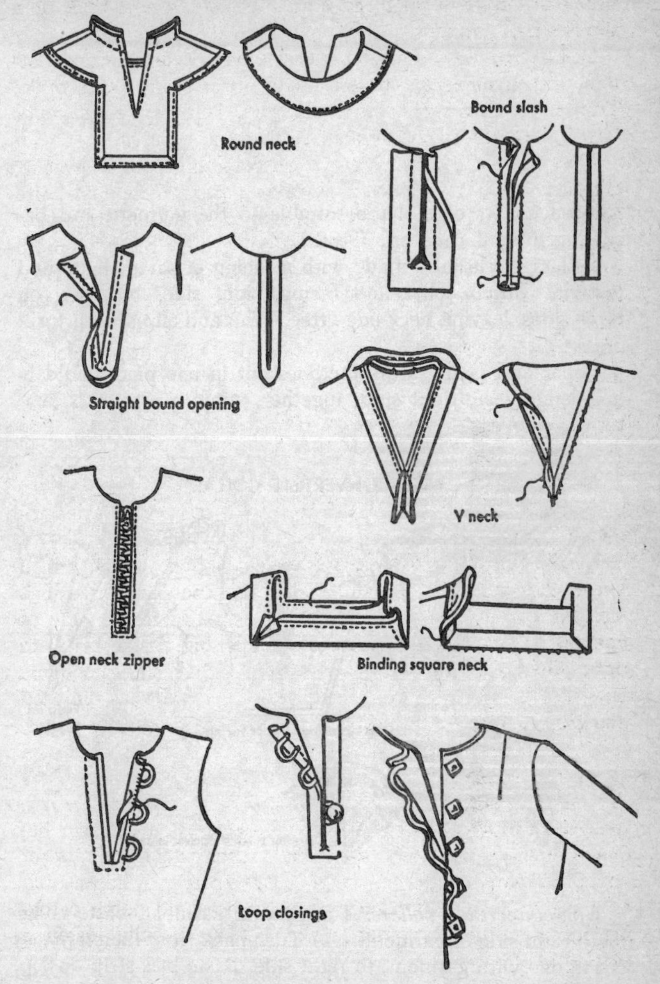
Round neck
Bound slash
Straight bound opening
Y neck
Open neck zipper
Binding square neck
Loop closings

# 28. COLLARS

CHOOSE collars of a shape suitable to the garment and becoming to you. (See pp. 58-62.)

Collars are usually made with a facing of same shape and material. Stitch collar and facing, right sides together, on three sides, leaving neck edge free. Trim and clip seams; turn; press.

Collar and facing are sometimes cut in one piece. Fold in half lengthwise, right sides together, stitch across ends, and turn as above.

NON-CONVERTIBLE COLLAR

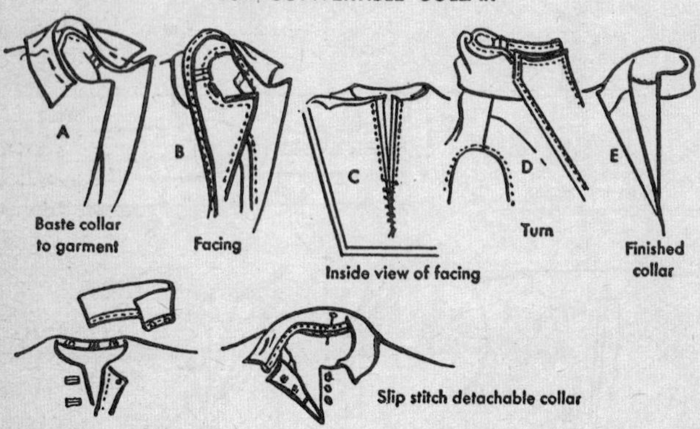


*Non-convertible collars:* To apply to garment, baste collar on to right side of garment. (A) Turn back front facing pieces cut in one with garment, to right side. Baste bias strip on top, in center part, between facings, and stitch through all thicknesses. Trim and clip seam, turn bias and facings to wrong side, turn edges (B) of bias under ¼ inch, stitching close to fold, then slip stitch bias to position on wrong side.

Or, collar is basted and stitched on right side of garment only from each end (C) to shoulder seam through front facing pieces turned back to right side over the collar. Under collar only is stitched to garment in center section between shoulder seams. Trim seams. Turn facing to wrong side. At shoulder seam, clip seam from top edge to stitching of under collar. Hem free edge of collar in center part over stitching on wrong side.

For collar of one thickness of fabric only, finish edge with lace, ruffling, hem, etc., before attaching to garment. Attach with bias basted over collar, stitched and turned to wrong side, where it is hemmed to position. Or attach with French seam (see pp. 108, 109).

*Detachable collar:* Face and turn collar as above. Encase raw edges at top in a 1½-inch bias strip with bias edges turned in ¼ inch on each side. Stitch bias on to collar. Place collar on garment and slip stitch bound edge to inside of garment about ½ inch down. Or, sew in snaps for easy permanent joining.

*Convertible collars* are worn straight up or turned down. Make a straight bound opening at neck (see p. 153); stitch outside of collar to wrong side of neckline, through blouse facing; press seam up. Turn under free edge of collar facing and hem to seam line on right side.

Or, for heavier fabric, stitch under layer of collar to neck edge, right sides together, before turning back blouse front facing, and trim seam allowance. Turn collar up, clip seam, turn under raw edges of collar and blouse facing, turn facing to wrong side, slip stitch top layer of collar to top of facing. Roll collar to natural position, hem free edge in center section of upper part of collar down.

*Notched collar* is a type of convertible collar. Face collar and turn. Stitch to right side of garment, turn under blouse facing edges ¼ inch; stitch, and turn blouse facing to right side. Stitch outside edge of facing along fold starting at bottom, pivot at top corner and stitch across to edge of facing. Stitching line should meet line of stitching for collar. Clip seam of facing, especially close at corner; turn facing to inside. Turn collar up so that seam is on back inside edge, facing down, and press seam. Baste bias strip over seam, ends under facing, and hem both sides by hand. Catch facing to garment.

For heavier materials, as wool, use the tailor's method. Sew the under collar to neck, right sides together. Clip seam line in at front edge of collar and at shoulder. Press seam open between clips and turn collar up. Attach upper collar to separate front facing; clip seams to press open as above. Baste facing to garment, right sides together, carefully. Turn collar up. Stitch along outside edge from bottom of facing up; pivot at corner across to collar seam line, up and around collar, down to garment seam line, across and down edge of facing. Clip seams, trim corners, turn facing and collar to inside. Roll collar to normal position, clip seam, hem free edge down.

*Standing shirt collar:* Face collar, turn. Cut out two strips for a band for the standing part, insert raw collar edges between two, right sides together, and stitch on seam line through all thicknesses. Trim seam to ¼ inch, turn band pieces down, press. Baste and stitch inner band to inside of shirt, right sides together. Turn under edge of outer band and baste in position on outside over seam. Stitch.

To finish collars, use decorative stitches or shell edge. For lace or embroidered edging in double collar, apply between two layers of collar before stitching around sides. When collar is turned, lace will form an edging.

# 29. YOKES

YOKES are often emphasized with stitching or by making the yoke of a different fabric. Yoke can be tucked, shirred, smocked, or decorated in a great many ways.

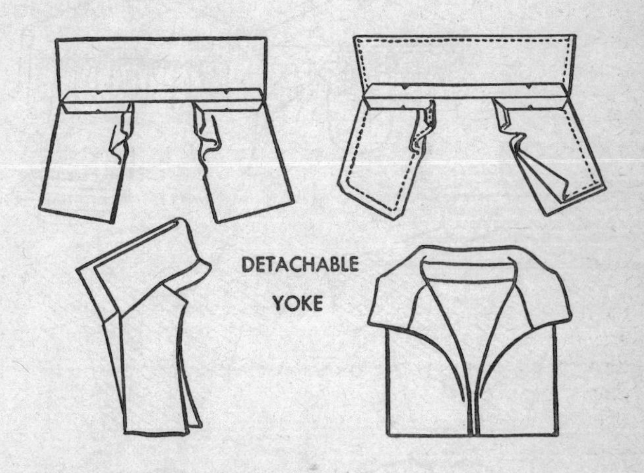


*Stitched-in yokes:* Attach yoke to garment with plain seams.

*Overlaid yokes:* Turn yoke edges back and attach over garment edge in lapped effect. Stitch close to edge, or back ¼ inch, as desired. Where this type of yoke is done with transparent materials, it is often a good idea to stitch over paper and then tear the paper away.

For lace yoke, finish edge of garment to which lace is to be applied and sew on lace by hand.

Or, stitch lace and garment together, and overcast a lace edging to garment over seam. This is done when lace has no finished edge.

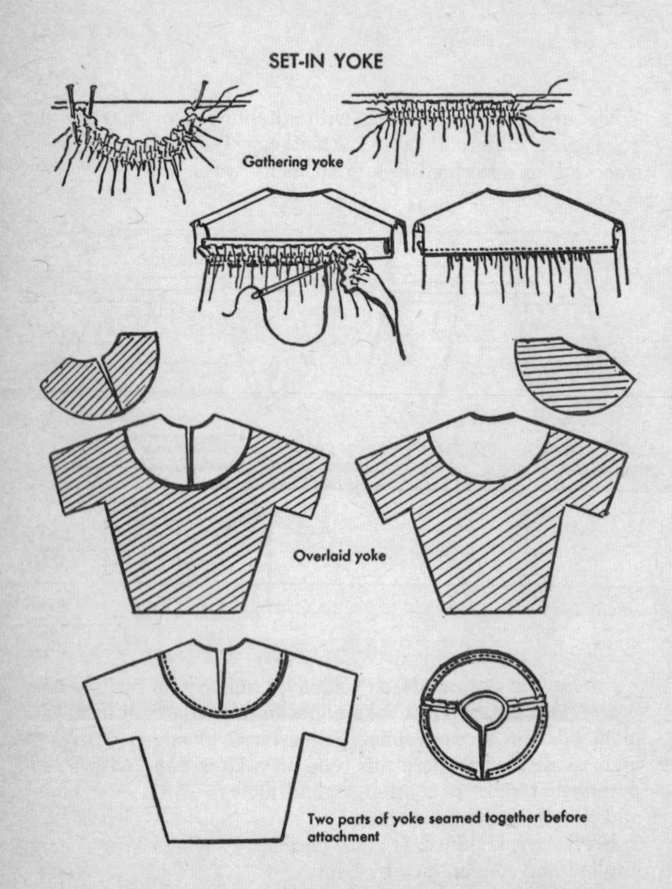

*Detachable yokes:* Made with button closing.

*Skirt yokes:* Attached as blouse yokes above, with plain or lapped seams.

# 30. SLEEVES

SLEEVES can be the telltale mark that a garment is homemade. So make sleeves carefully and set them in with special attention given to pressing top of sleeve. One-piece sleeve is folded right sides together and underarm seam is stitched. Two-

TYPES OF SLEEVE

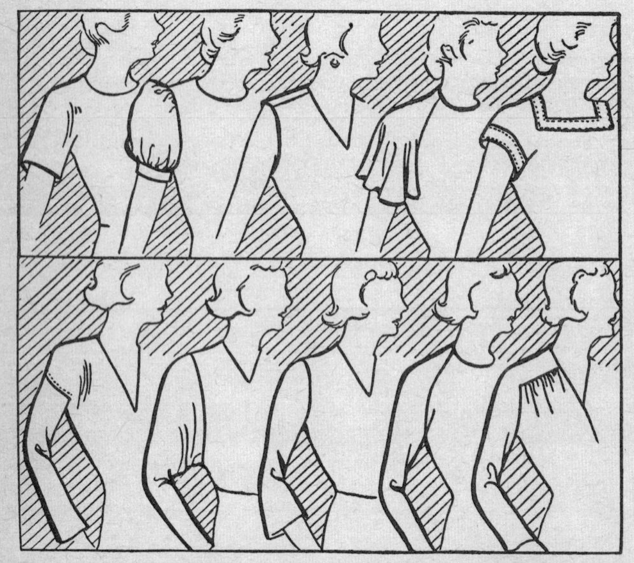

*Top row:* Kimono, Puffed, Sleeveless, Cape, Drop    *Bottom row:* Drop shoulder, Dolman, ¾ Set-in, Raglan, Epaulet

piece, or tailored, sleeve is placed right sides together, and stitched along underarm and side seams. Press seams open, turn right side out. Put in elbow or shoulder darts or gathers before sewing up seams.

*To set in sleeve with little fullness:*

1. Make sleeve. Drop, right side out, into armhole from wrong side of garment.

2. Match notches, V and VV, underarm seam, shoulder. Put in all pins perpendicular to edge, points down. Baste around bottom between notches.

3. Divide area between shoulder and notch in half and pin. Subdivide into halves again and pin. Continue until all fullness is pinned in.

4. Baste on seam line with short stitches, keeping left thumb on fullness and flattening fullness down as you ease it on to needle. Stretch armhole tightly as you work. Remove pins.

5. Check appearance of seam on right side for rounded smooth line. Press seam towards sleeve after stitching and press on a tailor's hem to give rounded appearance.

*To set in sleeve with a lot of fullness:* Work as above with this change. On seam line do a row of tiny running stitches and two more, ¼ inch above and below first line between notches at top. When setting in sleeve, pull up gathers between notches to fit. Or do machine gathering.

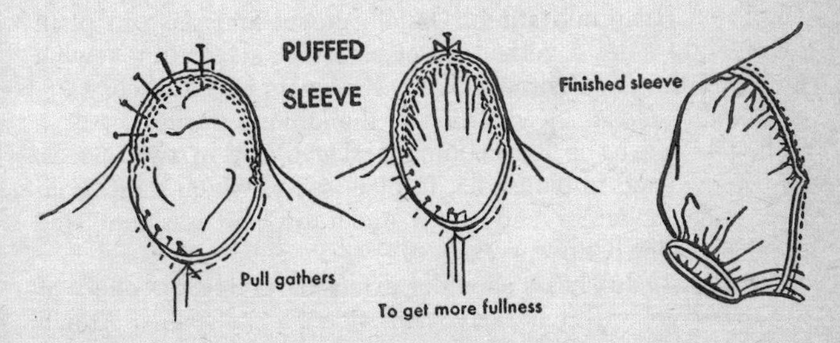

*Finishing the armscye:* Finish sleeve seam with pinking, overcasting, or a second row of stitching outside first and seam allowance trimmed. Finishing with an overedge stitch on the zigzag machine will give a smooth, strong finish.

THREE WAYS TO FINISH ARMSCYE

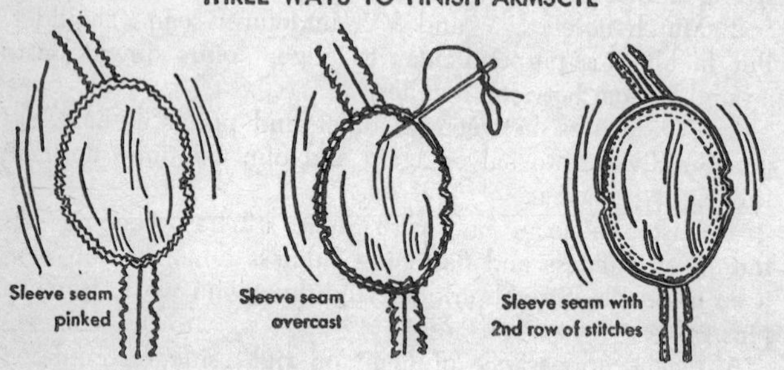


*Kimono sleeve:* This is cut in one with blouse. Sew under and side seam in a continuous line with double row of stitching for strength. Clip around underarm curve, and overcast or blanket stitch clips to reinforce.

Or, slash at underarm, and set in a gusset for more ease. Turn under seam allowance at slash, clipping where necessary and baste back. Pin over gusset as for lapped seam (p. 110), baste and stitch. Or join gusset and slash in plain seam, right sides together. Pivot carefully at corners, sewing to within ⅛ inch of corner. Overcast corners to reinforce.

*Dolman sleeve* is a variation of the kimono sleeve.

*Raglan sleeve* is like a kimono sleeve but in two pieces. Sleeve is joined to blouse flat in plain seams which slant. Fold right sides together and stitch underarm and garment side seam together. Clip curves.

*Epaulet sleeve* has a shoulder extension giving the effect of a narrow yoke. Stitch sleeve and side blouse seams. Attach

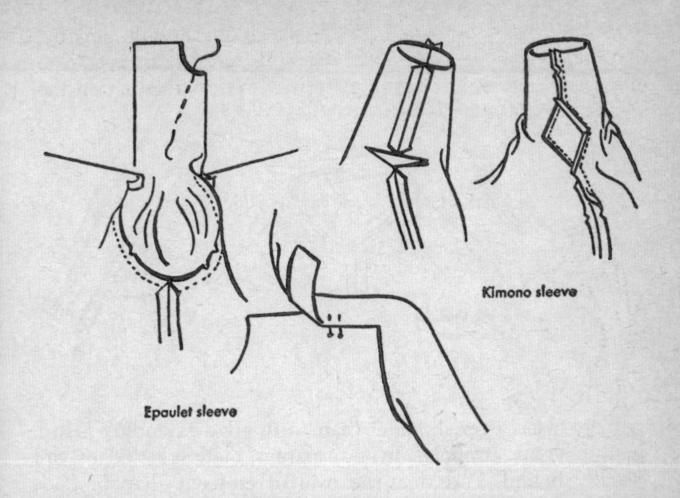


sleeve to garment armhole, right sides together. Attach strap part to shoulders in lapped seam.

Or, pin in entire sleeve to garment starting with epaulet and from shoulder seam, around armscye, and finishing at the back. Baste and stitch as a continuous plain seam. Top stitch on right side.

*Puffed sleeve* is gathered at top. Set in sleeve, pulling up gathers to fit.

*Shirt sleeve* is put in after yoke is attached to shoulders. Join sleeve to armhole in stitched fell seam and then underarm seam same way. Girl's soft shirt may be attached with plain seam under the arms.

*Shoulder pads:* Pattern pieces for making them are given in most patterns. Or, they may be bought at notion counters. Cotton or crepe dresses can have a little ruffle of taffeta sewed into seam at top of sleeve. Wool usually has triangular pad. Cut a square and fold diagonally. Stuff with cotton wadding, more thickly in center, turn in raw edges and slip stitch to-

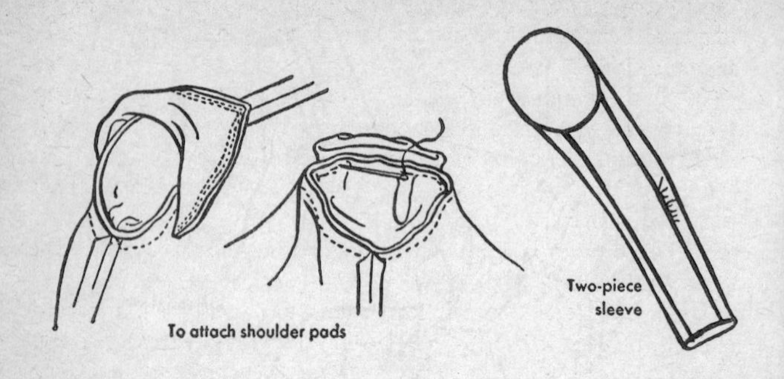


To attach shoulder pads

gether. Insert over shoulder seam with edge extending ½ to ¾ inch beyond armhole. In transparent materials, edges are usually bound. Pads may be oval or crescent shaped. Pads may be made of crinoline, or have a crinoline interfacing. Sometimes the pad is stitched on two sides, turned inside out, and the raw edges are then turned under and slip stitched or bound. The exact size and shape of pads is dependent on the style of the garment and the amount of attention to be called to the shoulders.

*Tight sleeve:*

1. Make bound opening exactly like straight bound neck opening (p. 153). For loop closing, sew loops on garment before applying facing.

2. Hemmed finish: Clip seam at the top of the opening. Fold seam allowance of the back part in half to make a narrow hem, and slip stitch to position. Turn full seam allowance of the front edge and the bottom to the wrong side, and slip stitch all around, mitering the corners. Finish with snap fasteners.

If seam allowance is not wide enough, stitch seam binding to the edges. Turn sleeve opening back on seam lines to wrong side and slip stitch binding to position. Reinforce top of opening by overcasting the clipped seams at the top of the opening together. Do not allow stitches to show on the right side. Fasten with snaps.

3. Slash opening about 2½ inches. Apply a straight strip two inches wide and five inches long around opening, right sides together. Stitch a V, tapering to nothing at the top. Fold strip in half and hem on wrong side over stitching. Front part forms overlap.

4. Close with zipper, following directions (p. 154) for neck zipper.

*Cuffs* are made like collars. Where cuff is to have a button closing, be sure it exactly fits the edges of the sleeve opening. When cuff and sleeve are cut in one, make sleeve seam a little wider at cuff end so cuff turns back over sleeve easily.

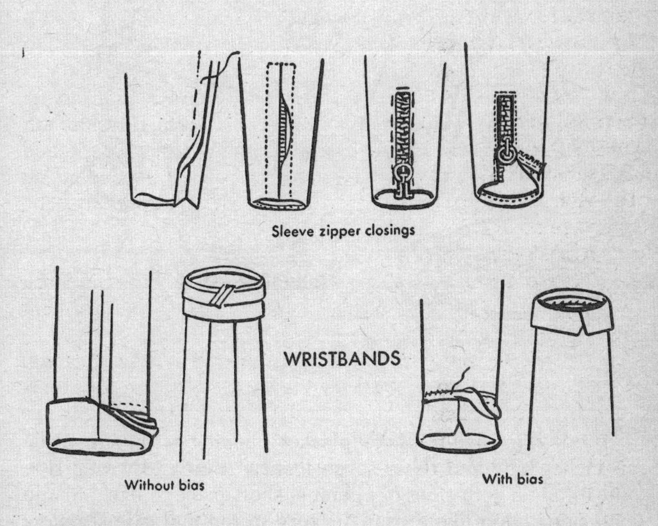


Sleeve zipper closings

*Wristband:* Piece is cut twice as wide as finished cuff plus seams, and as long as wrist plus seams. Fold in half, right sides together, and stitch ends. Turn right side out after trimming seams, and press. Stitch one thickness to right side of sleeve, press seam up towards wristband, hem free edge over seam on inside.

Or, apply on right side. Place bias strip over, stitch all together. Turn bias to inside and hem to position.

*Fold back band.* Make cuff. Attach right side to wrong side of sleeve through one thickness. Fold to outside and hem free edge over seam.

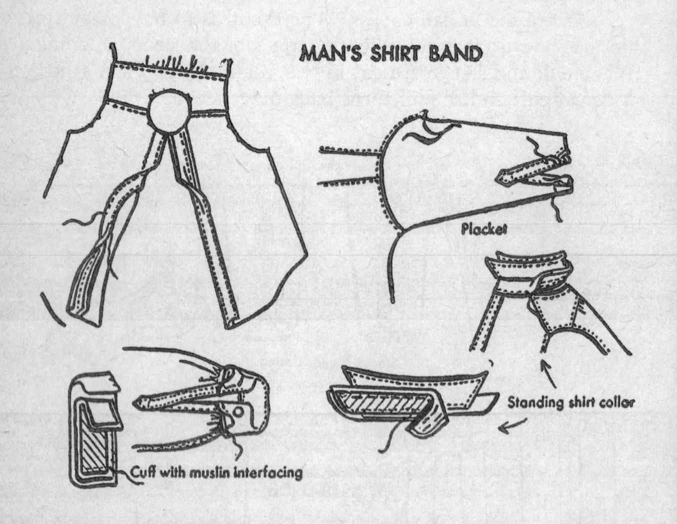


*Man's shirt band:* Make placket opening with one piece 5½ inches long and other seven inches. Attach to wrong side and stitch on both sides of opening, short piece to back. Shape long side at top like a triangle, turn in top and side seam allowance. Bring short, then long, piece to outside, fold them in half, baste edges over seam line on both sides. Stitch underlap (shorter one). Baste placket in finished position, stitch around and across shaped top. Rip basting, push underlap out of way, stitch overlap along edges and across. Now apply cuff to wrong side through one thickness, gathering sleeve to fit; baste other edge to right side over stitching, with edge turned in, and machine stitch through all thicknesses with two lines. (When cuff is made, a muslin interfacing may be applied on wrong side of one cuff piece, with two cuff pieces in position, right sides together, for stitching. This is for body, not for stiffening.) Make buttonhole and sew button on.

# 31. *BELTS*

BELTS are usually cut on the straight of the goods. Often they are shaped to fit the waist: the bottom edge is made longer than the top edge. Sometimes one end is shaped like a triangle. Several rows of stitching may be applied for decoration, as well as to give a stiffening effect.

*Single belt:* Finish edges all around with a hem or binding. Add decorative stitches, if desired.

*Double belt:* Cut out strip of desired length and twice finished width plus seams. Fold lengthwise, right sides together, stitch around, leaving an opening for turning. Trim seams close at corners, press seams open before turning. Turn belt right side out. Turn under raw edges and slip stitch.

To add stiffening with this method of constructing the belt, fold strip right sides together, place a piece of grosgrain, taffeta, muslin or belting on top, and stitch all three together. Continue as above.

*Two-piece belt:* Turn under seam allowance all around, insert stiffening under turned edges of one piece, baste and stitch two pieces, wrong sides together.

*Set-in belt:* Join belt to bodice and skirt with plain seams and top stitch. Or, turn seam allowance of belt under, and apply to garment in lapped seam. Where set-in belt is shaped, stitch very carefully around points and curves or the finished effect will be poor.

*Inner belt:* Sometimes a skirt is finished without a band at the top. Cut a piece of belting, ½ inch longer than waist, turn back ends ¼ inch, and hem. Attach hooks and eyes to ends to just fit around waist. Top of skirt is lap seamed to belting, letting skirt extend a little above belting. Where you do not want stitching to show on right side, turn top seam allowance of skirt over belting on wrong side and catch stitch.

*Drawstring:* Waistline often has casing stitched over it for belt. See pp. 134-135 for casings.

*Skirt belt or waistband:* Turn belt, right sides together, stitch two short ends. Trim close at corners, turn right side out, press. Apply one thickness to wrong side of skirt, stitch. Turn free end over stitching on right side and stitch. Or, apply one thickness on right side, hem free edge on wrong side.

Wide sashes are usually cut on the bias, and finished with a narrow hem or picot edging.

Bound buttonholes are made before seaming and turning belt.

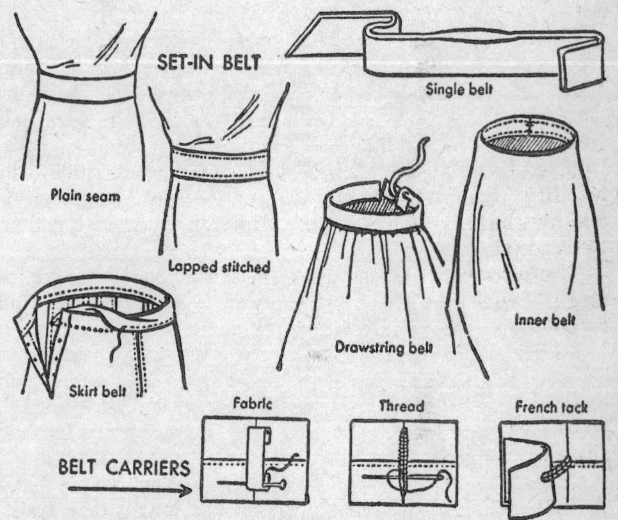


*Belt carriers:*

1. Fabric tube turned under at ends and tacked on either side of waistline.

2. Thread carrier. Several vertical stitches are taken over waistline, and then worked over with blanket stitches.

3. French tack. Like thread carrier, but done between garment and inside of belt so that nothing shows on right side.

# 32. *BUTTONS, BUTTONHOLES, FASTENINGS*

MARK place for buttons, buttonholes, fastenings, hooks, snaps, etc., very carefully. Use a cardboard gauge, and run a line of basting through where the centers of the fastenings will be. Use heavy thread except on very sheer fabrics. Linen thread is good for especially hard wear. Snaps, hooks and eyes, and two- or four-hole buttons are sewed easily on a zigzag machine, or may be sewed by hand as follows:

*Snaps* are sewed through the four holes with over and over stitches. Fasten thread on under side with backstitches. Mark the spots for the matched pairs. For a series of snaps, carry thread under garment from one snap to the next.

*Hooks and eyes:* Use overhand stitches under hook and around loops at base of hook. Overhand loops of eyelet. To make a worked loop for the hook, make two or three vertical stitches and work blanket stitches over, as in the belt carrier (pp. 171, 193-195).

*Lingerie straps:* Sew a short piece of ribbon to shoulder seam. At the other end attach a snap fastener with other half of pair sewed on to seam of dress. Or work a thread strap with heavy thread. Catch thread in shoulder seam and run needle through hole of snap fastener, about ¾ inch away from stitching at shoulder. Make several stitches like this to desired size and work over thread with blanket stitches. Sew other part of snap to seam.

*Weights:* Enclose weighted tape in a narrow hem, tacking tape through hem at beginning and end so it does not get out of place. Round weights may be covered with a piece of fabric a little larger than the weight. Gather edges over weight and sew edges securely together. Or, sew weight inside a little square pocket of fabric. Sew weight to garment with French tack (pp. 79, 172), or with dressmaker's chain-stitched tack, a series of chain stitches connecting two pieces of material. Another way is to let weight hang, attached to cloth with chain-stitching. This is used at seams and hems of tailored coats and jackets, for curtains and draperies, and for special details with soft materials.

*Fabric loops:* Sew a bias strip folded lengthwise, right sides together. Trim seam and turn right side out by attaching the end to a bodkin or small safety pin, or by sewing several overhand stitches with needle and strong thread at one end, drawing needle through and pulling strip after needle. Cut tubing into desired equal lengths. Apply it in a circle or in a U shape. Space carefully and sew ends in place by hand. Where garment is faced, apply loops between garment and facing. Stitch through all thicknesses securely. Fancy cord, bought at notion counters, can be used in same way. Fabric loops make attractive decorative edgings and can be used purely for decoration and also as a button fastening.

*Corded fabric loops:* Insert cord between edges of strip near lengthwise fold. Cord is twice as long as strip. Catch cord at middle to one end of the strip, folded in a little. Stitch close to cord with cording foot, making beginning and end of tube wider. Trim seam, turn right side out by pulling cord. Tube will turn onto uncovered part of cord. Or, sew a casing over fine cord. Cut heavy cable cord the length desired, push edge into casing, and catch the two cords together through the fabric, a short distance from end. Pull the smaller cord at other end to turn casing right side out over the heavy cord. Make loop as above, or apply in continuous loops without cutting into strips. These loops are firmer and heavier than plain fabric loops. Good for soft and lightweight fabrics.

*Frogs:* Frogs are decorative closings which match or contrast with garment to give interesting and dramatic effect. Decide on your design first, trace it on paper, and sew tubing

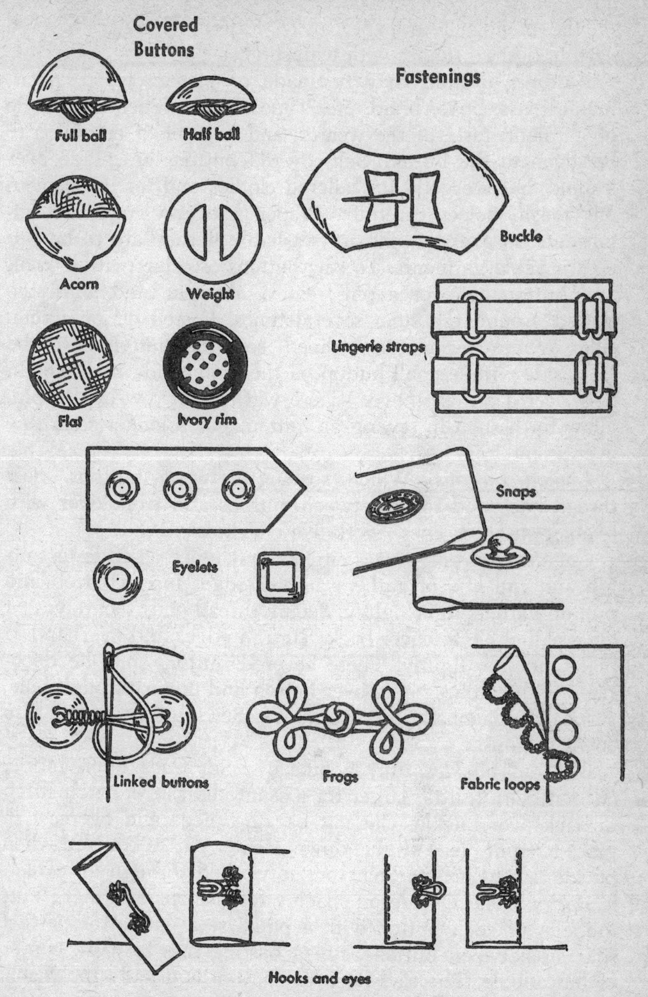
Covered Buttons
Full ball
Half ball
Acorn
Weight
Flat
Ivory rim
Fastenings
Buckle
Lingerie straps
Eyelets
Snaps
Linked buttons
Frogs
Fabric loops
Hooks and eyes

on the tracing. Tear paper away. Fasten tubing or covered cord in desired shapes with whipstitches.

*Buttons:* Buttons may be made of plastic, wood, pearl, metal, glass, bone, braid, etc. Type chosen depends on style of garment, taste of the wearer, and amount of emphasis to be given to the button. Self-covered buttons are made over a mold and are good for tailored clothes and for inconspicuous finish. Select carefully. Proper size and color are important. Be sure buttons are washable if they are to be put on washable garments. To sew buttons on, start with a knot, sew button on over a pin, remove the pin, and wind the thread around the stem several times. Fasten off on wrong side. Where garment is unlined, sew the button onto the right side with a small button on the wrong side underneath. Sew over a pin as above. Where you cannot sew over a pin, allow for a stem in sewing on button. For a longer stem sew over a match.

*Linked buttons:* Watch spacing between buttons. Pass thread back and forth between buttons and work over with blanket stitches. These work like cuff links.

*Covered buttons:* Cut a circle about twice as wide as button and run line of gathers around edge. Insert button and pull up gathers to fit tightly. Secure thread ends securely. Cut out small circle to cover back. Turn in edges and overhand in place, not too tightly. These covered buttons may be decorated with stitches going over button and under through hole, vertically, diagonally or horizontally. Sewing centers will also cover buttons.

*Covered buckles:* Buy a buckle mold, trace it on fabric, cut out cloth a little larger for a seam allowance, catch stitch in back over buckle. Cut out backing piece and overcast in place to front piece or glue down. Center part is covered when buckle is attached to belt, tongue worked through an eyelet.

*Buttonholes:* Decide on spacing for buttons and mark buttonhole for each button with a pin. Use a gauge for perfect spacing between buttons, run a basting line to mark center of buttonhole. The size for a flat button is usually the diameter of the button plus its thickness. It is a good idea to try out sample buttonhole first, especially for unusual button shapes. Mark the length of buttonhole with chalk.

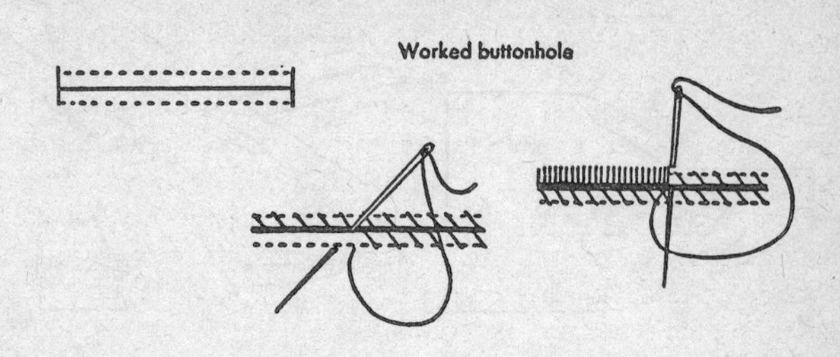


*Worked buttonholes:* Slash along chalk line marking length of buttonhole from center to each side. Use a long double thread with a knot and insert needle on right side of the fabric at the right side of the buttonhole and about ½ inch above it. Bring the needle out underneath the slash at the extreme right. Overcast the edges to prevent raveling, then work over with buttonhole stitch from right to left. Insert needle under slash and out below through loop of thread, which is drawn up to form a purl along edge. Stitches must be of even length and an equal distance apart. At edges, work a bar and blanket stitch over, or flare one edge with radiating stitches. When finished, cut off knot and the extra ½ inch of thread you started with. Used in men's clothing, children's garments, work clothes, wash garments. For women's clothes, use bound or piped buttonholes.

*Tailored buttonholes:* Mark the buttonhole and punch an eyelet at one end with a stiletto. Slash, overcast, and buttonhole stitch. Used for tailored clothes and men's garments.

*Eyelets:* Punch a hole with a stiletto or cut out a small round piece. Overcast edges and buttonhole stitch. A series of eyelets are sometimes worked along edges and then laced, as in peasant types of clothes. Very often used to bring a drawstring through a casing.

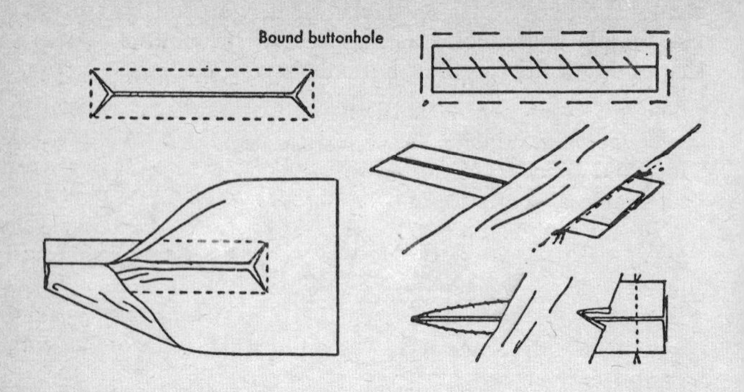


*Bound buttonholes:* Mark place for opening. Cut out an extra piece of fabric, 1½ inches wide and one inch longer than buttonhole when finished. Place right side down and baste through center over marking underneath. Do this very exactly. Stitch a box around line, ⅛ inch above and below center line. Cut through center to within ¼ inch on ends, then diagonally to corners. Turn binding through to wrong side, forming two little pleats that meet exactly in center on right side. Secure with diagonal basting. On wrong side arrange pleats at the corners and stitch through ends catching in the little triangles. On the right side outline buttonhole through original seam with tiny, invisible stitches. Facing is then turned over back of buttonhole, slashed, and overcast to position over buttonhole. Bound buttonholes are attractive and decorative. They are not good for garments that are frequently washed.

*Piped buttonholes:* Cut two lengthwise or bias strips, fold lengthwise, and stitch ⅛ inch from fold. Cut ⅛ inch from stitching. Accuracy is very important. Cut into strips ½ inch longer than opening. Place two strips so that the raw edges meet on the marked line for buttonhole. Stitch right through first line of stitching and backtack ends. Slit on marking between strips and diagonally to ends of stitching. Turn strips to wrong side, diagonal baste them together on right sides. On wrong side, stitch across ends, catching piping to triangle bases. Turn facing over, slit, and overcast to place. Used like bound buttonholes but particularly good for heavy wools.

*Corded buttonholes:* Sew cord in bias strips with cording foot and proceed as for piped buttonholes. Cording is used for firmness, emphasis, and decoration.

*Bound buttonholes without facings:* After buttonhole is complete, turn under the raw edges on the wrong side and hem.

*Buttonholer:* Machine attachment which makes worked buttonholes. Buttonhole is slit after stitching is done with sharp scissors or a razor.

*Tape bound buttonholes:* Good to make bound buttonholes for children's wear, and decorative for other garments if contrasting binding is used. They can also be used for underwear. Mark place for buttonholes and measure between marks. Cut a strip of material as wide as your measurement and bind both long edges. The strip should be longer than the number of buttonholes multiplied by their width. Use machine binder for speed.

Cut into sections, each one ½ inch to ⅝ inch wider than button. Turn the sections so that the bound edges meet, baste them together on paper, if desired, and stitch down the outside both long ends. Bind one long edge, then bind other edge together with edge of garment.

# 33. *FINISHING AND DECORATING*

THESE are the finishing details for a garment and can make the difference between a nice looking and a poor looking dress. Raw and turned edges are finished in a variety of ways. Many suggestions are given below. The important thing to remember in trimming is that trims must be suitable to fabric, kind of garment and cut of garment. Don't overtrim. It is better not to trim at all than to trim too much. Too much decoration is in poor taste.

1. Bias bindings and facings: See Chapter 24 for full explanation and illustrations. Bias may be applied with various designs and motifs. Bias strips folded through the center

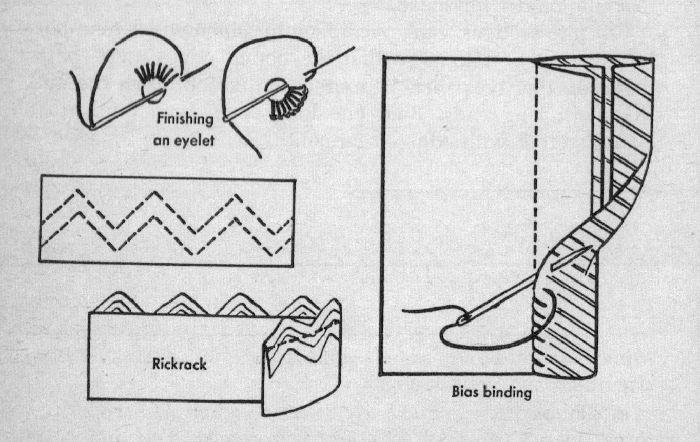

lengthwise may be fagoted together for edgings. They are used as trims, and are also turned completely to the inside and slip stitched to position so that they are not visible on the right side.

2. Rickrack comes in an assortment of colors and sizes. It will launder and iron more easily if stitched twice. To join rickrack strips, match the scallops in a hem felled seam. Four ways of applying rickrack are described below:

a. Turn edge of fabric under, twice with very light weight fabrics, and baste rickrack to wrong side so that half extends beyond fold. Stitch close to fold on right side, and, if desired, stitch again below first line close enough to catch inside edge of trim.

b. Apply rickrack to right side with tips of scallops beyond raw edge. Stitch through center and turn on line of stitching to wrong side. Stitch lower edge of rickrack.

c. Turn in narrow hem and baste. Apply rickrack to the right side so that half extends beyond edge and stitch through center. Various decorative stitches may be used in place of machine stitching.

d. Where rickrack is not applied to edge, baste it to a marked line and stitch it through the center with one or more rows.

3. Edges may be hemstitched and picoted. (See pp. 199, 112.)

4. Top stitch a finished edge by machine, in contrasting thread if desired. Hand done saddle stitching or other decorative stitch may be used, particularly on heavier fabric and on sports clothes.

5. Bands are applied as trims, often in the reverse manner to facings, that is turned to the outside. Bands may be ribbon or self fabric; flat, gathered, pleated or tucked. For professional results, use the machine edge stitcher or zigzag stitch. Miter corners. Bands are often used to mend worn places on a garment and in remodeling.

a. Double band. Make two bands, stitch all around on three sides, right sides together, trim seams, turn and finish

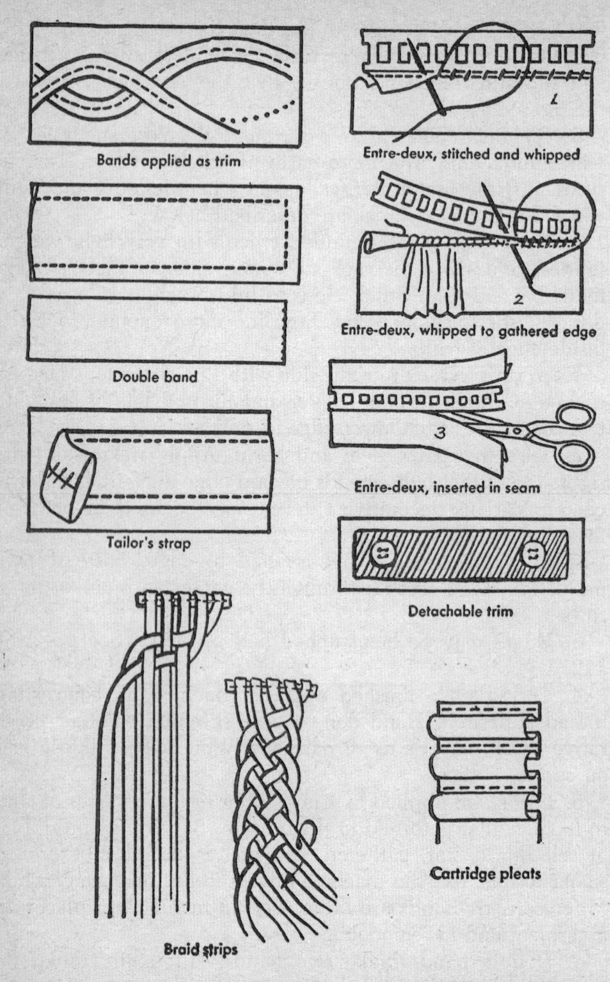


Bands applied as trim

Entre-deux, stitched and whipped

Double band

Entre-deux, whipped to gathered edge

Entre-deux, inserted in seam

Tailor's strap

Detachable trim

Braid strips

Cartridge pleats

fourth side by hand, turning in raw edges. Used for ties at the front edge of a garment or for bows and other neckline decorative finishes.

b. Turn in both raw edges of band and baste to position on garment. Edgestitch on both sides or catch by hand. Used horizontally or vertically on any part of garment for decoration.

c. Tailor's strap: Turn in raw edges of band so they meet in the center and overcast edges together. Baste to garment and edgestitch on both sides. Used for heavy materials, wools and velvet to decorate neckline, bodice, or skirt.

d. Bands are sometimes buttoned to garments for detachable trim. Make buttonholes in band, and sew buttons onto garment.

e. Entre-deux, known as seam beading and embroidery veining, is a narrow openwork band, which has fabric margins on both sides. It is often used as a trim between seam edges.

–Stitch entre-deux to right side, using cording foot to stitch close; trim margin to ⅛ inch, roll material over, whip. Or, trim both thicknesses and overcast.

–With very thin material, apply on right side, roll margin and fabric together, whip.

–Cut away margin, roll garment edge and whip to entre-deux through openings.

–Where edge of garment is to be gathered, roll edge and whip, pulling up thread every fourth stitch or so to gather. Whip gathered edge to entre-deux.

–To insert veining in a seam, fold seam allowances back, baste folds to both sides of veining and stitch. Trim seam of garment very close, and hem inner edge of veining to stitching.

6. Commercial embroidery edging is applied with one of the methods described under ruffles, (see p. 133). Miter corners carefully, retaining curves, trim and overcast raw edges. Or, lay in several pleats at corners.

7. Braid can be applied with machine braiding foot which holds braid in place and stitches through the center. If fabric

puckers, sew over paper and tear paper away later. Make a hole to push braid to wrong side of fabric, and fasten the ends. The machine underbraider is a little more difficult to use. Braid is used for decorative effects.

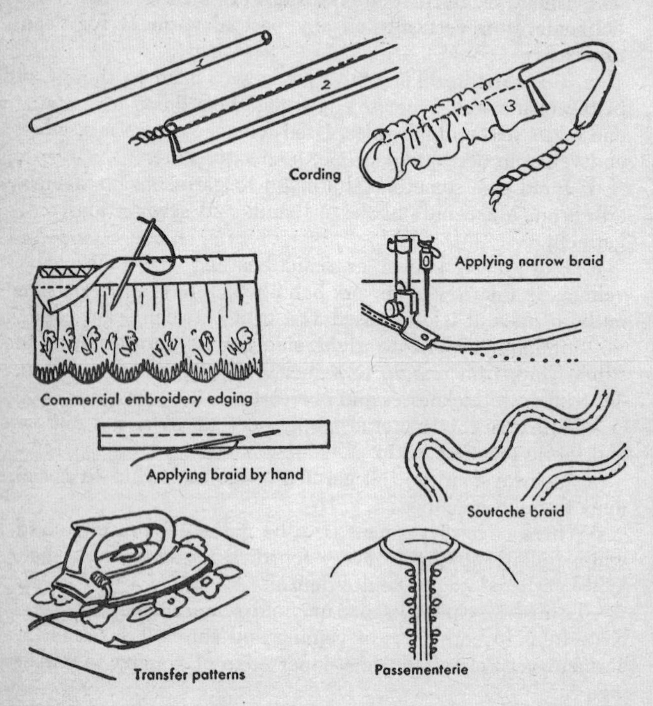


a. Apply wide braid as a binding, encasing raw edge of garment. Stitch fabric and both braid edges together.

b. Narrow braid is applied to right side, stitching at one side, and leaving other side free.

c. Braid may be applied by hand, with tiny stitches on one side and longer stitches, about ¼ inch, on wrong side. To make stitches invisible on right side, take a stitch through material and then through under side of braid.

d. To transfer braiding patterns to material, use hot iron transfer patterns. Where hot application will spoil the fabric, stitch through several layers of paper and through the fabric, without any thread. Apply braid with one layer of paper and tear paper away later.

e. Soutache braid is applied with braider or by hand. It is sometimes inserted inside a seam like cording to give a similar effect.

f. Passementerie is braid in fancy motifs. Use it judiciously, so that garment is not overtrimmed. Heavy passementerie may be hemmed by hand to garment through its finished edge.

g. Some braids can be applied with methods described under rickrack.

8. Cording and piping with contrasts, as described under seams, make good edge trims (see p. 110). Stitch bias strips as above and turn. Fold again lengthwise and overcast edges together. Baste to garment in a straight line or a shaped motif and stitch. Or, make bias strip in cord, baste and stitch with cording foot. Apply as described under seams. (See p. 110.)

9. Fringed edge:

a. Draw a thread; stitch or overcast close to drawn thread; pull out all threads below.

b. Wind strands of yarn or thread around piece of cardboard. Stitch across top, cut through bottom. Tear away paper below stitching, stitch turned edge of garment to top of fringe. Pull out remaining paper. If desired, whip over top, dividing fringe into groups of threads.

c. Tied fringe. Make fringe as above, whipping threads over top to divide into groups of two. Tie from the left, first pair with one thread of second. Tie threads together in groups of twos, one thread from each group across entire row. For second row, tie two threads of first pair, then continue as before across row. Make as many rows as desired.

d. Another method is to make fringe with needle threaded with double strands of yarn. Make a stitch in garment edge, pulling needle through loop before tightening thread. The needle is rethreaded for each stitch. Make fringe as full as desired and tie as described on page 185.

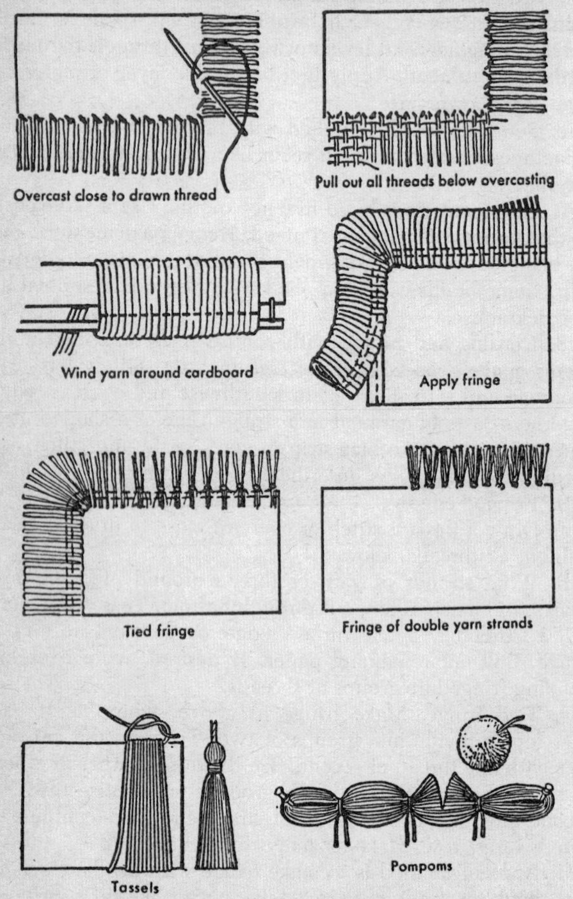

Overcast close to drawn thread

Pull out all threads below overcasting

Wind yarn around cardboard

Apply fringe

Tied fringe

Fringe of double yarn strands

Tassels

Pompoms

10. Tassels: Wind yarn around cardboard to desired thickness and tie with separate piece at top. Cut yarn across bottom, pull out cardboard, tie another strand around about ½ inch from top, leaving one long end to wrap around tassel several times. Thread a needle with this end, and insert needle in center to hold firm.

11. Pompoms: Wind yarn around cardboard about half as wide as the finished pompom is to be. Make yarn thickness about as wide as the cardboard is. Pull out cardboard. Tie through center. Cut both ends. Trim to a round ball.

12. Self-trim edgings:

a. Saw-toothed edge: Cut straight strips 2½ inches wide. Fold lengthwise through center. Cut a pattern of heavy paper and trace on material. Stitch on marking, cut off excess fabric and clip to points. Turn right side out, baste, press. Turn in raw edge of garment. Apply edging with one of methods described under ruffles, or with facing stitched on right side over edging, turned to wrong side and slip stitched.

b. Pointed edging: Cut lengthwise strips 1¼ inches wide. Cut into squares and fold diagonally once and then again. Baste onto right side of garment, edges together, overlapping points. Baste bias facing on top, stitch all together, trim seam, turn bias to wrong side, slip stitch to position.

c. Looped edging: Make lengthwise strips about 1¼ inches wide. Fold lengthwise and stitch about ¼ inch from edge. Turn inside out, press. Cut pieces exactly the same size, put ends together to form loop and baste to garment with even spacing, using same method as for pointed edging.

d. Scalloped edge: Draw scalloped design on paper and trace on fabric. Cut out two strips, sew around curves, right sides together. Trim, clip, turn, baste scallops, and apply to fabric as above. Miter corners so that two scallops joined make one wide corner scallop.

e. Cartridge pleat: See p. 126.

f. Ruffles: See p. 133.

g. Bindings, facings, bands: See pp. 136-40.

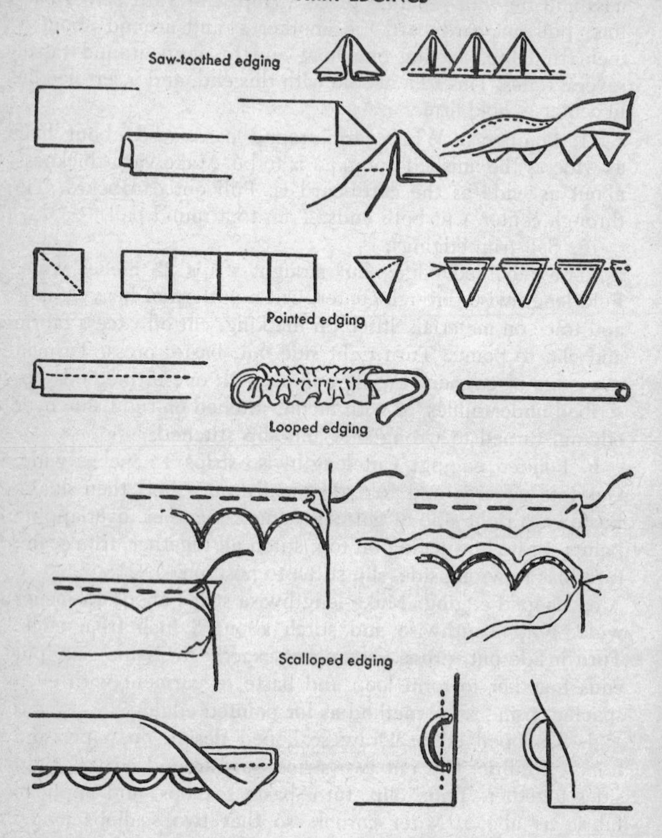


h. Braided strips: Cut out bias strips, fold in half, right sides together, and stitch ¼ inch from edge. Turn inside out with safety pin or bodkin, press. Take several strips and attach to one piece at top. Braid over and under, beginning at right. Stitch to garment.

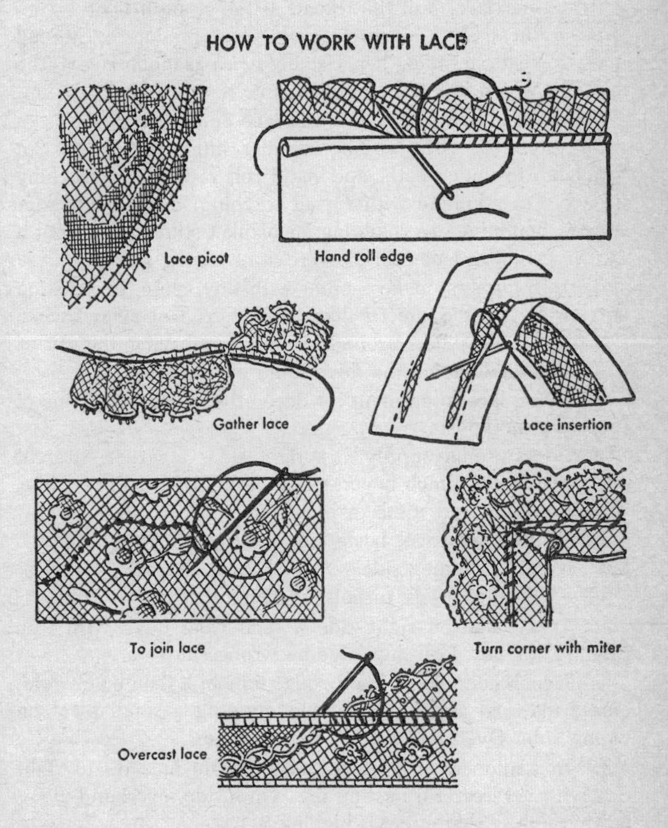


13. Lace: All-over lace, cut like fabric, must have its edges finished.

a. Hemstitch and picot or sew on lace picot edging by hand with tiny running stitches. Roll raw edge on wrong side.

b. Stitch near edge and hand roll edge to inside.

To gather lace, pull the thread at the straight edge to desired fullness, or whipstitch over edge, pulling up thread every few stitches to gather. Usually twice as much lace as the space to which it is to be applied is used.

To make a lace insertion, baste lace onto right side. Use a satin stitch (p. 197) or fine running stitch at joining. Cut away fabric underneath, and hand roll raw edges, catching in lace. Or, appliqué with zigzag stitching, the machine zigzagger, hemming, overhanding, or blanket stitching. To put a lace insertion in lace fabric, overcast or zigzag stitch.

To turn corners, make a miter with tiny, close, overcasting stitches so that the effect is like a fine cord. Cut away excess. Or, make little pleats around corners, preserving the curve.

To join lace, match the design and overhand.

Applying lace to garment for decorative effects: Use one of following methods:

a. On raw edge, apply lace right sides together, straight edge of lace 1/16 inch beyond seam line. Stitch on seam line, turn back hem and stitch or hem by hand.

b. On finished edge, baste lace to edge and stitch. Attach lace on right or wrong side.

c. Overhand loosely to finished hem.

d. Apply lace on right side ¼ inch from edge with tiny running stitches. Roll raw edge on wrong side.

e. French hem: Turn in raw edge ¼ inch; ½ inch below fold, crease material and bring to fold, forming a small pleat on wrong side. Overhand lace to folded edges.

f. On scalloped or irregular edge, baste lace on to right side with very careful basting line. On inside, overhand along basting line so that effect is like fine cord.

g. With entre-deux, hand roll hem, catching in margin and lace.

APPLYING LACE TO GARMENT

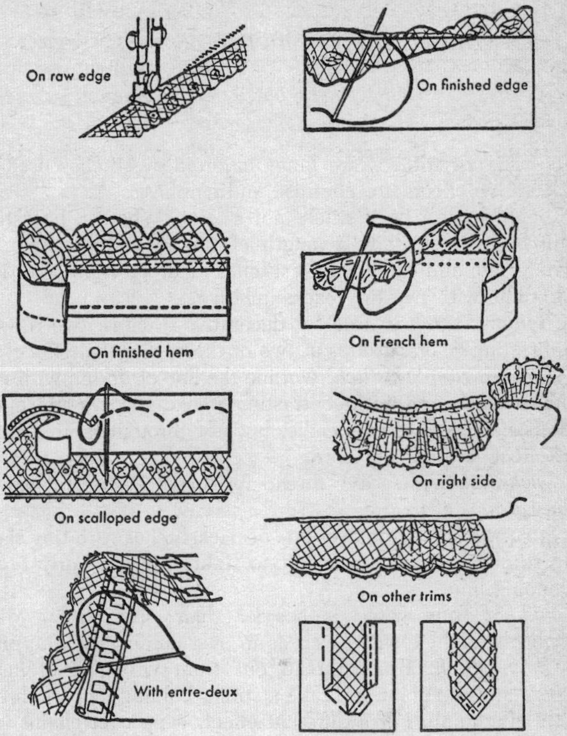

On raw edge

On finished edge

On finished hem

On French hem

On scalloped edge

On right side

On other trims

With entre-deux

14. Other trims: Tucked, pleated or shirred sections.
–Lacing woven through holes punched with a stiletto.
–Bows, ties, flowers, detachable collars and cuffs, jabots, etc.

# 34. *DECORATIVE STITCHES*

DECORATIVE stitches are fancy embroidery stitches used for decorative effects, for contrast, and emphasis.

Begin with a back stitch, not a knot. Where a backstitch will be visible, allow a length of thread to fall across the wrong side and catch it into stitches made on right side. Finish a line with two tiny backstitches.

*Running stitch* is used for decorative designs; two rows in contrasting colors, groups of two or three, diagonal effect, etc.

*Twisted running stitch:* Outline the line of design with running stitches, and with contrasting thread go over and under stitches, using a blunt needle, but not through fabric, to get an effect like twisted cord.

*Backstitch* with heavy thread for flower stems and to emphasize tops of hems.

*Stem stitch* is made over line of backstitches with tiny slanting stitches working from left to right. Gives a fairly heavy trimming line.

*Padded stem stitch* is heavier than stem stitch. Make stitches straight towards you as in overhanding or whipping.

*Chain stitch:* Bring thread out from wrong side, insert needle at same point and take a stitch, holding loop of thread with left thumb. For a different effect, whip over chains in a contrasting color. Used for stitching in a line especially on peasant type clothes and undergarments.

*Magic* or *checkered chain* is made like chain with two contrasting threads in needle. Keep one color to left holding thread under thumb, make stitch with other color. Bring second color to the left for the next stitch and hold under thumb. Continue. Stitches of chain are in alternating colors.

## DECORATIVE STITCHES

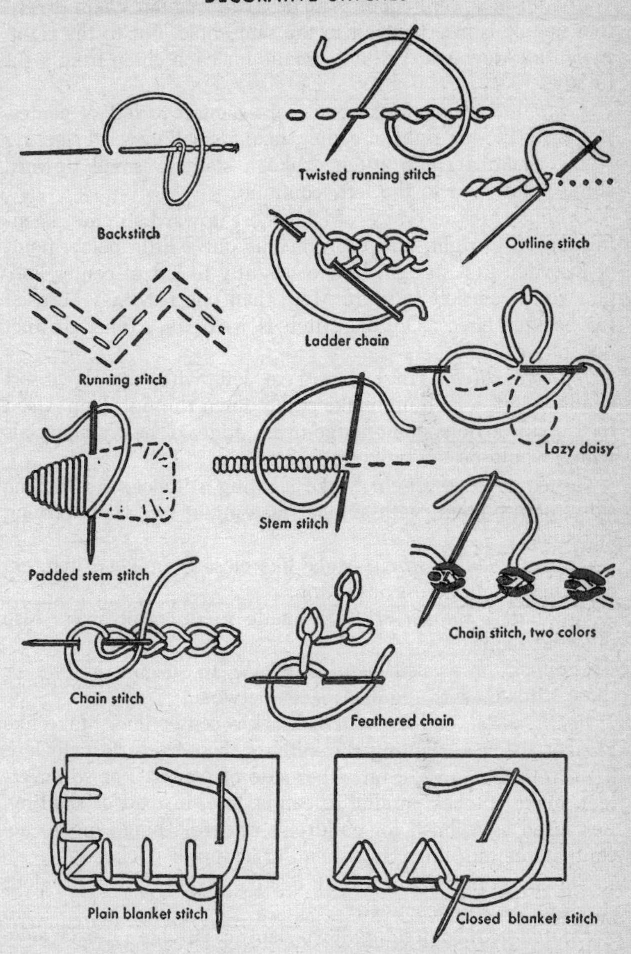

*Lazy daisy* is an elongated chain in a flower design.

*Ladder* or *square chain* is made like a regular chain except that needle is inserted, not in the same hole, but to the right. A slanting downward stitch is made for each chain from right to left.

*Feathered chain:* Make one loop, slanted to left of center. Below and to the right of center, take a small upward slanting stitch; make a chain stitch. Take a slanted, small upward stitch below and to the left; continue.

*Outline stitch or crewel:* Make short upward stitches, keeping thread to right, and bring needle out a little below point of insertion in a straight line, or slightly to left of center line. Or, work from left to right. More than one row may be used for heavier effect. Outline stitch is used for a fine, distinct decorative line.

*Blanket stitch:* Hold thread to left with thumb, insert needle about ¼ inch up, make stitch down through loop. Used for thread carriers, dainty edge trims, edges of heavy materials which would be too bulky to fold under.

*Closed blanket stitch:* Make slanting stitches, first to one side, then to other, with stitches meeting at top, thus forming a triangle.

*Crossed blanket stitch:* Make like closed blanket stitch, except that stitches cross at the top.

*Graduated blanket stitch* is made in different sizes. Also different slants.

*Grouped or spaced blanket stitch:* In groups of two or three stitches, with regular spaces between.

*Featherstitch or briar stitch:* Mark a center line. Make like blanket stitches, slanting the stitches, first from right to left, then from left to right on either side of center. For stiffer effect, make stitches parallel to center line, instead of slanting. Best used as a finish for children's underclothing, and to accentuate certain lines, as at hem, or at top of pockets.

*Closed featherstitch:* Insert needle at bottom of previous stitch so the stitches meet.

*Double featherstitching:* Two slanting stitches on each side.

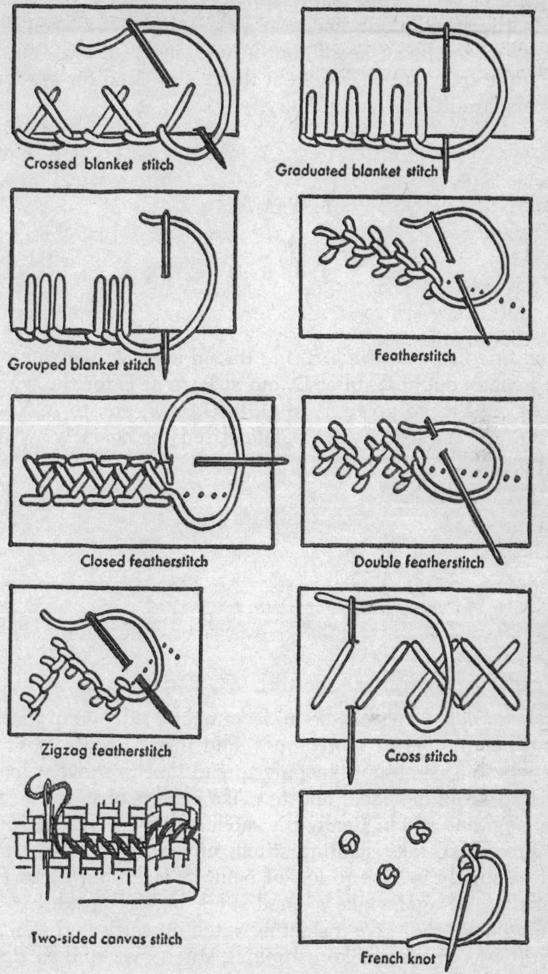
Crossed blanket stitch
Graduated blanket stitch
Grouped blanket stitch
Featherstitch
Closed featherstitch
Double featherstitch
Zigzag featherstitch
Cross stitch
Two-sided canvas stitch
French knot

*Zigzag* or *serpentine featherstitch:* Mark zigzag or curved line, featherstitch along line.

*Cross stitch:* Bring needle out at one, insert at two, out at three, in at four, out at five, in at three, etc. Used for borders, samplers, traditional embroidery.

7 5 1 4

8 6 3 2

*Two-sided canvas stitch:* Bring thread from wrong side out at A, in at B, out at C, in at D, out at B, in at E for the whole line. At end, R, go up to T, to Q, to U, to P, etc. to A, Y, A, Z, C, Y, C, Y, B, X, B, X, D, etc. Used for coarsely woven materials and needle point.

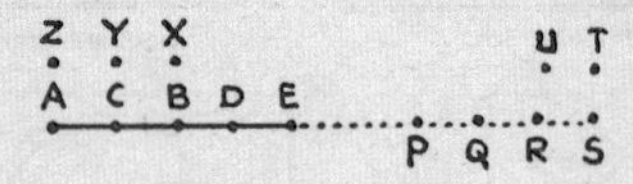


*French knot:* Bring needle up from wrong side, wrap thread around needle one or more times, and insert needle close to point where it came out, keeping thread taut to prevent looping. Used to fill in spaces and to make centers of flowers.

*Herringbone stitch:* Really the catch stitch, used for decoration. From left, take slanting stitch, upwards, and bring out needle a small distance to left of point of insertion. Cross the line made and again take a small stitch back. Repeat.

*Chevron stitch:* Make a slanting stitch upwards and a small backstitch as above. Make a running stitch over and to right of the backstitch. Slant next stitch down, repeat. A to B, under to C, over to D, under to B, E under to F, over to G, under to E, H.

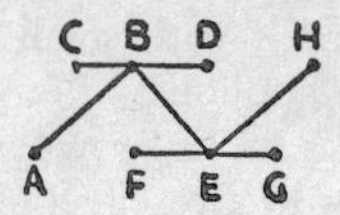


*Satin stitch:* Parallel close stitches to give raised effect. Good to pad design first with running stitches. Used for leaves, flowers, borders. Satin stitch can be made on the zigzag machine without padding.

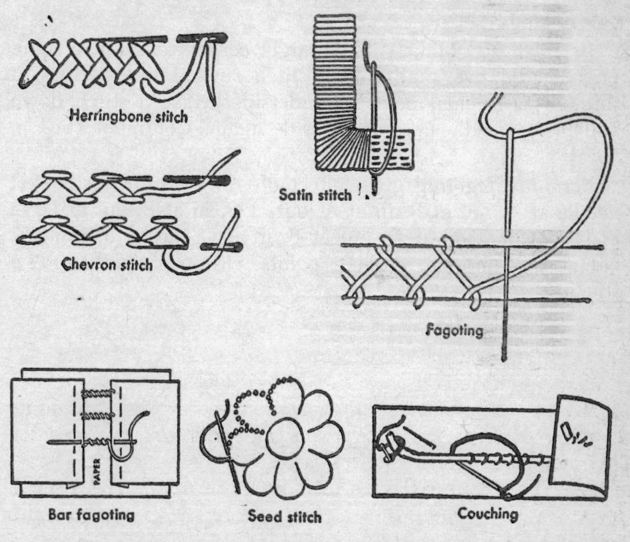


Herringbone stitch

Satin stitch

Chevron stitch

Fagoting

Bar fagoting

Seed stitch

Couching

*Seed stitch:* Pairs of backstitches. Make one backstitch, slant needle under for second. Used to fill in spaces and decorative narrow hems.

*Couching:* This is actually sewing on a thread or cord for decoration. Fasten a heavy thread on wrong side, leave loose on right side. With a second thread, usually finer, tack it in place at regular intervals with small stitches. Used often to outline an edge, as in appliqué.

*Brick couching:* Use several rows of plain couching, alternating tacking stitches to give effect of bricks.

*Puffy couching:* Weave a heavy thread in and out of a line of machine or hand stitching.

*Fagoting:* Cut fabric at desired place for fagoting. Turn edges under, and baste both sides to paper the proper distance apart. Bring needle out at left, slant to right under fabric and bring needle up; pass needle under thread and down to left. Continue. Used for openwork seams, collar and cuff edgings.

*Bar fagoting:* Make stitch straight across from left to right, pass needle over and under stitch several times, draw it through at original point to underside. Make a stitch down and bring needle up to right side again. Continue. (See p. 197.)

*Bermuda fagoting* gives effect of series of squares. Insert needle at A, out at B, in at A, out at B, in at B, out at C, in at D, out at C, in at D, out at B, in at C, out at B, in at C, out at E. Continue, binding points with two tightly drawn stitches.

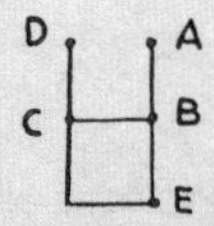

*Hemstitching:* Draw out several threads of fabric at line to be hemstitched. Start at right, pass needle under three or four threads, draw up through a loop and take a small stitch down through fabric. Continue. Double hemstitching is done on both sides. Used as a trim on garments and on table linens and doilies.

*Diagonal hemstitching:* Do line of plain hemstitching at one side. For second side, catch half the threads of two groups together, and take a stitch up through fabric.

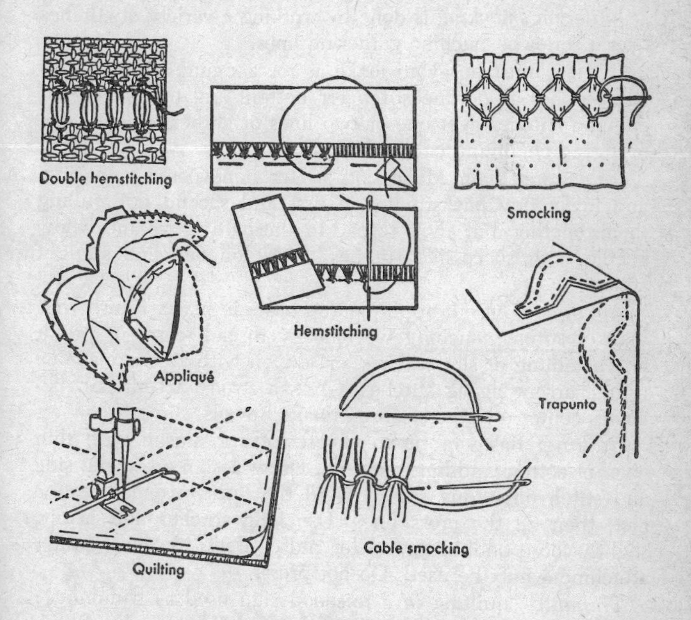


*Smocking:* Worked over groups of dots that form the corners of squares. Start at first row, make a small stitch over dot from right to left, repeat at second dot, and pull two dots together with another small backstitch at first dot. Pass needle under fabric to second dot in second row. Make a small backstitch, another at third dot and back to second to pull two together. Go back to first row. Continue. At end of row, fasten thread and start again at left for third and fourth rows. For this smocking, known as honeycomb smocking, you will need twice as much material as the finished effect, that is eight inches for a four-inch smocked section. Smocking is a lovely hand finish which may decorate almost any type of garment.

*Imitation smocking* is done by working a variety of stitches over a series of machine gathering lines.

Gathers must be even; make as for gauging. (See p. 11.) Use stitches as outline stitch for bottom and top rows, and chevron stitches over one or two lines of gathers in between, or zigzag chain and cable stitches.

*Cable smocking:* Make dots as for honeycomb smocking, and make tiny backstitches in first and second dot pulling them together, but allow thread to alternate above and below needle with successive stitches. Work on one line straight across.

*Appliqué:* Cut out appliqué and baste in place. Finish with blanket stitch; couching with heavy thread, cord, or braid; fine hemming or slip stitches, or sew on with zigzag machine using narrow zigzag stitches. Gives a strong accent and becomes center of interest on garments, towels, slip covers.

*Quilting:* Baste fabric to cheesecloth or muslin with thin layer of cotton wadding between. Draw design on wrong side and stitch on wrong side. Do all the lines in one direction first, then all the cross lines. Use long stitches and heavy, slightly loose bobbin thread for puffy effect. Machine quilter attachment may be used. Do not press.

*Trapunto* (quilting in a raised design used as trimming): Mark line of design on lining of cheesecloth or muslin. Stitch by machine or hand running stitches through both sides of design. Pull a heavy yarn through between lines of stitching, between outside fabric and lining, pulling out yarn and reinserting around curves or at points. At wider part of the design, insert extra padding of yarn or cotton wadding, pushing in with a pencil or orange stick, so that each section is completely padded. The padded parts stand out in relief. Do not press. Also called Italian quilting. Very dressy for rich fabrics, such as velvet. Used for slip covers, too.

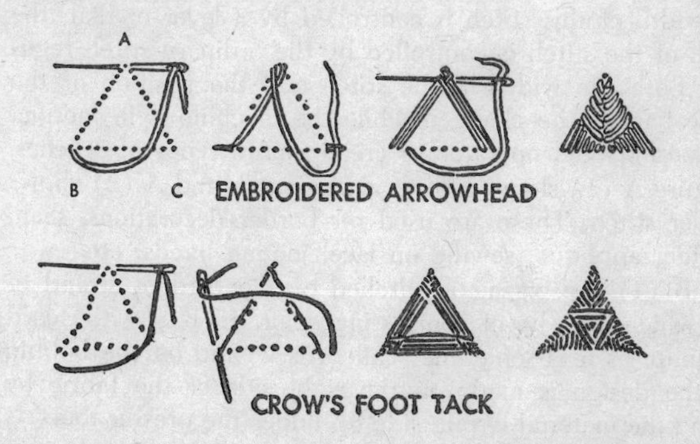


*Embroidered arrowhead:* Tailored effect and reinforcement at top of pleats, darts, short seams. Mark triangle with chalk, start at B up to A, make a tiny backstitch, down to C, and under to B. Continue in same manner to fill in triangle, taking very precise stitches side by side, and not allowing them to overlap. Press from inside over something heavily padded, for example, a folded towel.

*Crow's foot tack:* Mark triangle as for arrowhead, start same way but make backstitch at all corners and go back to B, marking line from C to B. Work around triangle in same manner, each stitch coming just inside previous one. The threads will automatically draw in to make crow's foot. Used like arrowhead.

*Bar tack:* Make several long stitches at ends of opening at right angle to opening. Make stitches over bar from left to right, catching in material, or use blanket stitch. Make small bar tacks, perpendicular to this, at either end. Used for tailored effect and reinforcing edges that may pull out, as the ends of a pocket.

A wide variety of decorative stitches may be obtained on the machine, particularly on the zigzag machines. On the zigzag machine the needle can be made to move from side to side, creating a stitch which resembles hand embroidery. The width of this stitch is controlled by a lever or dial; the length of the stitch is controlled by the ordinary stitch regulator. Both the width of the stitch and the position of the needle bar can be changed while the machine is in motion. This permits the operator to create many types of stitches.

Figure A (1) shows a short zigzag stitch and A (2) shows a wider stitch. These are used for border decorations, seam finishing, appliqué, sewing on lace, joining bands, etc.

In B (1) the zigzag is stitched over a cord or strand of yarn which may be of contrasting color. In B (2) the cord or guimp, as it is sometimes called, is wound on the bobbin and the design is made on the right side of the fabric by placing the material wrong side up under the presser foot.

Adjust your stitch regulator so that you make the shortest possible length stitch to produce the satin stitch shown in C (1). The lever which controls the width of the stitch may be regulated to produce a wide satin stitch for use on coarse linen, for example, or a very narrow stitch for dainty designs or edges, as on flowers, where the fabric is cut close to the stitching. In C (2) a narrow satin stitch is made on the sides of a wide zigzag stitch to give a braid effect trimming. Satin stitch can be made over cord or guimp to give a raised or padded effect.

The scalloped edge shown in D (1) is made by adjusting the width of the stitch while the machine is in motion. Cut the material away close to the stitching for a scalloped edge. A variation of the scallop is shown in D (2) where straight satin stitches are inserted between scallops as they are made. This makes an attractive border trimming.

## DECORATIVE STITCHES WITH THE ZIGZAG MACHINE

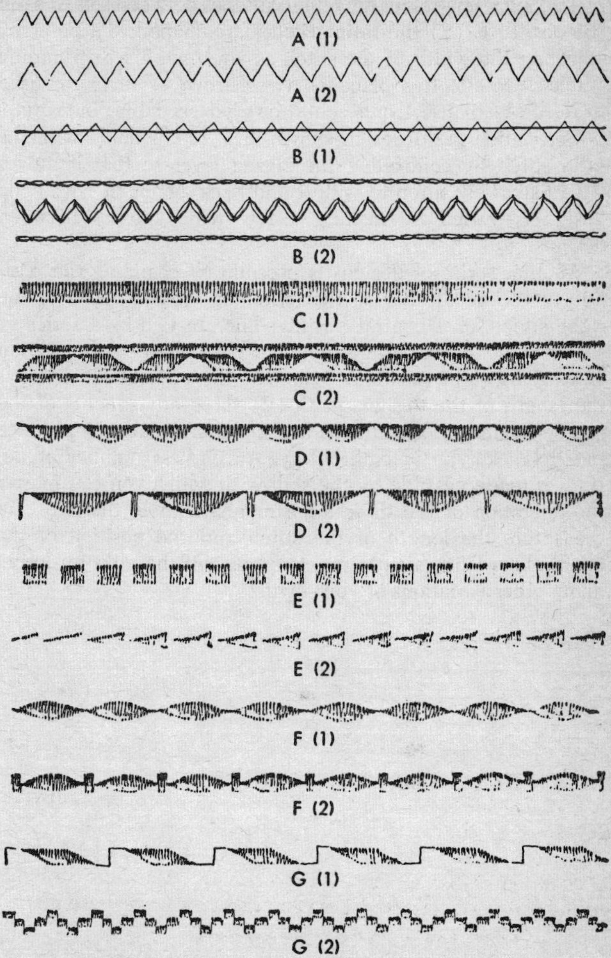

A (1)

A (2)

B (1)

B (2)

C (1)

C (2)

D (1)

D (2)

E (1)

E (2)

F (1)

F (2)

G (1)

G (2)

In E (1) wide satin stitches are blocked in little squares by making a few regular machine stitches between sets of satin stitches. In E (2) the satin stitches are shaped to a point by adjusting the width of the stitch as you sew. These trimming stitches are effective placed between rows of tucks, or used to decorate blouse fronts, children's yokes, table linens, etc.

Coronation braid design shown in F (1) is made with the satin stitch by controlling the zigzag lever so that it moves from narrowest stitch to widest and back again. In F (2) the design is varied by making a few wide stitches between designs.

Another series of designs is possible by changing the position of the needle bar so that stitching will be either to the right or left of a central position line. In G (1) a series of satin stitches is made alternating from extreme left position to extreme right position. Speed of the adjustment controls the length of the design. In G (2) three adjustments of the needle position, left, middle and right are made to produce the rickrack type of embroidery. An endless number of designs is made possible by the skill with which you can master the operation of the three adjustments, namely the width of the stitch, the length of the stitch and the position of the needle bar. With a little practice you will be able to design many other variations of your own.

# 35. *REMAKES AND REMODELING*

REMODELING is every woman's way of making the most of what she has.

First go through your wardrobe and try everything on. Do this with the proper attitude, that is, put on a good girdle, change your shoes, freshen your face and comb your hair. You will then be able to get an idea of how the garment really looks when you wear it. Now check fit critically; waistline, general hang or balance of dress, hem, set of sleeves, becomingness. Sort your wardrobe into separate piles: those things needing no change, those things needing refitting, those things needing vital changes. Don't, however, take any drastic steps until you are sure of what you are doing.

The easiest kind of refitting adjustment is taking in the side seams. When doing this, the safe way is to do the whole seam, for example, from waist to hem. Pin in the changed seam line on the right side, remove the dress, put in a line of pins on both sides of seam, removing first pins, then turn to wrong side and continue; when you fold the material, the two lines of pins will give you your new guide line. Be sure side and center hang straight to floor.

It is often better to increase or add new darts than to change basic seams. Where there are wrinkles, a fundamental rule is to make the seam towards which the wrinkle is pointing wider. Several narrow skimpy pleats are often combined into one or two larger pleats. Pleated skirts are shortened at the waist, not at the hem usually. Where pleats do not fall straight, the skirt is lifted at the waist.

Necklines often have to be cut lower. In this case, fold and cut both sides at once for evenness. Cut out a facing shaped

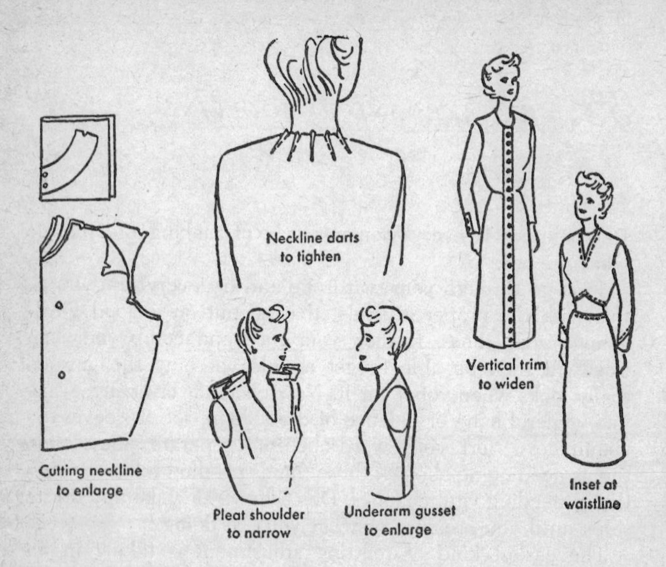


like the new neckline, on proper grain. Too low a neckline can have a vestee or yoke added. Too loose a neckline needs a few back neck darts.

Skirts may be shortened or lengthened (very common alterations) in the usual way for turning hems. Where creases show after lengthening, several rows of machine stitching or decorative bands may be used to cover them. Piecings must often be made. A false hem may be added without difficulty (see p. 116), with nothing showing on the right side. Or a decorative band may be applied with a lapped seam, piped if desired. Or, one or more pieces of contrasting material may be inserted if the skirt is cut above the hem. Where contrasting material is used, it is a good idea to use some of the same material in another place, so the total effect will be unified.

Seat bagginess means redoing skirt side seams and waistline seams. Often a lining in the seat will cure this problem. Tightness through the hips is cured easily by raising the skirt. This, of course, implies that the placket is removed and reinserted after the new waistline seam is stitched, and that the hem is changed.

Where the bodice is too long, a new waistline seam is necessary. Where it is too short, a piece has to be set in at the waist. This can be very attractive and decorative. Short skirts also may be lengthened at the waist with a set-in band or yoke.

A too loose waistline may be adjusted with gathers or body darts. Too tight a waist may need let-out seams, gathers, or darts. Bust tightness is usually fixed by letting out underarm seams or setting in a gusset. Vertical trimming bands can be used, or back and front closings can be let out and the skimpy effect resulting can be camouflaged with some decorative effect, such as a ruffle.

Vertical trimming may be used through the entire length of a dress for widening, through center, or side centers. Ribbon and narrow remnants are often used for this.

When shoulder is too long, rip out sleeve and reset or add dart or pleat in center of shoulder seam. A sloping shoulder needs a deeper outer seam. A short shoulder can have a yoke, gusset, band or epaulet set in on top or between sleeve cap and blouse. Or a panel can be set in blouse center back or front.

Twisted sleeves have to be reset in armhole. Changing the kind or position of the shoulder pad is often a great help.

In remodeling, some good general rules are: to combine fabrics of similar kind and texture; to use interesting, but not startling contrasts; to throw away badly worn fabrics; to sometimes cut close to old seam lines and throw away seams so that new seams will be clean cut; to repeat lines, such as curved yoke and pocket; to decorate piecings to accent, rather than to try to hide; to think of using the wrong side of the fabric if it is possible. Rip, clean (wash if possible) and carefully press an old garment. Dye if desired. Don't throw anything

## BOY'S MACKINAW FROM MAN'S OVERCOAT

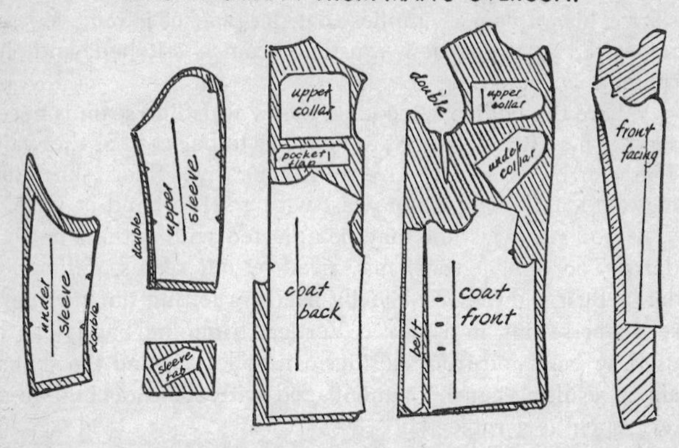


## SUIT DRESS FROM MAN'S SUIT

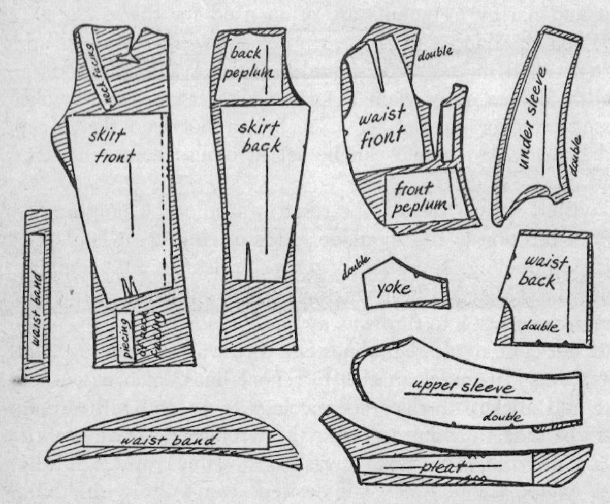

away until you are sure you won't need it. Don't start to work until you are sure of the finished effect you want. Pattern books and departments for ready wear are full of ideas. A new pattern, as much like the idea you have in mind as possible, should be bought and used for recutting and reconstructing. Some ideas and suggested projects follow:

1. From an old dress, make a jumper. Rip out sleeves, lower neckline to square or round shape. Cut out facing for neck and sleeve. Refit seams and redo hem if necessary.

2. From an old dress, make a blouse, dickie, vestee.

3. Make a skirt and bolero from an old dress.

4. Make children's clothes from old adult's clothing.

5. Make street length garment from evening clothes.

6. Add new collar and cuffs, or new collar and sleeves. Adding a yoke will often transform a dress. Pockets can be added or changed to match.

7. Cut out woman's or child's suit from man's. Use sleeve pieces to cut out new sleeves, facings for new facings, etc.

8. Change sleeve length, insert panels, use slot seam effect, add ruching, braid or other decoration.

9. Make one new dress from the best parts of two old ones.

10. Add pockets, collars, cuffs, decorative stitching, tucks, pleats, new buttons, new belt, piping, ruffles, cape, overskirt, etc.

11. Make a playsuit or bathing suit from an old summer dress.

12. Make dickies, halters, beach bags, jabots, tiny hats, belts from scraps and remnants.

13. Make a mackinaw for a schoolboy from a man's old winter overcoat with belted back.

14. Make a suit dress for street wear from man's suit with belted back and patch pockets.

15. Make a street dress from man's serge suit.

16. Make dickies from parts of men's old shirts.

STREET DRESS FROM MAN'S SERGE SUIT

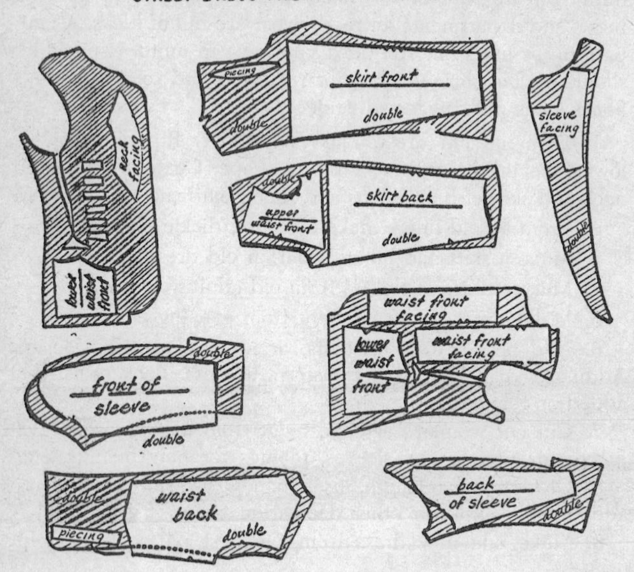


*Make-overs from Suits*

Man-tailored or dressmaker style—which shall the new suit be? Texture of the cloth and cut of the old suit coat are the best answers to that question.

This old suit had a belted back, patch pockets, and soft wool, lending itself best to a peplum-style jacket with an inset belt.

A four-gore skirt is about the only style that can be made from one pair of trousers; but a pleat set in at the center front adds to the grace and comfort of this skirt.

Here's a two-faced cloth that was good for a turn-about.

DICKIES FROM MEN'S OLD SHIRTS

**From good parts of men's old shirts, make a variety of dickies and a back shield.**

This old, shabby overcoat had a checked outside, worn and snagged, but a plaid inside without a mar. Just right for a boy's mackinaw.

The old overcoat was ripped apart, and because the cloth was so thick, it was sent to a cleaner for washing.

Only extra expense was for cotton lining, buttons, and buckle.

Will a man's suit make over into a dress? This trim outfit is the answer although it called for a bit of camouflage art. The waist front had to be pieced crosswise. So piecings were made in line with the inverted tucks, and the seams, extending from ends of tucks to armholes, were hidden by the rantering stitch.

A slit at the lower edge of the sleeve to match the tucks at waist front, and a seam running from the slit to the shoulder give the sleeve piecings a "meant-to-be" look.

The scrap-bag furnished round black braid for the plaited belt. Dickies of different styles and different colors offer all sorts of chance for change.

# 36. *TAILORING*

Constructing a suit or coat should be no more difficult than constructing a dress, once the basic elements of sewing are mastered. Your differences will be in interfacing, interlining, and lining.

You will need an interfacing of lightweight canvas or muslin. Sometimes canvas is used for the front and collar, and unbleached muslin for the rest of the garment. The lining should be of rayon twill, rayon or silk crepe, satin or sateen. Sometimes novelty linings are used for their effect, for example: quilted cotton, plaids, prints, checks, stripes. In a winter coat you will want an interlining of a wool or part wool fabric, chamois, or a satin-back, wool-face fabric. You will also need seam binding or linen tape and weights for the bottom of a suit jacket.

Alter the pattern as usual. Sponge wool fabric (pp. 7, 56), and lay the muslin in hot water for a few hours and hang it without wringing. This is to shrink it and remove sizing. Cut the pattern, mark it accurately, sew in darts. The pattern will give you directions for cutting the interfacing, which is sewed to the wrong side of each section of the garment with padding stitches.

Lay the interfacings in position. Padding stitches are made like diagonal basting stitches. Work with matching thread, take stitches about ½ inch long, just barely catching through the outer fabric, down one complete row, up the next, without turning the garment around. The stitches must not show on the right side, nor be pulled so tight as to cause puckering or pulling of the fabric. The entire interfacing piece is padded in this way to give the finished garment body, as well as a well-tailored look. Pad all interfacings except at the back shoulder and neckline. This piece is caught in the seams.

The seam allowances of the interfacing are then trimmed away, and the edge is taped. The tape is basted on so that one edge is on or just barely over the seam line so that it will be caught into the seam when the stitching for the seam is done. Overcast or hem the inner edge of the tape to the interfacing. Tape is put on around the revers, down the front edges, around the collar, and over the seam joining the collar to the neckline.

Make bound buttonholes in the front. Collar and facings are then attached and the buttonholes finished through the facings. Press as you go along as always. When the garment is finished, the last step is the lining, which is cut out from pattern pieces which come with the pattern.

The lining is put together as is the garment. The center back has a soft pleat, which is pressed in place and caught with catch stitches at the neck edge, the waistline, and the hem across the width of the pleat. Lining is placed in garment, wrong sides together. The raw edges are turned under about ½ inch and the fold is slip stitched to the garment. All seams must be carefully matched first, at armhole, shoulder, sides, neckline. Baste long seams together, the lining to the garment. This prevents shifting as it is worn. The sleeve is turned wrong side out, and the lining slipped on, right side out, and slip stitched to place. Baste the seam of the lining to the seam of the sleeve, wrong sides together. It is a good idea to pin the lining all the way around, with pins perpendicular to the edge, before doing any slip stitching.

If an interlining is being used, it is basted permanently to the seams and interfacing, but left free at the bottom. It can also be placed on the wrong side of each corresponding lining piece, and stitched together at the seams. However, the latter method causes bulky seams.

# 37. *CHILDREN'S CLOTHES*

CHILDREN'S clothes are constructed like adult's clothes, but there are certain special points it is wise to consider. Sizes are usually chosen according to chest measurement, not age. Pattern sizes range like this:

Children's sizes, 6 months to 4 years

| *Size* | *½* | *1* | *2* | *3* | *4* | *6* |
|---|---|---|---|---|---|---|
| Hip | 20 | 21 | 22 | 23 | 24 | 26 |
| Chest | 19 | 20 | 21 | 22 | 23 | 24 |
| Waist | 19 | 19½ | 20 | 20½ | 21 | 22 |

Girls' sizes, 5 to 13 years

| *Size* | *7* | *8* | *10* | *12* | *14* |
|---|---|---|---|---|---|
| Hip | 27 | 28 | 30 | 32½ | 35 |
| Chest | 25 | 26 | 28 | 30 | 32 |
| Waist | 22½ | 23 | 24 | 25 | 26 |

There must be plenty of room for freedom of movement. Simplicity is the keynote for good-looking children's clothes. Make plenty of provision for growth by taking deep hems; putting in gathers and tucks which can later be let out; and adding tucks to shoulder straps which can later act as an extension. Children of very young age should be encouraged to develop independence, by giving them openings down the front and buttonholes large enough for them to handle. Plackets should be large and easily accessible. It is a good idea to reinforce points of hard wear, such as extra stitching around armholes, self-patches on elbows and knees, stay pieces under pockets.

It is a good idea to make outdoor clothes very colorful so that children are visible to motorists and to mothers looking for a child who is temporarily not where he is expected to be.

The best fabrics are soft, smooth cottons of firm and even weave. Durability is vital. Use flat, smooth seams and finishes in construction. No irritant should be allowed. Line any article that might possibly rub or create friction.

Babies need very fine soft materials and flat, non-irritating seams. Allow room for growth and movement. Almost all children's clothes should be washable and easily ironed. Watch for color fastness and shrinkage control. Avoid a lot of fussiness; decoration should be neat and serviceable, usually in narrow lines for best effect. Do not use deep yokes and very wide embroidery edgings. When making party clothes, consider your time, for the number of times this type of garment is worn is usually very limited. Therefore, don't finish seams as carefully, and try to use short cuts.

Don't cut down adult clothing for children without a thought. Children's clothing should be becoming and suitable.

If the fabric is definitely a grown-up one, then don't use it for children. Develop proper attitudes towards becomingness, neatness and suitability of clothes in your children early in life, and the habits will stick.

### *A Self-help Bib for a Small Child*

The simplest yet one of the most useful and indispensable items of a small child's wardrobe is a bib for use at mealtime. The process of learning to eat brings many mishaps, and clothes need to be well protected with bibs designed for the purpose. Makeshifts, such as towels or napkins tied or pinned about the neck, roll up in the way and are an actual hindrance.

Bib for child

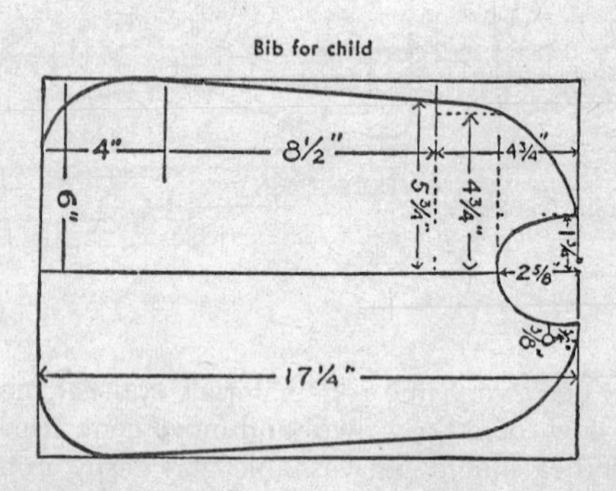


A bib should fit up well about the neck, hang straight and smooth across the entire front of the dress or suit, and cover the lap. The best material is absorbent but not bulky, and like other materials recommended for little children needs to be soft and comfortable in texture. Cotton ratine and light-weight terry cloth are examples of suitable material.

A bib can be even more than a protector of clothes. If

designed so that a child can put it on and take it off with little or no help it can be just as effective in teaching self-reliance as is learning to handle a spoon or cup.

The self-help design shown here is cut from a piece of cotton ratine 18 by 12 inches, making it possible to get three bibs from one-half of a yard of 36-inch material. The neck is cut deep and round so as to fit closely.

First, the sides and lower edge are bound with a strip of bias binding; then the neck is finished with another strip of bias, which extends into strings about 19 inches long at each side. After these have been stitched, each is run through an eyelet on the opposite side and a wooden bead or ring attached to each end as a pull.

As the bib is put on, the neck opening can be pulled out so that it slips easily over the head. Then as the child pulls on the beads the bib is drawn up to fit. There is no troublesome tying of strings, no bothering with bib clips.

# 38. *MAKING YOUR HOME MORE BEAUTIFUL*

CHOOSE fabrics for home sewing carefully. Consider the effect you want and critically examine materials for draping qualities, texture, strength, washability. Plan colors and try to visualize your finished room. Looking at magazines specializing in home decoration, and visiting furniture departments of retail stores will give you many good ideas.

Work carefully. Develop a pride in craftsmanship. It is poor economy to botch something and have to replace it very quickly because it does not stand up in wearing quality, or because it does not look well.

Review other parts of this book on fabrics, ruffles, pleats, headings and casings. You will need more than a nodding acquaintance with these techniques. And provide yourself with a flexible steel rule for measuring accurately. Know your machine attachments. The foot hemmer, ruffler and edge-stitcher will be of invaluable assistance.

*Flounces:* Slip covers, bedspreads and other articles for the home are usually made with some kind of flounce attached to a top piece. To attach flounces, see p. 133 on attaching ruffles.

*Circular flounce:* This is cut on the bias. Make a crosswise fold and put a pin into one corner to hold the fabric secure. To one end of a string, tie a pencil. Hold the string firmly at the corner with the pin, and with this homemade compass, draw a circular line about an inch down from the selvage to the fold. From the point thus made on the selvage, measure down the desired length of the flounce plus one inch for seams, and from this point make a second circular line with the pencil. Cut out as many flounce pieces as are necessary

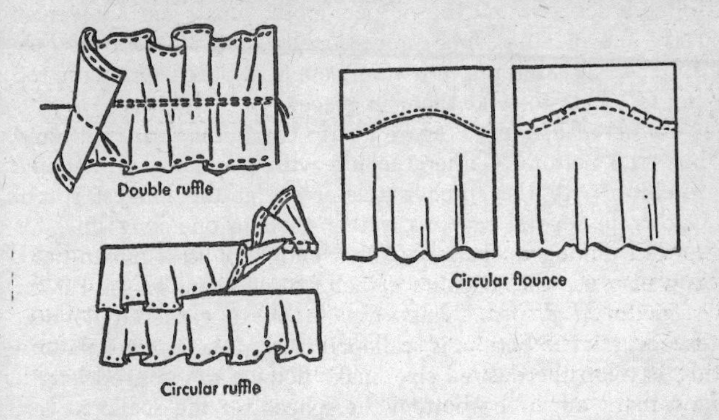


and seam them together. Narrowly hem the bottom or make a shell hem. The top raw edge is then attached to the spread, slip cover, etc.

*Godet flounce:* Cut out a straight piece the desired width and length (seam pieces together for long length) of the finished flounce, plus seam allowance top and bottom. Finish bottom with a hem or any desired decoration. Slash the flounce almost the whole width at even intervals and insert triangular godets. The bottom width of the godet should be a little less than half the depth of the flounce. Cut out the godets by marking them on the fabric thus:

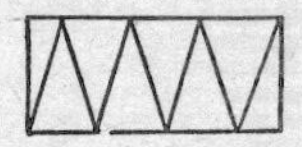

The godet should be cut so that a line from the top angle perpendicular to the bottom is on the lengthwise of the goods. To insert the godets, see p. 128.

*Pleated flounce:* Prepare a strip two to three times the finished length of the flounce, depending on the amount of fullness desired, and the proper depth, plus seam allowance. Have the pleating done professionally or do it yourself (see pp. 124-129), but put in bottom hem first. Stitch across the top of the pleats to hold them in place.

*Gathered flounce:* Prepare a strip twice finished length and hem the bottom. Gather the top with two lines of machine stitching with the stitch regulator set at the longest stitch. Gather in several sections, rather than in one long line, for ease in pulling up gathers. Wind ends around a pin to hold. You may use the machine gatherer attachment or the ruffler.

*Scalloped flounce:* This is made like a gathered flounce, except that the bottom is scalloped first. Make a paper pattern of a scallop the desired size, make flounce the desired length and mark off at the bottom the spaces for the scallops. Use the paper pattern to trace the scallops on the fabric and cut out. Sew bias binding on to scallops double, French style (see p. 136). Clip around curves, slash to points, turn bias over, baste and stitch.

# 39. *BEDSPREADS*

STANDARD-SIZE spreads are 72 x 108 inches for a single bed and 90 x 108 for a double bed. You may have to make some adjustments for your individual bed. It is a good idea to measure over the made-up bed, for blankets take up an amazing amount of room.

*Plain spread:* Use six yards of 36-inch fabric for a single bed and nine yards for a double bed. Six yards of 50-inch fabric will make a double spread. Cut 36-inch fabric crosswise into two three-yard pieces. Cut one lengthwise for two 18-inch strips. Seam one narrow width onto each side of the wide strip. Press seams open. Finish bottom with narrow hem. For a double bed, use a center strip of 36 inch and attach side strips of 27 inch each for standard-size spread.

*Spread with flounces:* Make a flat top piece to fit the top of the bed, of one center and two side strips, plus seam allowance at sides for attaching flounce. Make flounce of desired style, depth from top of mattress to floor plus two inches, and attach to three sides, usually in a plain seam. Circular flounce spread needs about 12 yards of 50-inch fabric. To measure the amount needed for a gathered flounce, measure length and width of bed. Add two lengths and one width together, multiply by two (for fullness) and convert to inches. Divide the figure by the width of the material, usually 36 or 50 inches, multiply your answer by the depth of the ruffle (with two-inch seam included), and since your answer is in inches, divide by 36 to get the number of yards needed. Add this to the amount needed for the top of the bed to get the yardage for the entire spread.

*Boxed spread:* Make flat piece to fit the top of the bed. At-

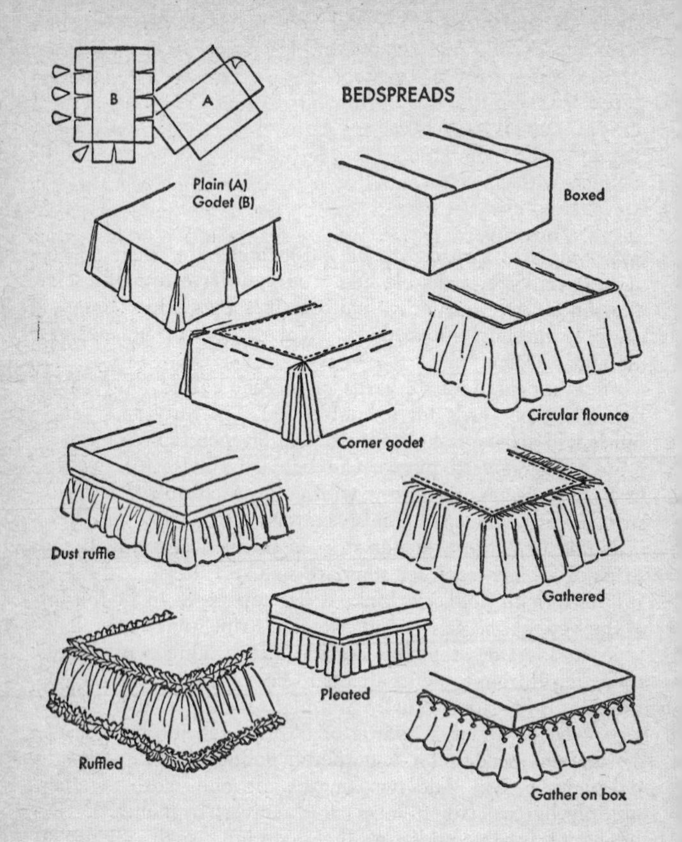


tach to it a strip about nine inches deep, and miter the corners for a careful fit (see p. 117). To bottom of boxed strip, attach desired type of flounce.

*Spread with dust ruffle:* This kind of spread is made in two parts, a separate flounce that is attached to the box spring ticking or sewed to a lining that fits under the mattress, and a short spread for the top of the bed. Make the lower section with any desired flounce, measuring the depth from the top of the box spring to the floor. Attach this to a foundation piece that fits the top of the box spring. This is made of muslin, usually, with a center piece and two narrower strips seamed on to the sides, as described above. Or, make the flounce with an allowance for a two inch lap over the box spring, and overcast the edge of this lap to the box spring ticking. Or, use tape snaps, sewing one tape to top edge of flounce and other tape to box spring ticking. Flounce is then snapped on and off for easy laundering.

The spread over the dust ruffle is shorter than a usual spread. For a plain spread, make as described above under plain spread, about 57 x 112 for a single bed and 72 x 112 for a double bed. The extra length is for tucking in the pillow. The spread should be long enough to cover the mattress and the top of dust ruffle completely. For a spread with a flounce, make as described above, but, again, much shorter. Finished flounce is usually nine to ten inches.

*Lining for spreads:*

1. Make lining of muslin exactly as you make spread, usually ½ inch shorter. Place finished spread out flat, wrong side up, put lining on top, wrong side down, turn in edges of lining and slip stitch to spread.

2. Or, make lining and spread exactly same size, put one on top of the other, wrong sides together, and finish edges together with binding, cording, braid, etc.

3. A third way is to put lining and spread right sides together, seam on both long sides and one short side. Turn right side out, turn in top edges and slip stitch by hand, stitch, or bind.

*Finishes for bedspreads:*

1. Pipe seams or insert cording (see pp. 110, 184), and finish lower edge in same way. To use self cording for the bottom edge, you need ½ to ¾ yard extra fabric.

2. On both sides, edgestitch decorative bands over seams.

3. Quilt top.

4. Use appliqué design in center of spread.
5. Use a double ruffle at bottom, possibly with a picoted edge.
6. Apply braid or ball fringe on edges.
7. Where there is not too much fullness, two front edges can be laced together at the corners.

PILLOW COVERING STYLES

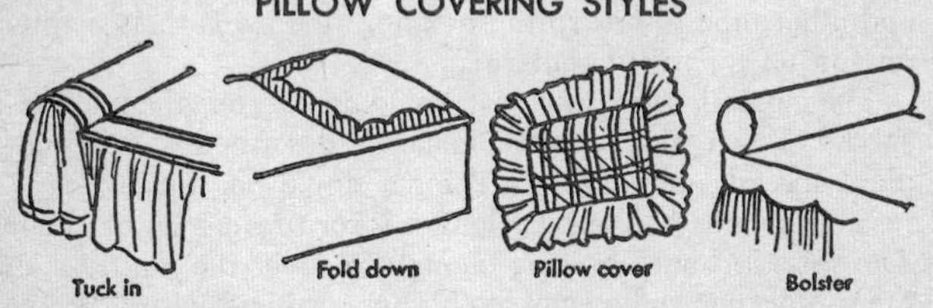


*Covering pillows on the bed:* Allow extra length on spread for tuck-in or make separate pillow sham as long as the width of the bed and wide enough to cover pillows completely. Finish edges in some decorative way. A pillow sham may be attached to the spread. Make the sham and line it, leaving one long edge raw. Attach to spread, wrong side of spread and right side of sham together, leaving sham lining free. Turn seam up, turn in raw edge of sham lining and slip stitch over seam. Or make seam as above, catching in all thicknesses, trim very close and seam again on right side ¼ inch from original seam.

*Bolsters:* Cut out a piece the width of the bed and about 30 inches wide. This piece may be quilted, if desired. Cut out two additional pieces, 6 x 30, and attach them at each end of the long piece with covered cording inserted in the seam (see p. 110). Put bolster roll on wrong side of fabric, arrange edges to meet and overcast. To finish ends, pull up cord tight, poke ends into the bolster after knotting or sewing to fasten them securely into place. Cover center with a tassel or large covered button.

*Decorative boudoir pillows* may be made by seaming two pieces of desired size and shape, right sides together, on three sides. Turn right side out, insert pillow, turn in raw edges and finish. Ruffles, cord, decorative stitches, braid, etc., may be used to finish edges.

# 40. *DRESSING-TABLE SKIRTS*

MAKE a pattern for the top of the table out of paper. Use this pattern to cut out the fabric, adding two-inch seam allowance. Put fabric on table, and tack allowance underneath. Make a gathered skirt, using twice the measurement around table, and the length from the table top to the floor plus hems. Hem bottom and top of skirt before gathering. Tack to the table, and cover the joining by gluing braid or ribbon over.

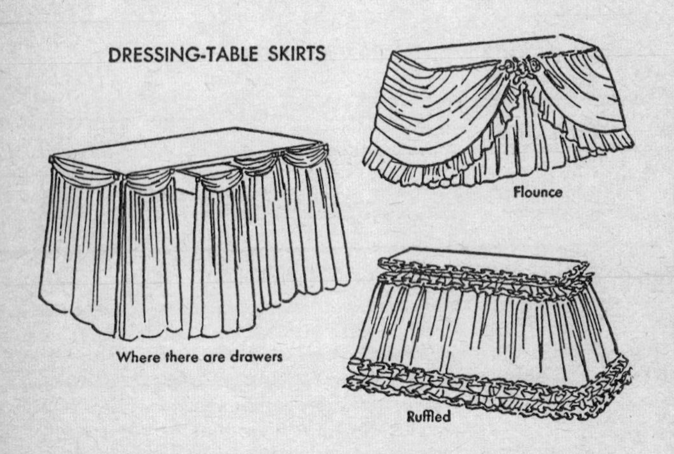


Or, stitch a 1½-inch to two-inch band to top of skirt, tack skirt on and turn banding over tacks to hide.

Where there are drawers, make skirt in two or more sections, depending on the style of the table, so that drawer may pull out.

For tiers, make a foundation skirt that fits table. Attach ruffles at even intervals down length of skirt.

Make these skirts as decorative as desired. Ribbons, bows, appliqué, ruffles, etc., are all suitable, but don't show poor taste by overdecorating. Remember that, if there is a great deal of material in the bedroom, you will do best with a wood table with no fabric on it. A mirrored or plastic fabric top is often a good idea so that powder and perfume can be easily wiped up.

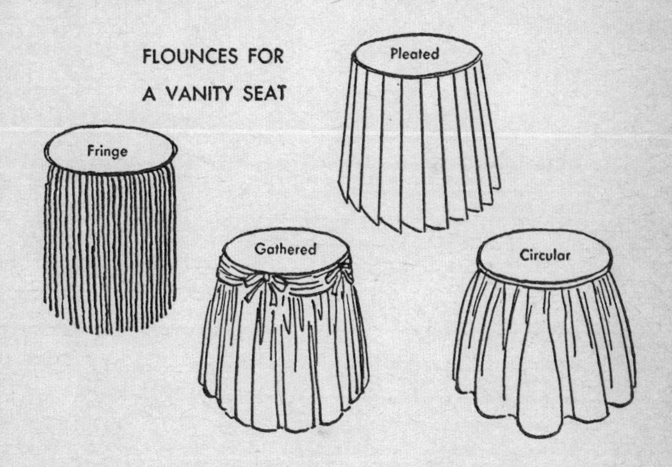


For the dressing-table stool, buy an inexpensive hassock and cover it. Make the top from a plain circle cut out to fit, and attach to a skirt. The top may be quilted. Or the top may be cut from a bias strip, stretched to fit on the outside of the seat, with the raw edge in the center gathered by machine to fit and then finished with a large covered button. For the skirt, make a plain sheath to cover the hassock and leave it plain or cover it with fringe. To put fringe on, start pinning it on at bottom and work your way up in order to get the best effect. The skirt may also be a gathered, pleated, or circular flounced.

# 41. *LAMPSHADES*

LAMPSHADES are made of paper or fabric stretched over a frame. Where it is hard to judge the size and shape of an uncovered frame, buy an inexpensive one of proper size and shape and recover it. Paper shades are made of wrapping paper, wallpaper, old maps, coated and treated papers. To make a pattern to fit the shade, paint the frame edge, or immerse in water if frame is rustproof, and roll over newspaper while wet. A perfect outline will be gotten with this method. Add seam allowance and cut out covering according to pattern. Join ends with paper fasteners or strong glue, like rubber cement, and overcast top and bottom with heavy thread to frame. Use a suitable decoration to cover stitches. To pleat paper shades, work with newspaper first until you get the proper size. Then cut out the covering, join under a pleat. Where lacquer or shellac is to be applied, crease pleats first.

To make an unlined gathered fabric shade, cut fabric length of frame plus two inches and 1½ times largest circumference, usually the lower edge. Seam. Hem top edge and gather by machine. Hem bottom edge. Wind wire frame with binding, then put on shade and turn over top edge, catching to binding on wire frame. Cover stitches with braid or ribbon. To line, make lining the same way, sew on to frame, seams facing out, apply shade on top.

Stretched shades are cut on bias. Stretch the fabric before cutting around shade, so that ends meet and lower edge is covered. Cut. Pin lower edge to frame, then pin around top, trying to get out all the wrinkles. Keep changing the pins, first on the bottom, then on the top, back and forth, until the shade is very smooth. Slip stitch the ends together. Overcast to the

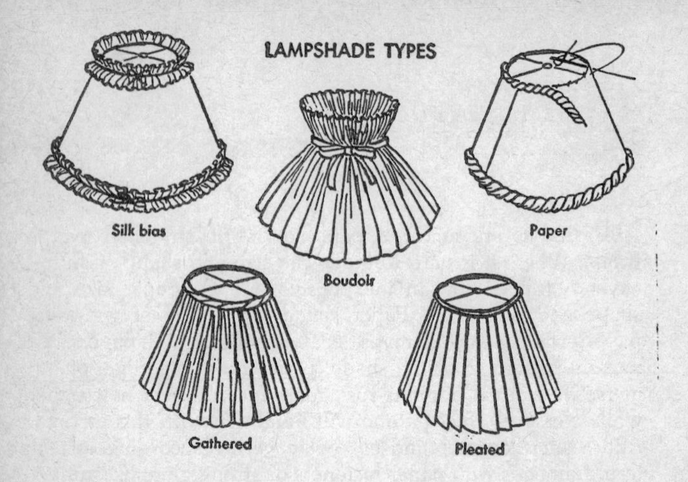


frame top and bottom with strong thread. Decorate as desired. This shade is lined first with a lining cut on a true bias.

To make a pleated shade, cut out a piece of desired depth plus two inches, make a one-inch hem at bottom. Pleat to fit and join ends under a pleat. Bind the top with narrow piping at bottom of binding if so desired. It is a good idea to work with a newspaper sample before working on the material.

For a petticoat boudoir shade, make a ruffle three times as long as bottom of frame and about five inches deeper than shade. Bind lower edge or turn up hem. Top edge is made with a three-inch heading. Join ends, pleat or gather shade and set on frame. Shade is usually finished with a bow or ribbon below the heading. Elastic thread used to make several rows of shirring is very pretty on a shade of this type.

# 42. *CURTAINS*

BEFORE you begin, examine your windows first and see if you can improve on the architecture with your curtain treatment. Short, narrow windows can be made to look longer and wider by extending curtains beyond edges of window and down to floor. Off-center windows can be made to look centered by carrying curtain fabric beyond edge of window on to wall. Place the fixture and rods first so that measuring will be more accurate.

To measure curtains, start from the bottom of the rod and measure to within one inch of sill, or to the bottom of the apron, or to within one inch of floor, depending on length desired. The curtain rod slips through a casing made at the top, and, if desired, a heading can stand above the casing. Casings are often made top and bottom so that curtain can be reversed for better wear. Curtain should be at least twice width of window, and wider for very sheer fabrics or for really full effect. The casing is made approximately twice the width or diameter of the rod. For a one-inch finished casing, add 2¼ inches, the ¼ inch for the first turn of the hem, and for one-inch heading add an additional two inches. Add at least three inches for finished hem at bottom and two inches as a shrinkage allowance. In sheer fabrics, hems are often made double. Measure lengths very carefully so that pairs are identical. Be sure center hems in a pair face each other. Hems may be done by hand or machine. Trimming is most easily done with ready-made trims applied to center and bottom edges. Cut off all selvages before starting to turn in hems.

After straightening the fabric and cutting the lengths, do

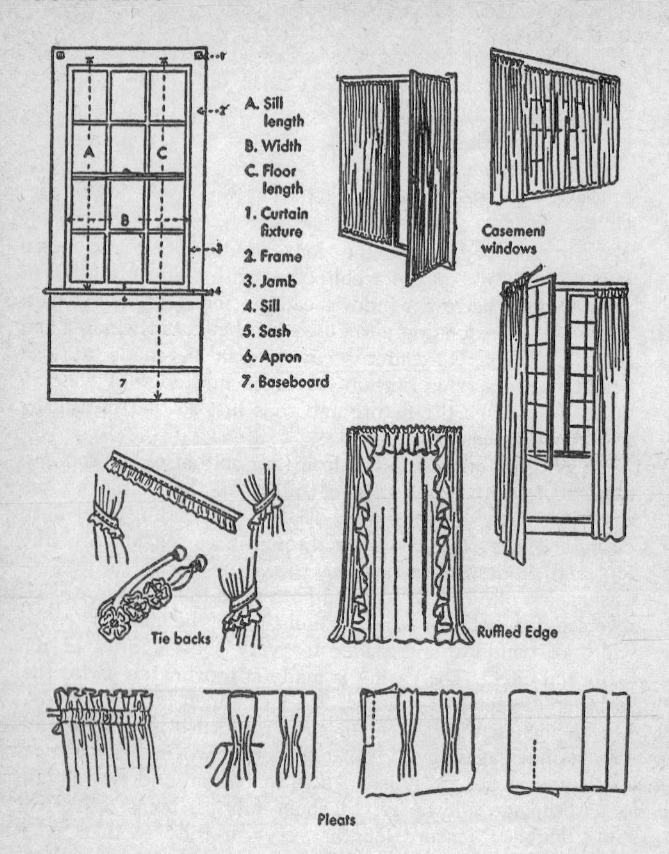


the outside narrow hems first, then make the center hems, which are approximately the depth of the bottom hem. Do the top hem (casing and heading) last, putting the shrinkage allowance into a tuck close to stitching line on wrong side, and finally apply the trimming.

*Sash curtains* are curtains for the lower part, or sash, of the window. The rod is placed at the top of the lower sash and the measurements are taken as already described, with the same allowances. A heading is usually allowed on a curtain of this kind.

*Cottage curtains,* also called Dutch curtains, are a combination of a sash curtain and a second curtain for the upper part of the window. For upper curtain, measure from bottom of top rod to four to six inches below sash curtain, or more where the curtain is to tie back.

*Casement curtains* are for windows that open in and out. Two rods are used, top and bottom, measurements taken from bottom of top rod to top of bottom rod. Casing and heading are usually used top and bottom.

*Tie backs:* The easiest tie back to make is a band about 4 x 12, folded in half lengthwise, outsides together, and stitched at the short ends. Trim seams, then turn to right side, turn in raw edges and top stitch all around.

For a ruffled edge, make a band as above, but insert ruffle between turned edges before top stitching. Or, seam short ends of band, right sides together, trim seams and turn. Stitch one thickness of band to wrong side of ruffle, turn free edge of band in, baste and stitch over seam on right side of ruffle.

For tie back with ruffle on two or three sides, cut out two pieces for the band, turn in raw edges all around and insert ruffle between turned edges. Baste carefully and top stitch.

*Pinch pleats:* Often a curtain is made with a pinch-pleated top instead of a heading and casing. The curtain is then attached to a rod with drapery hooks caught through the back of the pleat and hooked over the rod. There are usually four to five pinch pleats in one curtain, made from 1½ inches to two inches from the hemmed sides. Insert crinoline or lightweight buckram into top hem for stiffening; do not make a casing. Mark off spaces about three to 3½ inches wide starting from the center of the curtain, and make pinch pleats in this fashion.

Bring marks together, folding through the center as for a tuck, wrong sides together, and stitch the tuck from the top down to the hem line and across to the fold you have made. Backtack ends. Divide the tuck into three sections on the right side and catch by hand with over and over stitches at bottom of tuck. Be sure pinch pleats are evenly spaced.

*Ruffled valance:* Sometimes it is desirable to have a valance over the top of the curtain. An easy one is made by cutting a strip of fabric twice width of window and narrowly hemming it on three sides. Make a casing and heading on the fourth side and insert rod. The curtain is placed on a rod close to the window and the valance on an outer rod. This kind of valance is best over a ruffled curtain. Over a straighter curtain it would be best to gather the ruffle, instead of allowing the extra fullness to pull up in a gathered effect on the rod.

# 43. *DRAPERIES*

DRAPERIES are made in two lengths, to the bottom of the apron, and to the floor. Use at least one width of 36-inch fabric for each side of the window; one width of 50-inch fabric is not too much. Measure length, add four inches for top hem, two inches for heading, 3½ inches for lower hem. Straighten the fabric and cut into proper lengths. Watch design where there is a large print in the pattern. Match pairs carefully or the finished effect will not be good. Clip selvage, turn in 1½ inches to two inches on sides, two inches in center, 3½ inches on bottom, and five inches on top, turning only once, and catch stitch. The lining will cover the raw edges. The lining is made of sateen, about three inches shorter, and is turned in all around as in drapery. Top hem of drape is turned over crinoline or buckram for stiffening.

Place lining over drape, wrong sides together, and slip stitch edges, going over stitches every few inches for extra strength. Allow drapes and lining to hang 24 hours before tacking bottoms. Use plenty of pins to hold drape and lining together as you work. Do not attach the two at the bottom. Instead, French tack (see pp. 79, 172) them every four to six inches. Weights are often put into bottom hem to prevent curling of edges and to give proper effect. (See p. 173.)

To finish top, put in pinch pleats, as already described above. Stores have self-pleating buckram strips that are sewed to back of drapery heading, and, when pulled up, make pinch pleats quickly and well. Another type of heading is made with box pleats. (See pp. 125-127.) Measure four inches, then two inches, then four inches, etc., across top of drape. Bring four-inch markings together and stitch in pleats.

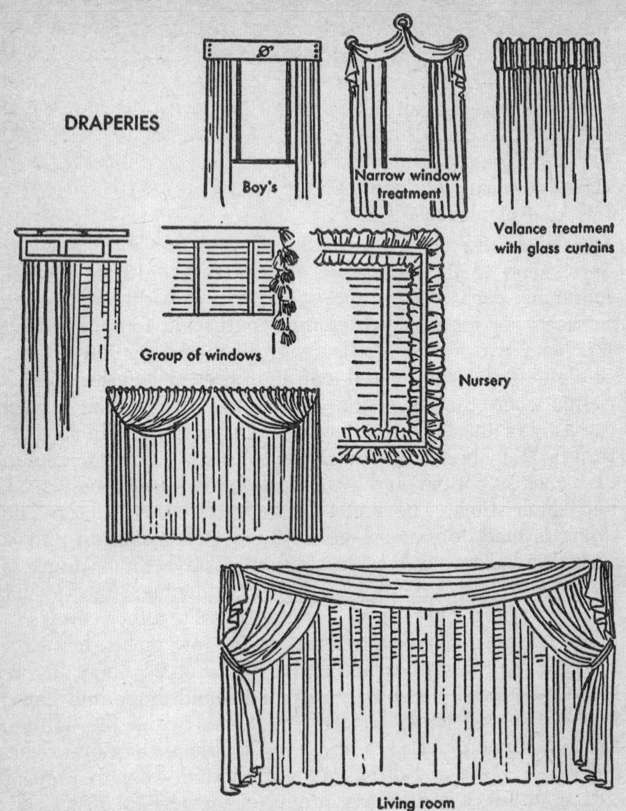


Make sure they are very straight and evenly spaced. Cartridge (pp. 125-127) and pipe-organ pleats are also used for drapery headings. Cut out pieces of cotton wadding, shape into a roll, and with a cording foot stitch strips of scrap material around them. Insert rolls into drapery heading, and stitch close with cording foot. Again spacing and evenness is important. A roll with four-inch diameter, with four-inch spaces between rolls, makes good proportion for floor to ceiling drapes. Sometimes a roll is used to form the pleats, but is not stitched in. Here you depend on the buckram to stiffen and hold the shape of the cartridge pleats. In this case, catch the top of the pleats to the drape with a few stitches to prevent any sag. Pipe-organ pleats are longer and closer together than cartridge pleats, but are made in the same way. Never press this kind of pleat flat.

# 44. *VALANCES*

VALANCES are decorative finishes for the tops of draperies. With rooms with low ceilings, start valance at ceiling. A simple valance has already been described (p. 234). Circular, pleated and gathered flounces can be used for attractive valances. A casing is made at the top for the outer rod on which the valance is placed. Valances are usually lined. They may even be sewed onto the top of the curtain or drape for an informal room.

Other valances are sewed onto stiff boards or wood. Sometimes these are called cornices to distinguish them from soft valances with no stiffening in the back. The boards are cut straight or are shaped (lumber yards will cut out wood

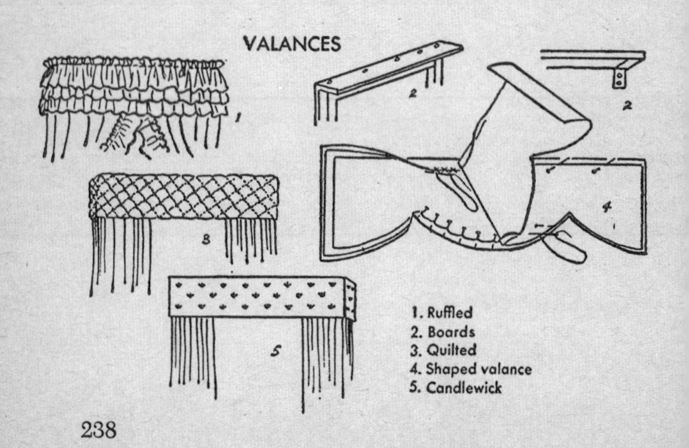

pieces to your measurements), and are attached to the window frame with brackets. The depth is usually from six to twelve inches. The fabric, either matching or contrasting, is cut to fit board, plus one-inch seam allowance all around. Cut lining piece and buckram to size without seam allowance. Fold back seam all around on valance piece and press, creasing sharply. Insert buckram under turned-back edges and baste. Turn in edges of lining ½ inch and place over valance, wrong sides together (lining will be a little smaller than valance), and baste edges together. Whip a piece of twilled tape to top and tack this tape over the top of the wood board, using ordinary tacks. The valance should go straight across the board and around back to the wall. These two short side sections are called the returns. Allow fabric for this when cutting.

Valances may be quilted, decorated with appliqué, ball fringe, or braid. They may be scalloped at the bottom, using a pattern made out of paper to shape the scallops. Reread directions for making scalloped flounce, p. 220.

For swag effect, use a width of fabric with ends cut diagonally. Hem edges and drape over tie-back pins or through rings. Experiment before cutting to get proper effect.

# 45. *SLIP COVERS*

SLIP COVERS can hide a multitude of sins in upholstered furniture and add new life and smartness to a room. To measure pieces for covers, take length and width measurements for each part of the piece separately and note them down. Measure from highest point to lowest (B-C) and add one inch extra allowance for each seam. Measure back (B-A), front (B-C), arms (G), wings (J-K), cushions (L-M-N-O-P), all separately. Add a good-sized extra allowance for a generous tuck-in on seat. Add all separate length measurements and divide by 36 to get the yardage. With 50-inch material, some small pieces may be cut from excess width left after large sections are cut, therefore 50-inch material is more economical. A typical comparison would be 5½ yards of 50-inch fabric as against eight yards of 36-inch fabric for a chair. You can make a plan on paper for the cutting layout to give you an idea of how the pieces should be cut. Allow extra material for patterned fabric that must be matched, about ½ to ¾ yards. Don't figure the amount too closely, give yourself a margin for error.

Material may be placed on piece to be covered and pinned and cut directly, but this is risky with an inexperienced worker. It is better to start with a pattern made from muslin or some other inexpensive, closely woven fabric. Lay muslin on chair back after cutting back piece of necessary width and length. Pin it to back, cut inside back piece and pin upper seam line together. Put in enough pins to hold material securely in place while working, so that there is no slipping. Cut out other pieces necessary to finish top of chair—for example, wings, arms, etc.—and pin in seams. Seams should

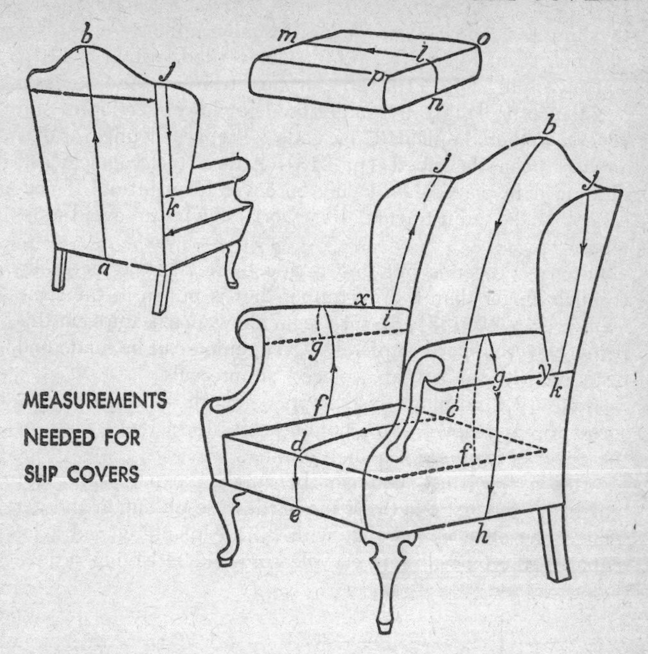


MEASUREMENTS NEEDED FOR SLIP COVERS

be about ¾ inch when finished, so that there is no danger of their being easily pulled out. Go on to seat and other parts, pinning them securely to chair, then pinning in seams.

When cover is all pinned together, carefully examine your work and repin where necessary. Look for wrinkles, tautness, too much fullness. Use tailor's chalk to mark seam lines and to make markings necessary to help you reassemble parts later. Trim seams to ¾ inch.

Separate pattern pieces and cut out material carefully. Be sure that grain lines are correct, otherwise slip cover may slip and pull out of place too readily. Center a printed pattern or stripes carefully. Transfer seam and assembly markings to slip-cover fabric. Join seams, usually upholsterer's seam (French seam in reverse, p. 109) or corded seam (p. 110). Narrow piping (pp. 110, 185), or moss trim may also be used.

Valance or flounce is usually used for lower section of slip covers, gathered, pleated, or godet. Prepare flounce as has already been described (p. 218). Attach the valance last, pinning it in place, then trying on cover for a fitting. If necessary, make adjustments, but work slowly to avoid mistakes.

Often a zipper is put into a side back seam. It naturally is much longer than a dress zipper, but is put in in the same manner (pp. 45, 145). Be sure seam allowance is ample at this point. Cover zipper completely. Or, opening can be made and fastened with large snaps, placed at intervals.

Make seat cushions last. Zipper for these usually goes across top and down two adjoining sides for a few inches, or the cover is made with a snap closing.

After a few tries, you can become an expert slip-cover maker. It's the first one that's the hardest, so plunge in and get going. The chances are that with a little planning and a lot of patience, you will get very pleasing and satisfying results.

# 46. *MENDING*

Mending can be fun if you treat it as an art and work for careful, durable, flat finishes. Study the weave of the fabric and try to duplicate it. Try to get as invisible a finish as possible except where you are making a decorative mend. In order to mend, you must have a basic knowledge of the hand stitches, although you will find that the running stitch is the one you will use most often. Stitches are usually short and fine. Rows of stitching are uneven to prevent definite lines from showing and to insure an invisible finish. Work from the right side most often to blend in your work.

Your work box contains much of the same equipment as for regular sewing, plus a darning egg, a hoop for machine darning, mending liquid, mending tape, rubber tissue, darning threads and needles, a crochet hook, buttons, snaps, hooks and eyes, tapes, and scraps.

Inspect your clothes regularly and try to prevent big jobs by the familiar stitch in time. These are likely spots to check:

1. Seams. Narrow seams may have to be stitched a little deeper to make them hold. If the edges fray, stitch a line near the edges and overcast them. Two rows of stitching prevent fraying and stretching.

2. Stitching. Rip out and resew broken or drawn stitching.

3. Hems. Rehem when necessary if threads catch or seem unusually loose. Check and restitch hems on household linens also.

4. Dangling threads. Catch and fasten off such threads before further damage occurs.

5. Bindings and facings. See if they are sewed on securely and restitch if necessary.

6. Pocket corners and placket edges. Reinforce with tape or stitching if they seem weakened by wear.

7. Fastenings. Check and resew buttons, snaps and hooks and eyes. Rework raveled buttonholes.

Patches are used where a hole has been made. Cut a patch on the straight of the goods and match it to the lengthwise and crosswise yarns in the garment. Match design and pattern in the fabric very carefully or the patch will stand out like a sore thumb. When inserting a patch into a washable garment, wash new material until color is the same as the color of the garment. The washing will also shrink the patch.

*Hemmed patch:* This is a strong mend used primarily for washable garments. Trim the tear to a rectangle. Clip diagonally at corners from ¼ to ½ inch, and turn edges under slightly beyond the ends of the clips. Crease sharply or press. Cut the patch about one inch larger than the hole, making sure to match the design. Baste the patch in place and slip stitch in place from the right side, catching the stitches in the very edge of the crease. Turn to the wrong side and turn the edges of the patch under ¼ inch, snipping a little off at the corners to prevent excess bulk. Slip stitch to place seeing that stitches do not show on the right side.

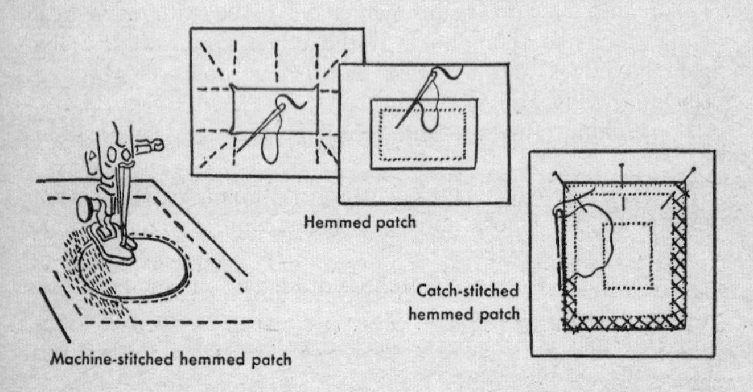
Hemmed patch

Catch-stitched hemmed patch

Machine-stitched hemmed patch

*Catch-stitched hemmed patch:* This is a variation of the hemmed patch and is used for heavy, less firmly woven materials, such as some drapery and slip-cover fabrics, bedspreads, and thin blankets. Cut the patch and machine stitch twice around the outside. Baste the patch in place and slip stitch on the right side. On the wrong side, catch stitch the raw edge of the patch to the article being repaired.

*Flannel patch:* This is used for flannel or other firm fabrics that do not ravel. Cut out patch as for hemmed patch and baste in place. Catch stitch on wrong and right sides without turning in edges of patch or hole.

*Lapped or underlaid patch:* This patch is used when sturdiness is more important than appearance. Make hole rectangular or round, round for greatest amount of stretch as in knit goods and elastic garments. Cut away ragged edges and baste matched patch to position. Darn by hand, working the stitches in over the edges even beyond the joining, or stitch by machine where a stiffer and stronger mend is desirable.

*Thermoplastic or pressed on patches:* Straighten edges of hole, put in patch cut from hem, and from wrong side, press on mending tape over patch. Use another piece of mending tape in place from which patch was taken, as the hem. Follow exact directions given with the tape.

*Inset patch:* This patch is used for silks and rayons and other fabrics to be dry cleaned, rather than washed. Cut around damage, clip in corners, as for a hemmed patch, and turn edges under. Baste matched patch in place, leaving a small seam allowance, and making sure that patch fits into the hole exactly. Overhand, from the wrong side, the two folded edges together. Overcast raw edges and press patch flat. Or, the patch may be finished by machine. Baste the patch in place, using long slip stitches and contrasting thread, which will later be removed. On the wrong side, stitch by machine exactly on the line of hand stitching. Trim off extra material, clipping corners to remove bulk, and press. Work over machine line on right side with very tiny stitches to conceal the seamed edge.

Darns are used for worn places, tears and snags. Try to get yarns from the fabric itself, lengthwise ones from seam edges and crosswise ones from the hem. Some machines have a special darning arm or a darning foot to facilitate darning by machine.

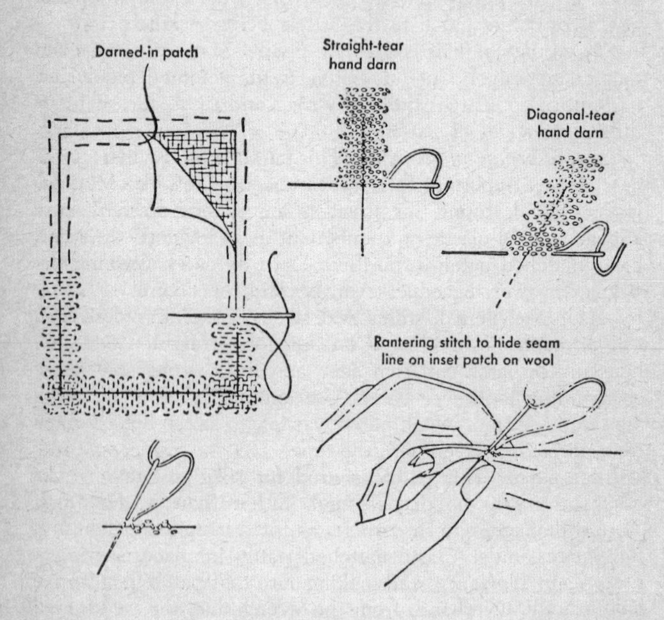


*Plain darns:* Used for hose and for small holes in woven fabrics. Trim away ragged edges. Use a darning egg for a stocking; otherwise keep the material flat. Run threads beyond the edges of the hole, taking very tiny stitches. Fill in the lengthwise threads, then run in the crosswise threads, as in weaving, over and under. Leave stitches loose at the end of rows to prevent a tight appearance.

*Straight tear:* Work back and forth over the tear, running stitches loosely and unevenly on all sides beyond the tear. Reinforce the tear by working over a piece of firm net on the inside. Finish by working vertical stitches on the inside.

*Three-corner tear and diagonal tears:* Made like straight tears. Any tear that is too ragged to be darned inconspicuously must be trimmed and patched with a suitable patch.

*Pattern darn:* This is used for materials with a distinct weave and tries to reproduce this weave. Study the weave carefully.

*Machine-darned tear:* Study the directions on your machine for darning. On some machines, a feed cover plate is used and the presser foot removed. Or, the feed may be lowered with no special cover used. The fabric is inserted in an embroidery hoop with the edges of the hoop wrapped to insure tightness. A machine darning foot is used with certain machines. Stitching is worked back and forth over tear. Darning over tears can be done quickly on the zigzag machine, for the needle moves from one side of the tear to the other. This kind of darn is used only when appearance is second to sturdiness.

In knit wear, two kinds of mends will take care of most of your needs. The knit stitch mend is inconspicuous and will have elasticity. The blanket stitch mend is easier to do but shows more and has no give. Make a cut in the worn spot and ravel the edges to give a squared-off area, with a straight line of loops at top and at bottom. Catch each loop as you unravel, working the needle into the side of the fabric. Pull in a crosswise yarn and work over it with loose blanket stitches, one for each knitting stitch. Pull in another crosswise yarn and work over it continuing until the hole is filled in.

For the knit-stitch mend or stocking-web darn, as it is also called, fill in the hole vertically with threads that catch the top and bottom loops. Work across the rows, putting the needle into two loops as shown in the illustration. Make stitches match looseness or tightness of stitches in the article you are mending.

Dropped stitches can be picked up with a crochet hook and fastened at the top with small overhand stitches. Large areas can be mended by knitting in a piece.

Special mends:

*Buttons:* To prevent strain on a button which receives much use, sew the button on with a shank.

Where cloth under a button has torn away, put a small inset patch on wools, rayons, and silks, and on cottons make a strong hemmed patch.

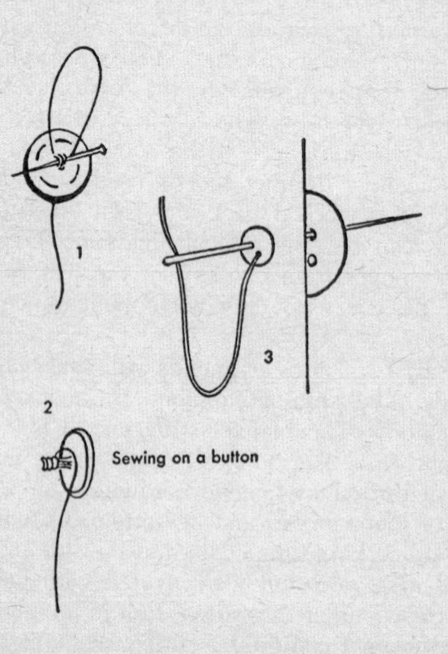

Sewing on a button

1. Make the shank by laying a pin or two across the top of the button. Sew several times over the pins and through the button and material.

2. Pull out the pins, lift the button, wind the thread beneath the button, and fasten off. Length of shank needed depends on thickness of the suiting.

3. For even greater protection, sew a tiny stay button directly under the top button but on the inside of the suit. Sew through both buttons at the same time and make a shank inside the top button long enough to allow the buttonhole to fit underneath without strain on the cloth.

Zigzag machines have the needle so spaced that it may be used to sew on buttons simply and rapidly.

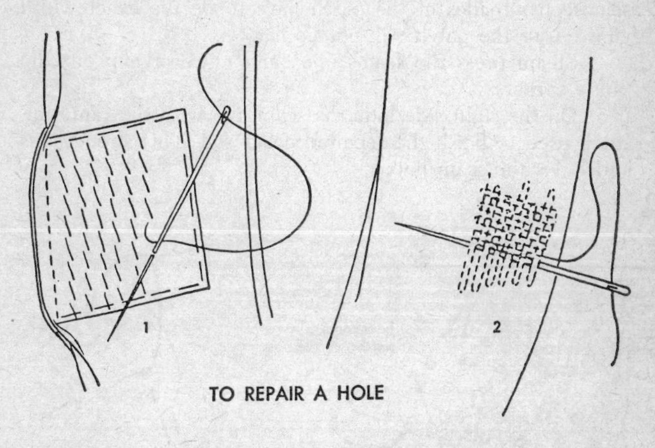


TO REPAIR A HOLE

*To repair a hole:* Set in a block of matching material. If you have no extra matching material on hand, enough can be cut from the inside facing of a vest or coat. Replace that material with another of similar color and weave.

1. Cut with the grain of the goods around the hole. If it is next to a sleeve seam, rip the seam open and let one side of the finished block go into the seam. Press the piece you cut out and use it as a pattern for cutting and matching the new piece to be set in. Cut the patch piece about ½ inch larger all around than the pattern so as to have ¼ inch for seams. Clip each corner of the hole diagonally. Turn the edges under ¼ inch. Baste and press lightly.

2. Lay the patch on the inside of the sleeve under the hole with the pattern matched exactly. Pin in place. With contrasting thread hem the folded edge around the hole to the patch. Take stitches about ⅜ inch apart through the edge of the fold. These stitches are to serve as a guide line for seaming by machine from the wrong side.

3. Now turn to the inside of the sleeve and stitch the patch in by machine on the line of the contrasting thread. The seams on all sides of the patch have to be the exact width allowed, or the patch will not lie flat.

4. Steam press the seams open and mitre or clip out the bulky corners.

5. On the right side hide the seam line with the rantering stitch used to finish the repaired collar roll. This strengthens and hides the seam line.

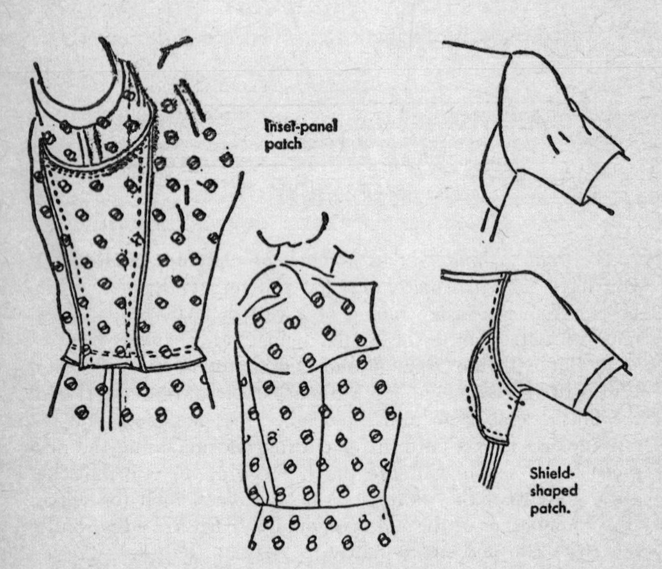

*Pinholes:* Work an eyelet where a heavy pin or brooch has left a hole.

*Underarm wear:* For a small patch, set in a shield-shaped matching piece of material, leaving a double seam allowance on the patch edge to make up for the seam allowance that is taken out of the bodice. To make a panel patch, cut out the underarm section from the sleeve down to the waist. Using this as a pattern, cut, match, and seam in a new piece.

*Worn spots:* Do preventive darning or reinforce the underside of a thin spot with a piece of matching or similar material. Make sewing as invisible and flat as possible. Worn elbows on long-sleeved dresses can be cut off making short sleeves.

*To mend a thin elbow:* Cut a piece of cloth or rayon lining large enough to cover the underside of the entire thin spot. Baste in place. Tack with rows of loose tailor's basting. Make the rows of basting parallel to the lengthwise grain of the cloth, about ½ inch apart—closer where the cloth is very thin.

On sweaters, decorative patches of felt or leather, or novelty patches that you can buy, are sewed on to the outside.

*Worn plackets:* To replace worn sleeve plackets, rip stitches joining the top of the placket to the sleeve. Continue ripping under the fly side, detaching from the sleeve and the cuff. Select a replacement material for the placket to match in shade, weight, and weave. Place the right side of the material to the inside of the sleeve opening. Match the end of the material to the bottom of the sleeve. The other end of the placket will be turned under and brought to a point. Stitch the placket to the sleeve, taking a ¼-inch seam. Fold over and top stitch over the seam, turning in a ¼-inch seam allowance. Slide the placket between the cuff, and top stitch. Stitch across the top of the placket holding the fly piece.

*Worn or ripped linings:* In replacing sleeve linings, stitch at wrist and fell into place by hand at the armhole. Be sure that after being felled the lining is smooth and not twisted. Small tears or holes are patched or darned. If the lining is

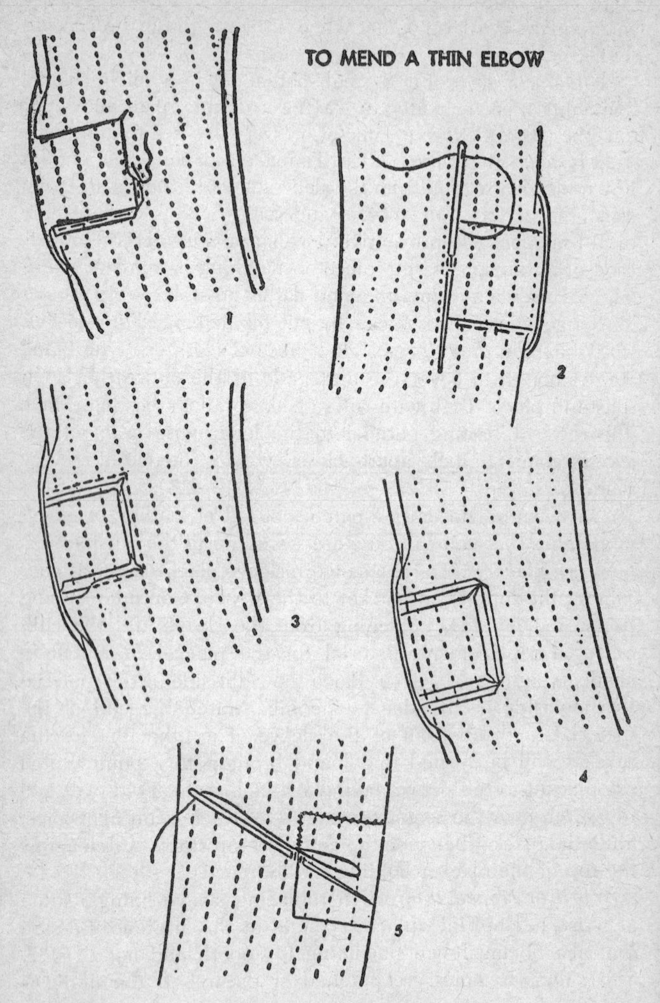
TO MEND A THIN ELBOW
1
2
3
4
5

worn at the underarm, rip at the seam, sew on a patch or shield, and restitch.

*Pulled out lingerie straps:* When the garment attached to the strap is torn, set in attractive diamond-shaped or triangular patches set in with Bermuda fagoting (see p. 198).

*Frayed, worn, or torn collars:* Where collars are only slightly frayed, a row or two of stitching close to the edge is sufficient. If parts of the collar show wear or rips, top-patch or darn the collar. Where the collar shows extensive wear along the outer edge, put on a bias binding. Stitch to the wrong side first, fold to the right side, and stitch along the edge.

Where the collar is well worn put on a new top collar. Stitch the top collar first to the top on the underside, fold to the right side, fold in the seam allowance at sides and bottom, and stitch into position.

In the case of heavy collars, generally worn, remove the entire collar and replace with a matching one, or replace the top collar with a new one if the under collar is in good shape. To replace the collar, machine stitch the top collar to the neckline of the garment, and fell down the under collar by hand.

*Turning collars:* In the case of lighter weight garments, badly worn or damaged collars are turned. The collar is removed with a sharp blade and turned. For collars without neckband or reversible shirt collars, seam underside of collar to neckline (A), fold top side of collar over seam and top stitch into position (B). For collars with neckband, seam collar to outside of neckband (A), close by stitching inner neckband down to collar with top stitch (B).

*Replacing collars:* Worn or damaged collars are removed and replaced with matching ones following the procedure outlined above. Replacement collars are obtained from unrepairable garments.

*Worn hems on coats and jackets:* The following methods are used to repair worn hems on the subject items:

If sufficient length is available, the hem is ripped, cut off above the damage and rehemmed (B). The new raw edge thus resulting should be bound (C) or turned under.

Worn or damaged material on the hem edges is darned.

Heavy garments are bound. The garment is spread on a

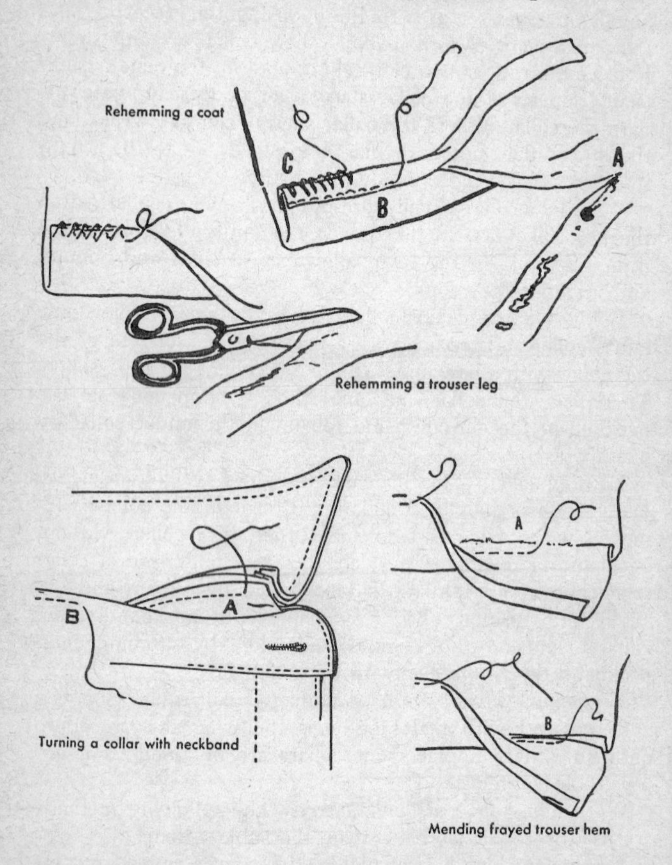


Rehemming a coat

Rehemming a trouser leg

Turning a collar with neckband

Mending frayed trouser hem

table with the inside up. Using a ¾-inch binding, place it along the bottom edge, beginning at the buttonhole end. Fold end of binding over ⅝ inch. Beginning ½ inch from bottom edge of the garment, backstitch across the ⅝-inch fold and continue stitching ½ inch from the bottom along the entire length. Stop stitching two inches from the bottom end of the garment. Cut off the binding ¾ inch beyond the inside lining on the button end. Fold the end of the binding over ⅝ inch. Continue stitching to the end of the binding and backstitch the fold. Turn the garment over so the outside is up. Fold the binding to the outside of the garment. Turn the binding under ¾ inch; make sure that the fold on the end of the binding is turned under before beginning to stitch. Backstitch the end fold and stitch along the entire length ¾ inch from the bottom of the garment. Stop stitching two inches from the end of the binding. Fold under the end of the binding ⅝ inch. Continue stitching to the end of the binding and backstitch the fold.

*Wear guards:* Wear guards protect trouser legs from the rub of shoes. To make them, use heavy tape about ⅝ inches wide or cloth cut from the leg seams. Turn down cuff, and baste the guard on just inside the leg, next to the fold that will be the bottom edge of the trouser. Stitch by machine

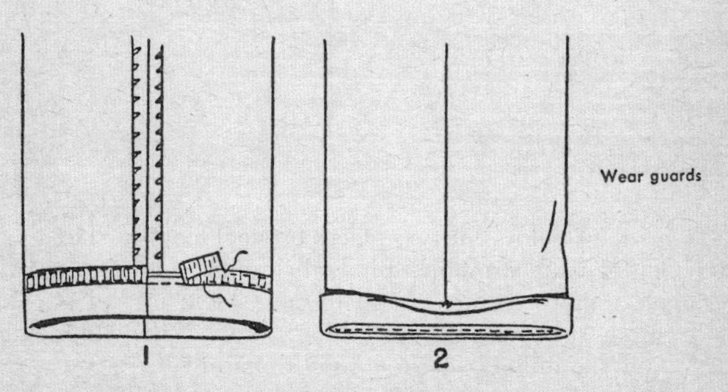


Wear guards

along both edges of the guard. Turn the cuff back and tack it into place.

To put the wear guard on to trousers without cuffs, first rip hem open. Baste, then stitch a guard on just inside the lower edge of the leg—on the hem side of the bottom crease (1). Then rehem the trousers (2).

*Shields:* When wear and perspiration cause holes under the arms of suit lining, tack in new shields to avoid staining of the outer material of the coat. Make underarm shields of fabric that matches or is similar to the jacket, or make shields of rayon lining.

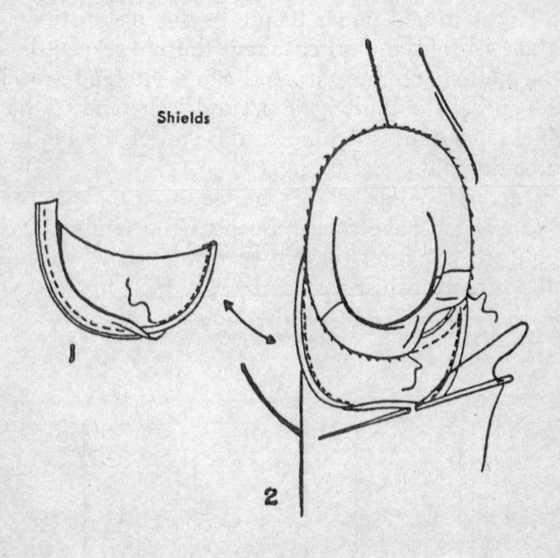


To make shields, cut two pieces of wool cloth to shape and sew under each armhole. Bind all around with rayon. Rip armhole lining just far enough to tack shield into place (1). Slip stitch shield to the coat lining around the outer edge (2). Sew the lining back in around the armhole.

*To lengthen trousers:* Pick out the tacks at the side of the cuff and rip open the lower edge. Spread the cuffs out full length. If the cuffs have never before been repaired or adjusted, there will be three sharp press lines. The top crease marks the length which the trousers have been, so measure from this line when you mark a new length.

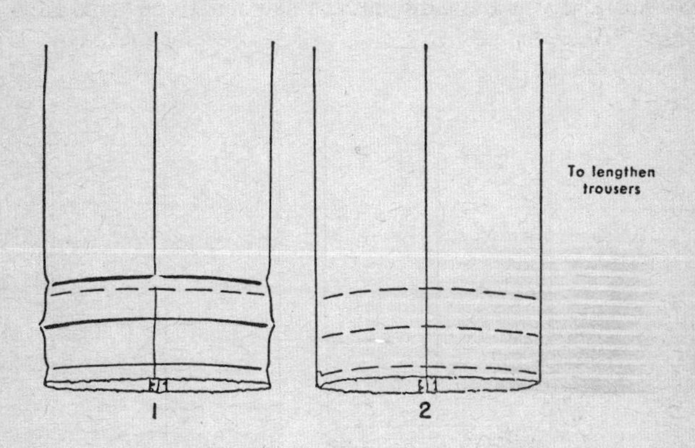


To lengthen trousers

Measure from the top crease the amount you want to lengthen the trousers (1). Mark around the leg with tailor's chalk. Then steam out the old crease lines. Make a new plain cuff or a French cuff, depending on how much you want to lengthen the leg. If you are adding one inch or less to the trouser length, finish again with a plain cuff. If trousers are lengthened more than one inch, finish with a French cuff.

*To make a plain cuff finish:* From the chalk mark, measure down 1¾ inches and mark a line around the trouser leg (2). Mark another line 1¾ inches below that. Pick up, fold, and baste along the middle chalk line. Pin the first and third lines together and baste. Steam press.

Now fold to form the new cuff along the line where the third and first chalk lines are basted together. Baste to hold the cuff in place and press. To finish the cut edge, which is turned up inside the trouser leg, turn the cuffs down again, baste and stitch by machine. Finish with a wear guard, then tack the cuffs at the side.

*To make a French cuff:* If it is necessary to lengthen the trousers more than one inch, use a French cuff. From the chalk line that is the guide for the new length (1) make two

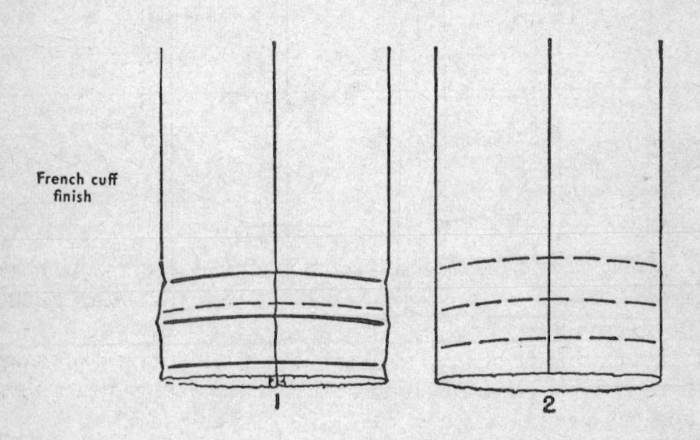


more lines, one 1¾ inches above the first line, and one 1¾ inches below the first line (2). Fold on the center line and baste. Lay this fold against the top line and baste. Fold and baste along the lower line, which marks the bottom of the cuff. Steam press.

Turn the cut edge up inside the pants and turn in so that it just meets the top fold. Trim off extra material. Join the two folds with hand stitches about ¼ inch apart so they won't catch on shoes. Put in a wear guard. Steam press and tack cuffs at the side.

*To shorten trousers:* Pick out the tacks at the side of the cuff and rip open the lower edge. Spread the cuffs out full length.

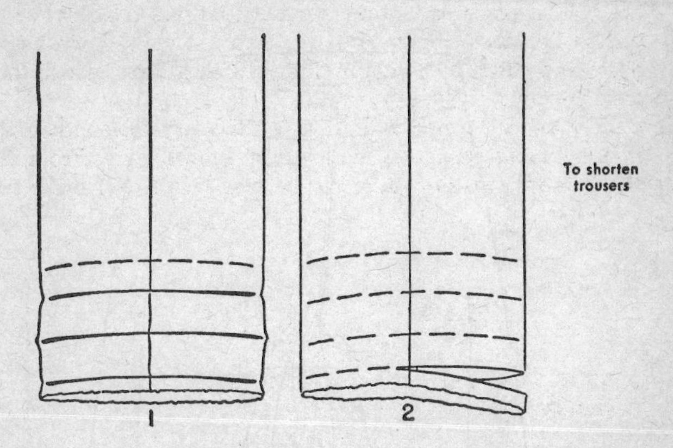


From the top press crease, which marks the old length, measure the length which the leg is to be shortened. Mark around the leg at the new length with tailor's chalk. Steam press to take out creases (1).

From this new line, measure down and draw two more lines 1¾ inches apart. Make a fourth line 1¾ inches below this, and cut away excess material below this line (2).

Finish as a plain cuff. Pick up, fold, and baste along the middle chalk line. Pin the first and third lines together and baste. Steam press.

Fold to form the new cuff along the line where the first and third chalk lines were basted together. Baste to hold the cuff in place and press.

To finish the cut edge, which is turned up inside the trouser leg, turn the cuff down again, baste and stitch by machine. Finish with a wear guard, then tack the cuffs at the side.

*To let out or take in seat:* Most trousers have a generous seam allowance at the back rise. This seam may be reseamed to make the seat smaller or larger. Do this before you rip out the old stitching, then rip the old seam and steam press the new seam.

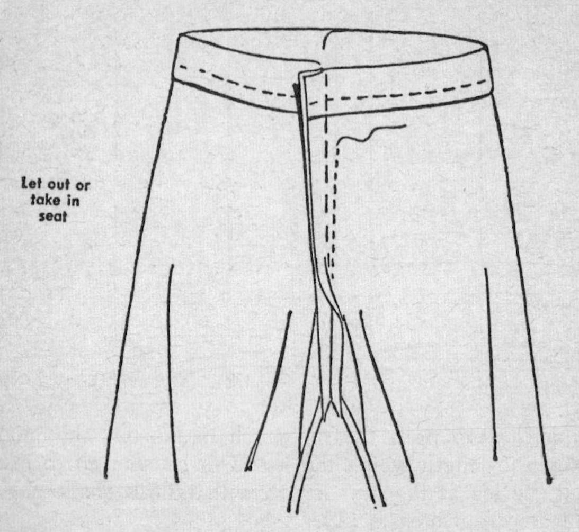


If there is any doubt about the fit, baste the new seam line, rip out the old stitching and fit the trousers before stitching.

*To let out too-short crotch:* Rip the inseams down from the crotch point about 12 inches. Open the back and front rise slightly—just so the seam allowances of the inseams are free. You will find plenty of seam allowance for this purpose if there have been no adjustments made previously.

Let out the seam as needed and resew, tapering off to meet the old stitching lines of the inseams. Press open, then reseam the front and back rise and press again.

*Frayed pocket edges:* If the edges of side pockets are slightly frayed, but not along the full length of the opening, rip the inside facing apart from the pocket edge a little beyond the worn part. Turn in the worn edges, slip stitch them together and finish as before.

If the edges are more worn, trim off the worn parts of both the facing and the pocket, but be very careful to keep a straight line. Reseam the facing to the pocket edge by machine, using a very tiny seam. Roll the seam line so that it is barely inside the pocket opening, then baste and press. Stitch the pocket edge by machine once or twice, depending on how it was finished in the first place.

*If the entire pocket edge is frayed:* If the pocket is worn along the entire edge, cut the bars at each end and rip the seams open for a few inches, just above and below the pocket. Rip the facing from the pocket mouth. Trim off the worn part. Make certain to keep a straight line. Reseam. If the facing is badly worn, rip the other side of it away from the cotton pocketing and turn that side out to the pocket edge. Reseam the facing to the pocket mouth with right sides of the two pieces together. Turn facing back into the pocket with the seam line just inside. Baste, press and stitch as it was before you ripped it. Resew the seams above and below the pocket. Bar pocket ends by stitching back and forth to strengthen.

*To replace inside pocket:* Turn trousers inside out and rip out stitching that holds pocket to waistband. Cut a paper pattern for the pocket. Mark the side that is to be laid on the fold when you cut the new pocket. Allow about ⅜ inch for seams when you cut.

Cut off the old pocket next to the two wool facings just inside the pocket mouth. This leaves in some of the old pocketing that is stitched back of the wool facing. If this part of the old pocket were ripped out, it would be more difficult to put in the new one.

*Worn hems on trousers:* If the bottom of cotton or wool trousers is frayed at the edge but has sufficient length to permit turning a new hem of 1½ inches and still retain cuff size, cut off the bottom and turn a new hem.

Where the length of the trousers does not permit cutting away the damaged part, open the hem and stitch a seam above the frayed edge. (See A.) Rehem so that the seam does not show on the right side (A). (See p. 254.)

If the inside hem is badly damaged, cut it off and apply a new facing (B). Then rehem the trouser leg (B).

Rehem cotton and wool trousers, where appearance is secondary, on a lockstitch machine. If appearance is of primary importance, wool trousers are felled by hand.

*Cuffs:* With a worn cuff, carefully take out the stitches along the edge of the cuff and open the seam on the edge. Trim the frayed edge off about ¼ inch, tapering off around the curve. Turn in trimmed edges about ⅛ inch and machine

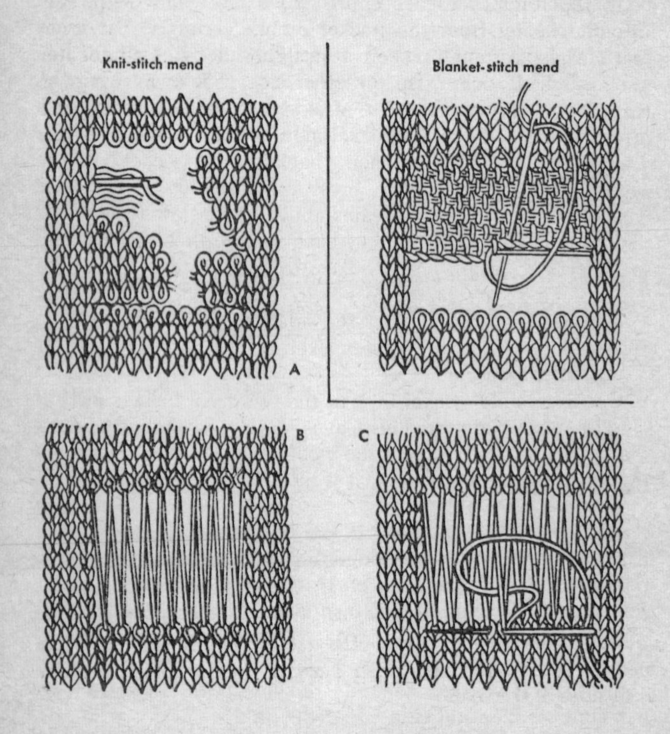

stitch. Stitch around the cuff and do a second line of top stitching like the original finish. The cuff will be shortened by such a small amount that it will not make a difference.

*Blankets:* Replace worn out bindings with new ones. An old blanket can be finished at the edge by trimming off the frayed part, running two lines of machine stitching and then finishing with blanket stitches.

*Gloves:* Mend with the same kind of stitch originally used in hand-sewn gloves. With leather gloves, use two needles to copy the original stitch. Thread both ends of the thread through needles. Make a stitch, bring the needle on the other end of the thread through the same hole, in order to get the same effect on both sides. Or, blanket stitch each side of a tear, then blanket stitch the two edges together where the original stitch is like a fine buttonholing stitch.

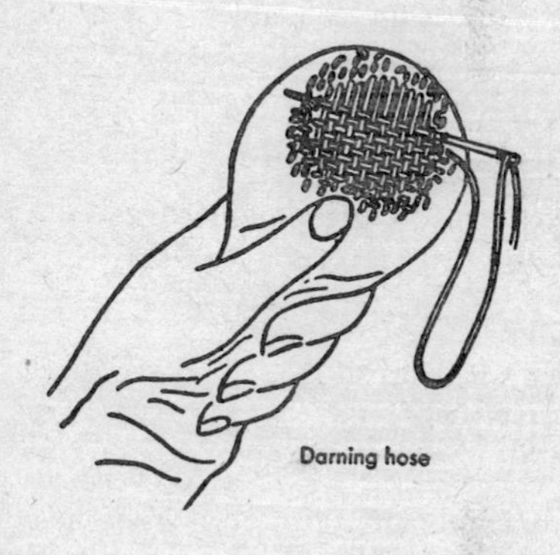

Darning hose

*Hosiery:* Mend a run with an overhanding stitch. Certain stores will do this for you. Darn holes over a darning egg.

*Bras, girdles, slips, overalls, and play clothes* can be mended most effectively with a zigzag stitch which catches both sides of the tear.

## *PRESSING SUGGESTIONS*

Pressing a garment gives it the finished, professional look which is so important. Therefore determine the proper temperature for the fabric and plan to press as you work.

Pressing is a basic part of sewing. It is not the same as ironing because it depends on pressure and steam to do the work rather than on the movement of the iron. The process is principally one of lifting the iron and putting it down on a damp cloth.

Here is the equipment you will need:

- an ironing board
- a sleeve board
  - (the sleeve board will do for most work if a regular ironing board is not available)
- an iron
- two press cloths
  - one of heavy muslin
  - one of light muslin
  - (all starch and sizing should have been removed by laundering)
- sponge
- pan of water
- small camel's hair brush
- tailors' cushion
- velvet board

Keep the ironing board open near your machine as you sew. Everything you do will work more easily if you press as you work.

Make certain that your ironing board is smooth, soft and well padded. You can make your own pad with old turkish towels, but make certain that all the starch has been laundered out of the muslin covering.

Except for ordinary cottons and linens, press everything on

the wrong side. Woolens, silks and rayons will require a press cloth between the iron and the material. Rayons require very little heat and may be damaged by a hot iron. Silks may take a slightly higher temperature. Cottons, woolens and linens require a hot iron.

Always press lightly to avoid causing a shine. If a shine does appear, it can usually be removed by rubbing with a rough, damp cloth. Napped materials may be stroked with a fine wire brush, the type that is used in cleaning suede shoes. This is used to raise the nap to its original position.

Buttoned materials should be pressed from the wrong side with extra padding (turkish towels will do) to allow space for the buttons.

Embroidered material should be pressed on the wrong side with extra padding underneath.

Curtains, laces, dotted swiss cottons and novelty fabrics particularly, should be pressed from the wrong side.

For woolens, use a heavy dry cloth over the material, and a lighter cloth (which has been wrung out of water) placed on top of the dry cloth.

Linens should be very damp and ironed with a hot iron.

Napped materials are pressed on a velvet board or by running the material over a damp cloth placed over an upended iron. Steam is used to remove wrinkles from napped fabric garments wherever this is feasible.

Double napped fabrics may be pressed by turning the end of the flexible velvet board over both sides of the fabric, and steaming through it.

Whenever you move the iron, try to follow the grain of the material as closely as possible.

Press each seam, tuck and dart as you finish it. This not only gives you a neater job but makes working much easier. Never join one seam to another before it has been pressed. You may dampen the seams with a brush and place a cloth over them. A damp sponge is used to dampen the press cloth itself.

If you are afraid the iron may leave an impression, dip

your brush in water and run it down the seam, then press over the damp cloth. Fabrics which may show the marks of the seams through, are pressed with strips of paper under the seam edges.

Press darts toward the center front or the center back of the garment. When this cannot be done, slash and press open, then overcast. Press underarm darts downward.

Press hems by placing a damp cloth over the skirt.

Press small pieces over a sleeve board. If no sleeve board is available, you may use a rolled magazine or a rolled towel.

Tops of sleeves are pressed with the tip end of the iron.

When sleeves have already been stitched into the armscye, press by moving the iron toward the sleeve over a sleeve-board or over a sleeve cushion. Insert a damp cloth between the iron and the sleeve.

Press pleats, after hem is sewed and pleats have been basted, over a slightly dampened cloth.

When the garment is finished, give it a final pressing. Smooth out, shrink in and blend all the joinings so that the finished dress has all the smoothness of a professionally finished product.

## STAINS—AND HOW TO REMOVE THEM

### *Stain Removal*

Remove stains as soon as practical, before they get a chance to set. Follow these steps: (1) Determine, first, the cause of the stain. (2) Determine the type of fabric—particularly whether it is washable or non-washable. Consider the fiber, the color, the type of dye. (3) Then determine the method you will use. (4) Test any chemical you plan to use on a seam or other sample of the fabric. If you plan to wash the material, remove stains before washing. Remember: Hot water will set some stains such as egg, blood or meat juice. Soapy water will set some stains like tea, coffee and the juice of most fruits.

In general there are three basic methods of removing stains from non-washable fabrics: (1) Sponging or swabbing with solvents like carbon tetrachloride or benzine. (2) Bleaching with hydrogen peroxide, oxalic acid or Javelle water. (3) Dry cleaning with a paste made of absorbent powders like French chalk, white talcum powder or Fuller's earth.

The following chart lists accepted methods of removing the most common stains:

| *Stain* | *White Cottons or Linens only* | *Any Washable Colored Fabric* |
|---|---|---|
| Adhesive Tape | Soak fresh stain in cold water. Wash in warm suds. For stubborn stains, use salt water solution (¼ c. salt to 2 c. water). | Sponge with carbon tetrachloride. |
| Blood, Sugar | | Sponge with cold water. Wash in lukewarm suds. |
| Candle Wax | Crumble off excess wax. Place stained portion on blotter and press with hot iron. Sponge with carbon tetrachloride. | Same method as for cottons and linens. |

| *Stain* | *White Cottons or Linens only* | *Any Washable Colored Fabric* |
|---|---|---|
| Chewing Gum | Rub with ice, scrape off gum. If stain remains, sponge with carbon tetrachloride. | Chill with ice and scrape off gum. Sponge with carbon tetrachloride or other solvent. |
| Chocolate, Cocoa | Sponge with carbon tetrachloride; then with warm water. If stain persists, work in pepsin powder, allow it to remain for 30 minutes, then sponge off with water. | Wash in lukewarm suds. Remove cream spots with carbon tetrachloride. |
| Cod Liver Oil | For fresh stains, sponge with carbon tetrachloride; then wash in warm suds. Bleach old stains with hydrogen peroxide. Rinse well. Or use solution of 2 tablespoons of banana oil in a cup of soap jelly. | Wash in warm suds. For old stains use carbon tetrachloride or other solvent, or hydrogen peroxide bleach. |
| Coffee or Tea | Pour boiling water from height of 2 or 3 feet through stain, from reverse side. If stain persists, bleach with hydrogen peroxide. Rinse well. Do not use soap first; it may set the stain. | Sponge with warm water. If stain persists, apply warm glycerin, let stand ½ hour, rinse well. Wash in warm suds. |
| Cream or Ice Cream | Soak in cold water. Remove. Treat as fruit or chocolate stains. Wash in warm suds. Rinse well. | Sponge with cold water. Wash in lukewarm suds. Use carbon tetrachloride if stain persists. |
| Eggs or Meat Juice | Soak in cold water. Wash in hot suds. Avoid hot water first; it may set stain. If persistent, sponge with carbon tetrachloride. | Sponge with cold water. Wash in lukewarm suds. |

## *STAINS—AND HOW TO REMOVE THEM*

| *Stain* | *White Cottons or Linens only* | *Any Washable Colored Fabric* |
|---|---|---|
| Fruits or Fruit Juices | Pour boiling water from height of 2 or 3 feet through stain from reverse side. If stain persists, use hydrogen peroxide. Rinse well. Avoid soap; it may set stains. | Sponge with cool water. If stain persists, apply warm glycerin, let stand a few hours, rinse well. Wash in warm suds. |
| Grass | Rub with cooking fat or oil and wash in hot suds. Bleach remaining stain with hydrogen peroxide. Rinse well. Alternative: Use alcohol. | Wash in lukewarm suds. Sponge with alcohol or hydrogen peroxide. Rinse well. |
| Grease and Oil | Rub in soap and wash in hot suds. If stain persists, sponge with carbon tetrachloride or other solvent. | Sponge with carbon tetrachloride or other solvent. Wash in lukewarm suds. |
| Ink | Rub in glycerine. Rinse in cold water. | Apply paste of absorbent powder. |
| Iodine | Hold in steam of teakettle or wash in hot suds, or moisten and expose to sunlight. | Wash in lukewarm suds. |
| Iron Rust | Soak in oxalic acid solution. As soon as stain disappears, apply weak ammonia solution. Rinse well. Or apply lemon juice and salt and dry in the sun. | Apply commercial rust remover. Follow manufacturer's directions. |
| Lead Pencil | Use soft eraser. If stain persists, rub in soapsuds. | Immerse in chloroform or alcohol. Brush with soft cloth. |

## *STAINS—AND HOW TO REMOVE THEM*

| *Stain* | *White Cottons or Linens only* | *Any Washable Colored Fabric* |
|---|---|---|
| Lipstick or Rouge | Rub in glycerine or vaseline. Wash in hot suds. If stain persists, bleach with hydrogen peroxide. Avoid soap; it may set stain. | Soften with vaseline or lard. Sponge with carbon tetrachloride. Wash in warm suds. If stain persists, bleach with hydrogen peroxide. |
| Mildew | Wash in hot suds, apply lemon juice and salt, dry in the sun. Bleach old stains with hydrogen peroxide. Rinse well. | Wash in warm suds. If stain persists, bleach with oxalic acid. |
| Nail Polish | Apply acetone or nail polish remover, or alcohol, or lacquer thinner. Wash in hot suds. Bleach out remaining color. | Same method, except for acetate rayon. Sponge acetate fabric with carbon tetrachloride, apply a drop of banana oil, remove dissolved polish with cloth. |
| Paint | Scrape off fresh paint and wash in warm suds. If stain has dried, soften with oil, lard, or vaseline; then sponge with turpentine or banana oil. Wash in warm suds. | Follow methods for cottons and linens. |
| Scorch | Moisten, expose to sunlight. Repeat several times. If stain persists, bleach with hydrogen peroxide. Rinse well. Woolens and silks may respond to water alone. | Can seldom be removed. Brush woolens with fine sandpaper. |
| Tobacco Juice | Sponge with cold water. Work in glycerine. Let stand for 30 minutes. Wash with soap and water. | Sponge with denatured alcohol. |

The clothes you make and the clothes you buy will look nicer and last longer if you care for them properly and intelligently. Listed here are some suggestions for clothing care:

1. As soon as you remove garments, hang them on hangers which are properly shaped.

2. Never hang clothes in a closet while they are still wet.

3. Clothing should be hung in a dry, cool, well-ventilated place.

4. Where possible, avoid wearing the same clothes for two successive days. Allow the wrinkles to work out.

5. Brush frequently to remove dust and lint. Brush in the direction of the nap.

6. Avoid damage to your clothes through perspiration. Shields attached to underarms, astringents used where practical, will give some protection.

7. Remove stains and dirt as soon after they appear as possible. Never store an uncleaned garment for the season.

8. Remove dust from serge with the sticky side of adhesive tape.

9. Remove dirt from suede with emery cloth.

10. Remove shine from blue serge, black silk, etc., with cheesecloth dipped in vinegar.

11. Dry raincoats by hanging immediately in a dry, cool, well-ventilated place.

12. Avoid friction points that will wear out furs and good clothes—rubbing jewelry or handbags, tight joints, etc.

13. To brighten furs, shake thoroughly, but take care to avoid breaking leather.

14. Hosiery should be washed before the first wearing and after every wearing in lukewarm water and mild flakes. Keep sheer stockings in a lined box to avoid rubbing.

15. Felt hats should not be hung on a rack when wet. Brush after each wearing with a soft bristle brush.

16. Straw hats exposed to rain should be pushed out, with sweatband turned out, and allowed to dry resting on the sweatband.

17. Shoes should be kept in a cool, dry place. Polishing helps to preserve them. If dried too rapidly, shoes will shrink.

18. Before washing, sort clothes into packs which require approximately the same kind of laundering.

19. Soak clothes overnight, if possible, to loosen dirt. Do not soak unless colors are known to be fast.

20. Woolens, silks and rayons, should be washed in lukewarm water and never rinsed in cold water. A few drops of vinegar in the rinse water for silks will add lustre.

21. Bathing suits should be rinsed, after each wearing, in lukewarm water and mild soapsuds. Avoid hot iron. Never pack away suit while any part is wet.

22. Foundation garments should be laundered in accordance with manufacturers' directions. Usual solution is lukewarm water and mild soapsuds. Avoid rubbing, twisting, wringing and excessive soaping.

23. Lace curtains should be measured before being washed. Avoid rubbing. Squeeze and work in suds. Dry curtains on stretchers or spread a sheet on the floor.

# DICTIONARY OF FABRIC WEAVES

**ALBATROSS** *(wool, cotton)*. Plain weave. Soft, light, sheer. Pebbly surface. Cotton has slight nap. Used for infants' wear, negligees, nuns' dresses.

**ANGORA** *(cotton warp mohair filling)*. Plain weave, high finish. Used for men's coats.

**ANTIQUE SATIN.** Satin weave. Heavy, dull luster. Used for draperies, upholstery, bedspreads.

**ASTRAKHAN** *(wool, mohair, cotton)*. Woven or knitted. Soft, thick, spongy. Usually with cotton back, wool or mohair face. Lustrous, curled, thick pile yarns. Used for coats, trimmings.

**BALLOON CLOTH** *(mercerized cotton, silk, linen)*. Plain weave, strong, coated with rubber to be waterproof. Durable, smooth high luster. Used for shirts, dresses, treated for airplanes, balloons.

**BASKET WEAVE** *(2 threads or more interlaced at right angles)*. Weave looks like a basket. Used for women's dresses, draperies.

**BATISTE** *(wool, high quality mercerized cotton, spun rayon, silk, linen)*. Plain or Jacquard weave. Soft, sheer, often printed. Hard texture, luster. Used for lingerie, handkerchiefs, infants' wear, ladies' collars, dresses, heavier types for foundation garments.

**BEDFORD CORD** *(wool, rayon, cotton, silk)*. Wide ribs run lengthwise. Warp yarns float on back. Similar to piqué. Used for suits, topcoats, riding clothes, slacks, uniform, draperies, upholstery.

**BENGALINE** *(silk, rayon, combed cotton, wool)*. Rib runs crosswise. Filling is coarser than the warp, slightly heavier than poplin, compact texture. Used for dresses, coatings, ribbons, draperies, men's shirts.

**BIRD'S-EYE** *(linen, cotton, rayon. Also a worsted fabric)*. Clear finish with small indentations on the face suggesting a bird's eye. Used for diapers, towels.

**BOLIVIA** *(wool, may also have mohair, alpaca, etc.)*. Satin weave. Soft, velvety nap. Tufts run in diagonal or vertical rows. Used for coats, suits.

**BOMBER CLOTH** *(cotton)*. Firm twill weave with two fine warp yarns to one heavy fill yarn. Used for draperies.

**BOUCLÉ** *(wool, rayon, cotton, silk, nylon, linen)*. Two fine yarns twisted with a thick yarn. Covered with loop at intervals to give nubby effect. Woven or knitted. Various weights. Used for draperies, coats, suits, dresses, sportswear.

**BRILLIANTINE** *(silk, worsted, rayon, mercerized cotton, mohair).* Varies with fiber and finish. Silk is light, loosely woven, slips easily. Cotton has a fine yarn in the warp and a loosely twisted yarn in the fill. Used for dresses, linings, suits.

**BROADCLOTH** *(worsted or wool).* Open twill weave. Close uniform texture. Pile is permanently pressed down in one direction. Smooth, lustrous, velvety. Used for dresses, women's suits and coats.

**BROADCLOTH** *(mercerized cotton, spun rayon).* Fine crosswise rib made by weaving several warp yarns together. Used for men's shirts, shorts, pajamas, summer jackets, women's and children's dresses, gowns, pajamas, draperies, tablecloths.

**BROCADE** *(silk, rayon, cotton, nylon).* Embossed effect obtained by Jacquard weave. Low relief. Fill yarns float over the warp. Used for draperies, upholstery, dresses, ties, blouses, corsets.

**BROCATELLE** *(silk, rayon, linen, cotton).* Jacquard weave. High relief embossed effect. Lightly woven. Stiff. Pattern is formed by the warp yarns. Used for draperies, upholstery, dresses.

**BUCKRAM** *(cotton, linen, sized to stiffen).* Mesh. Thicker ply yarn than crinoline. Heavy buckram made by gluing two fabrics together. Used for stiffening, shaping, bookbinding.

**BUNTING** *(worsted, cotton).* Loose, porous, thin. Used for flags, banners, curtains.

**BURLAP** *(cotton, jute, hemp).* Plain weave. Coarse, heavy. Used for sacks, floor covering, backing, furniture covers, draperies.

**BUTCHER'S LINEN** *(heavy cotton, rayon).* Plain weave. Strong, stiff. Looks like linen. Used for aprons, coats, dresses, children's clothes.

**BYRD CLOTH** *(mercerized cotton).* Close, firm, twill weave. Wind resistant. Usually finished to resist wind and water. Used for snow and ski suits, sport jackets, raincoats.

**CALICO** *(cotton).* Plain weave, light, coarse, inexpensive, usually printed on one side. Sized to crispness but this washes out. Used for dresses, skirts, curtains.

**CAMBRIC** *(linen, cotton).* Plain, fine, firm weave, bleached or dyed-in-piece goods. Smooth, soft finish. Used for handkerchiefs, children's dresses, slips, underwear, nightgowns.

**CANVAS** *(cotton, linen)*. Firm, heavy, plain weave. Stiff. Various types. Used for sails, flooring, awnings, shoes, art, needlework, furniture, covers.

**CAVALRY TWILL** *(woolen or worsted)*. Strong, rugged, has raised cord. No set weave. Hard texture. Used for slacks, sportswear, military suits and coats.

**CHALLIS** *(wool, spun rayon, cotton)*. Plain weave. Durable. Soft, pliable, light. Medium weight. Drapes well. Used for women's dresses, blouses, negligees, children's dresses, men's shirts, ties, draperies, linings.

**CHAMBRAY** *(cotton, linen)*. Plain weave. Smooth, lustrous. Changeable color effect obtained by weaving white filling with colored yarns. Variety of weights. Used for fine children's dresses, men's shirts, women's dresses, blouses. Heavier types for mattress ticking, work shirts.

**CHENILLE** *(cotton, wool, silk, rayon)*. A yarn with a pile all around. "Similar to a caterpillar." Used for rugs, women's robes, trimmings, bedspreads.

**CHEVIOT** *(worsted, spun rayon)*. Rough. Similar to tweed but with heavier yarn. Close. Used for suits, overcoats.

**CHIFFON** *(silk, nylon, fine highly twisted cotton, rayon)*. Plain weave, light weight, sheer. Difficult to handle. Drapes well. Durable. Difficult to launder. Soft or stiff finish. Used for drape over silk, fine dresses, blouses, scarfs, trimmings.

**CHIFFON CREPE** *(silk or rayon)*. Plain weave. Sheer, soft, crepe texture. Used for dresses, lingerie, handbags.

**CHIFFON VELVET** *(rayon)*. A soft, lightweight velvet. Used for quality dresses.

**CHINA SILK** *(silk)*. Plain weave. Threads are irregular. Used for linings.

**CHINTZ** *(cotton)*. Plain weave. Bright prints. Surface glaze remains after washing. Used for furniture covers, curtains, draperies, dresses, smocks, housecoats.

**CIRE SATIN**. Satin weave. High luster like leather. Usually in metallic colors. Used for dresses.

**COCHLE** *(cotton, rayon, wool)*. Shriveled effect. Used for dresses.

**CORDUROY** *(mercerized cotton, rayon)*. Ridges in the warp or fill or both. Yarn pile runs lengthwise. Used for slacks, suits, dresses, jackets, shirts, sportswear, draperies, bedspreads, upholstery.

**COTTONADE** *(cotton)*. Twill weave. Heavy, firmly woven. Speckled stripe alternating with dark stripe. Similar to covert. May be napped at back. Used for linings, work clothes.

**COVERT** *(wool or worsted in 2 shades of color, rayon, cotton)*. Twill weave, light weight, durable. White and colored yarns alternate in warp and filling. Speckled appearance, medium or heavy weight. Wool is used for men's topcoats, women's coats and suits. In cotton, used for men's shirts, women's dresses, sportswear, uniforms, draperies, bedspreads.

**CRASH** *(linen, cotton, rayon, wool, jute)*. Open weave, soft, lustrous, absorbent, rough texture. Durable. Usually white dyed in plain colors or stripes. Used for dresses, draperies, upholstery, towels.

**CREPE** *(highly twisted yarn, silk, rayon, cotton, wool, nylon)*. Woven with alternate right and left hand twisted yarns. Varieties have crinkled texture or smooth surface. Used for fine dresses.

**CREPE BACK SATIN** *(silk, rayon, nylon)*. Satin weave, crepe-twist filling. Reversible. Used for dresses.

**CREPE CHARMEUSE** *(silk, rayon)*. Satin weave. Dull luster. Drapes well. Used for fine dresses.

**CREPE de CHINE** *(silk, rayon)*. Soft, finely crinkled, smooth, lustrous. Used for dresses, blouses, lingerie, curtains.

**CREPON** *(silk, rayon, wool)*. Plain weave. Heavy, wavy lengthwise ribs. Used for dresses, lingerie, handbags.

**CRETONNE** *(cotton, linen, rayon)*. Plain, twill or satin weave. Firmly woven. Usually has bright large patterns. Used for draperies, furniture covers.

**CRINOLINE** *(cotton)*. Open, mesh of fine low grade yarns. Usually sized and stiff. Used for stiffening, linings, bookbinding.

**DAMASK** *(silk, rayon, linen, cotton, wool, mohair, nylon)*. Jacquard weave. Figured material in which the design is woven flat into the fabric. Firm, lustrous, reversible. Warp yarns float over the fill. Used for tablecloths, napkins, draperies, bedspreads, upholstery, evening wraps.

**DENIM** *(coarse, hard twisted cotton)*. Twill weave. Stiff, durable, smooth, resists water, snags, tears. Woven with colored warp and white fill yarns to give a speckled appearance. No. 2.20 denim weighs 2.2 yds. to the pound. Heavy denims have low numbers. Light denims are classified by ounces to the yard. Used for work clothes, upholstery, drapes, sport clothes.

**DIMITY** *(mercerized cotton, linen).* Plain weave. Thin, sheer, crisp, corded or check effect. Similar to lawn. Dyed, printed or white. Used for dresses, blouses, ladies' neckwear, lingerie, curtains, bedspreads, table scarfs, lampshades.

**DOESKIN** *(wool, rayon, cotton).* Satin weave. Fine napped, lustrous, soft finished. Used for suits, sportswear, uniforms.

**DONEGAL** *(wool, rayon, cotton).* Plain or twill weave. Yarns have colored nubs. Looks like tweed. Used for women's coats and suits, sportswear.

**DOTTED SWISS** *(cotton).* Plain or lappet weave. Sheer with crisp finish. Used for children's dresses and bonnets, women's dresses, aprons, blouses, neckwear.

**DRILL** *(cotton).* Twill weave. Heavy, firm. Right to left diagonal. Used for middies, women's uniforms, sportswear, work clothes, linings, slip covers.

**DUCK** *(cotton, linen).* Plain weave. Closely woven, durable. Varies in weight. Generally lighter than canvas. Used for sportswear, work clothes, awnings, tents, sails.

**DUVETYNE** *(wool, rayon, silk, cotton).* Twill weave. Suede finish, thick, lustrous, smooth, with deep nap on both sides pressed into fabric. Feels like felt. Used for women's coats, suits and dresses, men's sports coats.

**ELASTIQUE** *(rayon, wool).* Ribs in groups of two on face. Hard texture. Diagonal left to right. Used for suits, coats, slacks, military coats and suits.

**END-and-END CLOTH** *(cotton).* Plain weave. Pin check obtained by alternating different colored yarns. Similar to chambray. Used for shirts, children's wear.

**ÉPONGE** *(wool, rayon, cotton, silk).* Similar to ratine. Spongy, knotty surface. Used for dresses, women's suits, draperies.

**FAILLE** *(silk, rayon).* Has a crosswise rib weave. Fill is stronger than warp. Feels soft. Similar to grosgrain. Used for dresses, coats, blouses, curtains, draperies.

**FAILLE: TAFFETA** *(silk, rayon)*. Stiff, crisp, has fine crossrib. Used for dresses.

**FELT** *(fur, wool, cotton, rayon, hair)*. Thick, compact. Made by pressing loose fibers under heat and moisture. Used for hats, table covers, linings, etc.

**FLANNEL** *(wool, worsted, cotton, spun nylon, spun rayon)*. Simple plain or twill weave concealed by a dull finish. Soft texture. Napped. Used for suits and coats, dresses, skirts, jackets, shirts.

**FLANNELETTE** *(wool, wool and cotton)*. Printed and napped on one face only. Used for pajamas, baby blankets, diapers.

**FLAT CREPE** *(silk, rayon)*. Plain weave. Smooth, soft, slight crinkle, flat appearance. Used for dresses, lingerie, handbags.

**FLEECE** *(wool, wool and cotton, cashmere, camel hair, mohair, alpaca)*. Heavy, compact, soft. Has long nap. Durable but often bulky. Woven or knitted. Used for coats.

**FOULARD** *(silk, rayon, cotton, wool)*. Plain or twill weaves. Light weight with soft finish or fill. Drapes well. Usually printed with small figures. High luster. Used for ties, dresses.

**GABARDINE** *(wool, combed cotton, rayon)*. A fine, tight twill weave which gives single, diagonal lines over face of cloth. Hard texture, lustrous. Used for men's and women's suits, coats, raincoats, uniforms, men's shirts.

**GAUZE** *(cotton, rayon, silk)*. Similar to cheesecloth, but more closely woven, sheer, transparent. Used for bandages, trimmings, curtains.

**GEORGETTE CREPE** *(silk, rayon)*. Plain loose weave. Pebbled effect. Sheer, less crinkled, harder, less lustrous than Crepe de Chine. Used for dresses, blouses, negligees, lingerie, curtains, bedspreads.

**GINGHAM** *(highly twisted, mercerized cotton, rayon)*. Plain close weave. Fine or medium yarn. Dyed or printed in stripes, checks or plaids on both sides. Average texture 64 x 66. May be sheer. Used for housedresses, aprons, children's dresses, sportswear, pajamas, men's shirts, curtains, draperies, spreads.

**GLASS TOWELING** *(highly twisted linen, cotton, rayon)*. Plain loose weave. Usually has red or blue stripe or check. Used for towels, table covers, kitchen curtains.

**GRENADINE** *(hard twisted cotton, rayon, wool, silk)*. Loose leno weave. Dyed yarns produce stripe or check. Used for dresses, ladies' neckwear, curtains.

**GROS de LONDRE** *(silk, rayon)*. Close rib weave. Ribs run crosswise in alternate heavy and thin ribs. Used for dresses, evening dresses, blouses, curtains.

**GROSGRAIN** *(silk, rayon, cotton)*. Rib weave with heavy filling cords. Rounded rib runs crosswise. Hard finish. Used for ribbons, women's coats and suits, vestments, dresses, trimmings.

**HARRIS TWEED** *(wool)*. Imported from Scotland. Distinctive, homespun appearance. Used for suits, coats.

**HERRINGBONE.** Any fabric woven to resemble fish backbone. Staple. Used for suits, coats, dresses.

**HOMESPUN** *(wool, rayon, cotton)*. Plain loose weave. Undyed, crude, coarse, heavy, uneven. Looks home loomed. Used for drapes, slipcovers, women's coats and suits, men's sportswear, children's coats.

**HONEYCOMB or WAFFLECLOTH** *(cotton, rayon, wool)*. Honeycomb weave. Rough texture. Raised geometric pattern. Used for towels, novelty dress fabrics, bedspreads.

**HOPSACKING** *(cotton, wool, rayon, linen)*. Open weave, usually basket weave. Hard, rough, durable texture. Homespun appearance. Used for sportswear, draperies.

**HUCKABACK** *(linen, cotton)*. Huckaback weave. Firm, durable. Yarns float over large areas creating absorbency. Used for towels, quilting, draperies, shirts.

**JASPÉ CLOTH** *(rayon, cotton)*. Plain weave. Warp has threads of many colors, fill, one color. Gives effect of multicolored stripes. Firm, hard, durable. Used for draperies, upholstery.

**JEAN or MIDDY TWILL** *(cotton)*. Strong, twill or herringbone weave. Firm, clear surface. Finer than drill. Used for children's play clothes, work clothes, sportswear, linings.

**JERSEY** *(wool, cotton, rayon, silk)*. Plain knitted fabric. Originally made on a circular machine, now also made on a tricot machine. Vertical rib. Elastic. Used for undergarments, dresses, sweaters, sports shirts, gloves.

**LACES.** The warp and filling are twisted to make a fabric. Warp runs crosswise, filling lengthwise; made by hand or machine in many types. Used for ladies' neckwear, trimmings.

**LAMÉ** *(metal with silk or rayon).* Glittering metallic yarns used in background, pattern or both. Glitters. Used for draperies, evening wear, blouses, trimmings, millinery.

**LASTEX** *(rubber with cotton, wool, silk, rayon).* Yarns are wound around rubber core. Used either as filling or warp or both. Stretches. Soft, thin. Used for girdles, bathing suits.

**LAWN** *(fine cotton, linen).* Plain weave. Light, sheer, soft, semi-crisp. Used for children's clothes, dresses, blouses, lingerie, ladies' neckwear, curtains.

**LENO** *(cotton, silk, rayon, nylon, wool).* Open weave as for gauze. Used for curtains, wrappings.

**LINSEY-WOOLSEY** *(linen or cotton and wool).* Wool is the fill. Loose, coarse, usually highly colored. Used for sports clothes.

**LONGCLOTH** *(cotton).* Close plain weave. Similar to nainsook. Used for lingerie, children's wear, men's shirts.

**MADRAS** *(long staple cotton, rayon).* Plain or Jacquard weave. Has yarn-dyed woven stripes in warp. Thin, lightweight, tightly woven. Used for men's shirts, pajamas.

**MAROCAIN** *(rayon).* Plain weave, stiff, crisp. Closely set creped ribs. Heavier than canton crepe. Used for dresses, blouses.

**MARQUISETTE** *(cotton, rayon, nylon).* Fine, firm, open (leno) weave. Sheer. May be soft or crisp. Lacy effect. Used for evening wear dresses, children's dresses, curtains.

**MATELASSÉ** *(spun rayon, cotton, silk, wool).* Jacquard weave. Double fabric. Raised surface joined to back fabric gives quilted appearance. Back fabric shows long floating yarns. Used for upholstery, draperies, dresses, women's suits, evening wraps.

**MELTON** *(wool).* Twill or satin weave. Thick, close, felted, smooth surface. Usually in plain colors. Used for hunting equipment, coats, uniforms.

**MERINO** *(wool plus cotton).* Knitted. Used for undergarments. Not to be confused with Merino lambs which give finest wool.

**MESSALINE** *(rayon, silk).* Loose satin weave. Light, high luster. Used for dresses.

**METALLIC CLOTH.** Metal threads in the design. Used for dresses, draperies, pocketbooks.

**MILANESE** *(silk, rayon, nylon).* Knit, sheer, has fine diagonal rib, little elasticity. Runproof. Used for lingerie, linings.

**MILIUM.** Metal spray on fabric. Like aluminum foil in insulation, it radiates body heat back, makes thin fabrics warm. Silver colored on reverse side. Dry-cleanable. Used for coat linings. Light, warm.

**MOIRÉ** *(rayon, cotton, silk)*. A wavy line added in the finish, usually on a ribbed cloth. Used for draperies, formal dresses, suits, bedspreads, trimmings on taffeta, ribbons.

**MONK'S CLOTH** *(cotton)*. Loose, basket weave, coarse. Used for draperies, furniture covers.

**MONTAGNAC.** Has floating filling yarns. Soft, bulky, lustrous. Nap in small curly tufts. Used for coats.

**MOSQUITO NET** *(cotton)*. Net. Coarse firm mesh. Used for protective coverings.

**MOUSSELINE de SOIE** *(rayon, silk)*. Plain close weave. Crisp, sheer. Harder than voile. Used for trimmings, evening wear.

**MOURNING CREPE** *(silk)*. Plain weave. Dull finish. Used for dresses, lingerie, handbags.

**MULL** *(cotton, rayon, silk)*. Plain weave. Sheer, soft, lustrous. Softer than lawn. Similar to batiste in finish. For children's wear.

**MUSLIN** *(cotton)*. Plain weave. May be bleached or unbleached. Wide variety of weights. Sized. Used for making patterns, sheets, pillow cases, bedspreads, underwear, dresses, uniforms.

**NAINSOOK** *(cotton, mercerized cotton)*. Plain weave. Light, soft, slightly lustrous. Similar to batiste, cambric, longcloth and dimity except for finish. One side may be calendered. Used for infants' wear, lingerie, ladies' neckwear, blouses.

**NEEDLE POINT** *(wool bouclé yarns)*. Knots appear to cover the entire fabric. Close, firm, finely nubbed. Woven. Used for women's coats and suits.

**NET** *(cotton, linen, rayon, silk, nylon)*. Twisted mesh. Varies widely from fine to coarse, sheer to full. Used for draperies, trimming, curtains, millinery.

**NETTING** *(cotton, linen, nylon)*. Knotted in fisherman's knots. Used for draperies, sportswear, trimmings, bags.

**NINON** *(silk, rayon)*. Plain weave. Thin, smooth, crisp. Heavier and harder than chiffon. Used for evening dresses, scarfs, curtains.

**NUN'S VEILING** *(wool)*. Soft, thin. Hard feel, white or plain colors. Used for dresses.

**ORGANDIE** *(combed long staple cotton, rayon)*. Plain weave, sheer, stiff, crisp, transparent. Difficult to launder. Used for dresses, blouses, ladies' neckwear, curtains, bedspreads.

**OTTOMAN** *(rayon, silk, cotton)*. Heavy, has wide flat ribs running crosswise. Hard texture. Used for women's coats and suits.

**OXFORD CLOTH** *(cotton, rayon)*. Plain or basket weave. Two yarns in the warp and one heavier yarn in the fill give heavy feel. Used for shirts, pajamas, dresses, sportswear, draperies.

**PAISLEY CLOTH.** Overall scroll designs. For coverings, shawls.

**PANNE or SLIPPER SILK** *(rayon, silk, nylon)*. Stiff, dull luster, heavy. Used for dresses.

**PARACHUTE FLARE CLOTH** *(rayon, silk, nylon)*. Fine, soft, featherweight, high luster. Used for lingerie, blouses, parachutes.

**PERCALE** *(cotton)*. Plain, close weave. Higher thread count than muslin. Used for sheeting, curtains, dresses, men's shirts.

**PERCALINE** *(cotton)*. Plain weave. Light, high sheen. Finer than percale. Sized and calendered. Used for linings.

**PIQUÉ** *(combed, corded or mercerized cotton, rayon, silk)*. Wales or ribs run lengthwise. Used for ladies' neckwear, dresses, sportswear, bedspreads, draperies.

**PLISSE** *(cotton, rayon)*. Plain weave. Puckered chemically in stripes or checks. Used for dresses, lingerie, curtains, bedspreads.

**PLUSH** *(silk, rayon, cotton, mohair)*. Higher and less dense pile than velvet. Used for draperies, upholstery, corset linings.

**PONGEE** *(silk, cotton)*. Plain weave. Soft, mercerized finish. Average 72x100. Uneven yarns. For dresses, shirts, curtains, pajamas.

**POPLIN** *(silk and wool or worsted, cotton, rayon)*. Rib weave runs crosswise. Staple. With water repellent finish for outdoor wear. For dresses, blouses, shirts, suits, gowns, draperies, uniforms, etc.

**RADIUM** *(rayon, silk)*. Plain, firm, close weave. Smooth, supple, soft. Used for dresses, lingerie, linings.

**RATINE** *(rayon, silk, wool, cotton)*. Plain weave or knitted. Spongy, bulky. Nubbed fine and thick yarn twisted together with a fine yarn to give a nubby effect, coarse. Used for women's coats and suits, dresses, blouses, curtains.

**REP** *(silk, rayon, wool, cotton)*. Plain or rib weave. Rounded ribs run crosswise. Many warp yarns to each fill yarn. Used for draperies, upholstery, apparel.

**ROMAINE CREPE** *(silk, rayon, wool)*. Plain weave. Heavy crepe. Used for dresses, evening wear, lingerie, handbags.

**SAILCLOTH** *(cotton, linen, jute)*. Light canvas. Used for awnings, slipcovers, draperies.

**SATEEN** *(cotton, rayon, created by use of mercerized cotton or calendering)*. Satin weave with more filling on surface. High luster. Plain or printed. Used for draperies, bedspreads, upholstery, robes, slips, linings, pajamas.

**SATIN** *(silk, rayon, cotton, nylon)*. Smooth, lustrous, soft. In variety of forms. Used for women's apparel, linings, draperies, upholstery, bedspreads, trimmings.

**SATIN CANTON** *(rayon, silk)*. Satin weave. Soft, medium weight, high luster, crepe back, with pebbly ribs. Used for dresses, lingerie.

**SCRIM** *(coarse cotton, linen)*. Plain open weave. Lightweight, durable. Used for curtains.

**SEERSUCKER** *(cotton, rayon)*. Crinkled lengthwise. Crepe stripe effect. Light, crinkly. Need not be ironed. Used for dresses, housecoats, men's summer suits, women's uniforms, blouses, bedspreads, curtains, slipcovers.

**SERGE** *(worsted, silk, cotton, rayon)*. Has diagonal lines usually discernible on both sides. Heavy, clear, hard texture. Storm serge is coarse. French serge is soft; staple. Used for suits, uniforms, coats, dresses, upholstery.

**SHANTUNG** *(cotton, rayon, silk)*. Plain or twill weave. Has small, irregular raised lines in filling. Rougher than pongee. Used for dresses, ladies' suits, blouses, sportswear, pajamas, curtains.

**SHARKSKIN** *(worsted, rayon, cotton)*. Has small color effect designs in weave to resemble skin of shark. Basket or twill weave. Durable. Uses de-lustered yarn. Springy feel. For suits, sportswear.

**SURAH** *(rayon, silk)*. A lightweight twill weave. Lustrous. Woven in stripes, checks, or plaids. Used for dresses, blouses, ties.

**TAFFETA** *(silk, rayon, nylon, wool)*. High, crisp texture. High lustrous finish. Fine, firm, plain weave. Crossribbed effect. Used for dresses, lingerie, negligees, slippers, evening wear, draperies, curtains, bedspreads, pillows.

**TAPESTRY** *(silk, rayon, wool, cotton)*. Jacquard weave. Rougher than damask. Draperies, upholstery.

**TARLATAN or ARGENTINE CLOTH** *(cotton)*. Plain open weave.

Lightweight. Transparent, stiffened slightly. Used for curtains, displays, stiffening, fancy dress costumes.

**TERRY CLOTH** *(cotton, linen)*. Loops on face or back or both. Absorbent. Used for towels, robes, draperies, bedspreads.

**TICKING** *(firm cotton or linen)*. Any close weave. Usually striped, though it may have a pattern. Sized and calendered to stiffness. Finished to be water repellent and germ resistant. Used for mattress and pillow covers, upholstery.

**TRICOT** *(wool, worsted, silk, nylon, cotton)*. Knit. Lengthwise chain stitch. Slight elasticity. Strong. For underwear, dresses.

**TRICOTINE** *(rayon, wool)*. Twill weave. Diagonal rib. Similar to cavalry twill in wool. Used for sportswear, suits, uniforms.

**TROPICAL WORSTED.** Twisted yarns. Firm open weave. Weight 6-8 ounces per yard. Used for summer suits.

**TULLE** *(silk, rayon)*. Net. Close, hexagonal mesh. Used for evening dresses, veils, trimmings.

**TUSSAH.** See Shantung.

**TWEED** *(wool, worsted, rayon, cotton)*. Plain, basket or twill weaves. Rough texture with homespun effect. Monotone tweeds use two shades of one color. For suits, coats, skirts, dresses, sportswear.

**TWILLS.** Cloth with a diagonal line in weave. For clothing.

**VELOUR** *(wool, cotton)*. Satin or twill weave, soft, heavy with close nap or pile weave. Also in plush. For coats, dresses, draperies.

**VELVET** *(silk, rayon, cotton, wool, worsted)*. Close pile weave. Back is plain. Varies greatly in quality and type. May be transparent, brocaded, antiqued, heavy, light. Used for dresses, trimmings, draperies, ladies' skirts, coats, blouses, hats, bedspreads, upholstery, handbags, shoes.

**VELVETEEN** *(cotton, rayon)*. Yarns are floated and cut to form a pile. Used for dresses, ladies' coats, ladies' suits, negligees, children's coats, draperies.

**VENETIAN CLOTH** *(cotton, wool)*. Fine twill weave. Similar to Melton but medium weight. High luster. Used for men's wear, linings, topcoats, dresses.

**VOILE** *(wool, cotton, silk, rayon)*. Sheer, open weave. Light, transparent. Drapes well. Has pronounced ribs. Used for lingerie, ladies' neckwear, blouses, curtains, bedspreads.

## *BOOKLETS TO HELP YOU SEW*

The pamphlets listed below were prepared by various government agencies. They are available from the Superintendent of Documents, Government Printing Office, Washington 25, D. C. A check, money order, postal notes or special coupons must be sent in advance. Coupons may be purchased at the rate of 20 for $1.00 and used for the purchase of any government document.

A B C's of mending. Rev. 1946. 23 p. il. 10¢. Catalog No. No. A 1.9: 1925

Coat making at home. 1941. 27 p. il. 15¢. Catalog No. A 1.9: 1894

Dresses and aprons for work in the home. Rev. 1947. 1948. 16 p. il. 5¢. Catalog No. A 1.9: 1963

Fabrics and designs for children's clothes. 1937. 24 p.il. 10¢. Catalog No. A 1.9: 1778

Fitting dresses. Rev. 1946. 29 p. il. 10¢. Catalog No. A 1.9: 1964

How to tailor a woman's suit. 1946. 24 p. il. 15¢. Catalog No. A 1.38: 591

Making a dress at home. 1944. 24 p. il. 10¢. Catalog No. A 1.9:1954

Mending men's suits. Rev. 1946. 24 p. il. 15¢. Catalog No. A 1.38: 482

Pattern alteration. 1945. 40 p. il. 15¢. Catalog No. A 1.9: 1968

Slip covers for furniture. Rev. 1943. 26 p. il. 10¢. Catalog No. A 1.9: 1873

How to make your ironing equipment last longer. 1942. 2 p. 5¢. Catalog No. A 1.59: 11

Sewing machines, cleaning and adjusting. 1943. 24 p. il. 10¢. Catalog No. A 1.9: 1944

Stain removal from fabrics, home methods. Rev. 1942. 30 p. il. 10¢. Catalog No. A 1.9: 1474

## *PERSONAL RECORD OF MEASUREMENTS*

*(See illustration on page 66)*

Pattern Size ........... Style ...........

| | Your Measurement | Pattern Measurements | Adjustments + or — |
|---|---|---|---|
| 1. Bust | | | |
| 2. Chest width | | | |
| 3. Back or neck seam | | | |
| 4. Upper back width | | | |
| 5. Width across shoulder blades | | | |
| 6. Blouse length—center front | | | |
| 7. Blouse length—center back | | | |
| 8. Blouse length—over bust | | | |
| 9. Blouse length—over shoulder blades | | | |
| 10. Armhole depth | | | |
| 11. Shoulder height | | | |
| 12. Underarm length | | | |
| 13. Shoulder length | | | |
| 14. Sleeve length | | | |
| 15. Sleeve-cap length | | | |
| 16. Upper arm (or sleeve width) | | | |
| 17. Elbow | | | |
| 18. Waistline | | | |
| 19. Hips | | | |
| 20. Skirt length | | | |

## *INDEX*

## D

## T

## U



## V

W



Y



Z